NORWICH CITY
The Seventies

NORWICH CITY
The Seventies

EDWARD COUZENS-LAKE
FOREWORD BY GERRY HARRISON

AMBERLEY

Dedicated to Canaries everywhere. On The Ball City.

First published 2013

Amberley Publishing
The Hill, Stroud
Gloucestershire, GL5 4EP

www.amberley-books.com

British Library Cataloguing in Publication Data.
A catalogue record for this book is available from the British Library.

ISBN 978 1 4456 1821 0 (print)
ISBN 978 1 4456 1829 6 (ebook)

Typeset in 10.5pt on 13pt Sabon.
Typesetting and Origination by Amberley Publishing.
Printed in the UK.

CONTENTS

FOREWORD

Put simply – the players, managers and coaches of this Norwich City era made history. They set a high benchmark for the future, changed the perception of the club outside of Norfolk, and showed that dreams can come true. So any record or tribute to their accomplishments is richly deserved.

Basically, the achievements of the 1970s laid the foundations for all of Norwich City's subsequent development – almost literally in one area. At the beginning of the decade, there were apple trees on the back of the River End terrace; by the end there was a brand new £1.7-million-pound stand.

On the playing side, that development was much more dramatic; the transformation of a decent provincial outfit, which seemed always to be on the search to match some heroic cup memories and characters like Barry Butler, Terry Allcott, Ron Davies and Bill Punton.

Norwich City would become a club that could compete at the highest level. In the process, they seemed to turn tradition on its head – impressive League results, forgettable FA Cup performances, and what looked like a spell of exclusive rights to League Cup success. All achieved with a lot of panache and quite a bit of pain. This was a different Norwich City.

The pain came first.

'You'll be a good player when you're fit,' said new manager Ron Saunders to Graham Paddon. 'But I am fit!' complained an indignant Paddon. 'You wait,' said Ron, with one of his conspiratorial winks and a smile. Or was it a grimace? Ron Saunders' route out of the Second Division, where Norwich had been trapped for too long, was through discipline, fitness and a clear playing system. It took time to convince the doubtful and knock a winning combination into shape.

I once put to him the question: 'You were asked to come here and sort the club out. What did you do?' 'Sorted them out,' he replied. That was Ron – never one to give too much away.

Through the mist of sweat and toil, any number of heroes emerged: of course the Forbes-Stringer blockade; the midfield leaders, Graham Paddon and Doug Livermore; the goalscorers Ken Foggo, David Cross, the unlucky Peter Silvester, and that latecomer to the party, Jim Bone. The only concession to show business was Kevin Keelan – with his pre-match warm-up routine of a fag or two, a whisky gargle and playing Rod Stewart very loudly. These guys were pioneers, trailblazers and deserve a special place in the club's honour board.

A late winner at Carrow Road against Swindon Town after a tense game doesn't sound very exciting. But when it's in front of a crowd of 31,736, the goal is scored by the incomparable Duncan Forbes, and it means Norwich had one foot in the Promised Land of the First Division ... it may in some way explain the noise, the excitement of it all.

However, getting 110 per cent out of a small squad at a higher level was hard to maintain, even for a high-octane motivator like Ron Saunders. And when the manager and the board disagreed on the way forward, not even the glamour of a trip to Wembley disguised the rift. Ron went off to Manchester City and the club went for John Bond.

'Are you sure, John?' A question an anxious Sir Arthur South put to his new manager frequently. 'Trust me, Chairman,' he usually replied. And John Bond, a flamboyant risk-taker, physically imposing and always immaculate, was usually right. The one-time Sir Arthur, no mean businessman himself, wasn't so sure when he saw the bill for the Norwich Post House Hotel where all the new signings first migrated.

In they flooded – Mel Machin, John Benson, Ted MacDougall, Phil Boyer, John Sissons, Tony Powell, Colin Sullivan, Kevin Bond, plus a support coaching staff. The inevitable relegation (with Manchester United) seemed only a minor irritant in the drive to rebuild a team on the principles of possession and attack. The MacDougall-Boyer partnership was spectacular – good enough to get them both international call-ups. About the only time they didn't produce the goods was in that 1975 League Cup final, when eliminating Ipswich and Manchester United on the way to Wembley had raised expectations sky-high.

And then, of course, there was Martin Peters – whose surprise arrival helped see them over the promotion line (with Manchester United) when things were wobbling a bit. Anyone who saw Martin Peters play for Norwich was fortunate. Supposedly past his best, he didn't tackle and wasn't quick. That's a laugh! He seemed to win the ball by stealth and pop up at the right place before anyone else. He was a sort of real-life optical illusion. His control and passing were eye-catching, but you had to be quick to spot them because he'd usually moved things on. And he was rarely injured.

The outside world in much of the 1970s – with its strikes and political turmoil – wasn't a bundle of fun. But Carrow Road was a colourful mix of good football, controversies and smiles, great results, surprise results, comings and goings. Plenty of talking points, of course. If the local and national press couldn't get a story out of John Bond's Norwich they weren't trying very hard. Throw in a surging John Ryan run; a Jimmy Neighbour jink or two; some Colin Suggett inspiration; slick passing from Mick McGuire; the strength of David Jones; the emergence of Kevin Bond, and there was always a lot happening. That kid Kevin

Reeves was a revelation, young Justin Fashanu was an immediate favourite, and Peter Mendham looked very promising.

But nothing is more transitory than football. At the end of the decade, John Bond was being tempted elsewhere; Kevin Reeves, in at £50,000, was on the way out at over £1 million, already with an England cap to his name. Ken Brown, an essential background influence in the club's metamorphosis, was about to inherit some good players, but new difficulties in a changing game. And the Norwich City of the seventies was always going to be a hard act to follow.

Nor were all of the colourful characters limited to the dressing room. The exploits of Sir Arthur South and Geoffrey Watling are worth a book, with good legal counsel. And head groundsman Russell Allison, another experienced operator, held a unique position. He claimed he could say anything he wished to anyone at the club because he was so poorly paid they wouldn't sack him. Probably not true, but a good Norfolk approach to life – bold and straightforward. If you could handle the abuse he heaped on you, then Russell – with his builders' tea in filthy cups in his den beneath the stand – was a convivial host. His wide range of seaside postcards and historical club gossip was lively entertainment. His home-made Chablis, though, was best avoided, as secretary Bert Westwood discovered to his cost. But that's another story. And there were plenty of those in the 1970s – the decade when Norwich City took a giant step forward.

Gerry Harrison
Anglia TV 1969–93

INTRODUCTION

Is it just me or do those of us of a certain age still think that football was 'better' in the 1970s?

Maybe it was.

Match of the Day in colour; masses of parka-clad schoolchildren invading the pitch at Hereford; David Coleman's excited commentary at an FA Cup final ('Clarke! ONE-nil!'); Brian Clough calling Jan Tomaszewski a 'clown'; Holland's absorbing total football at two World Cup finals; Bobby Stokes; Kevin Keegan; Billy Bremner; perms; tight shorts; Jimmy Hill and Ossie Ardiles signing for Tottenham; Ron Saunders standing astride Mousehold like a Roman Emperor of old; Duncan Forbes going into battle with a glint in his eye; Jimmy Bone; Supermac; Martin Peters, aka The Ghost; Graham Paddon's long hair; and John Bond's big cigars.

Yes, it definitely was!

We all love our football now of course, and we love our team. But I do think that the game is missing something today that it had in abundance back in the decade that taste didn't as much forget as lock securely in a wooden chest and cast into the middle of the deepest ocean.

Because the game was fun then. It made you smile. The players smiled. The fans smiled – that's when they weren't kicking the 'you know what' out of each other of course, but if you just put your rose-tinted spectacles on you can forget all of that and just concentrate on the football. It was colourful, exciting, and full of character.

It was certainly all of that if you were a Norwich City fan. We had it all: promotions, relegations, Wembley Cup finals, managerial ins and outs, World Cup winners, and million-pound transfers. And a cat that played in goal. How could all of that not be fun?

I wanted to take a look back at that decade as a Norwich fan, to either introduce to, or remind those born and bred on a diet of Bellamy, Sutton, Huckerby and Holt *et al.*, of names who should equally be revered and certainly not forgotten.

Saunders, Keelan, Forbes, MacDougall, Peters and Bond, to name but a few. The players, the matches, the goals and the incidents.

It isn't, by any stretch of the imagination, a definitive, blow-by-blow account of the clubs ups and downs throughout that time, and was never intended to be. But it is a snapshot look at some of the players, games and incidents that cropped up along the way. And yes, it doesn't include all of those that I would have liked to have included – but then it was quite a busy time in and around Carrow Road!

So grab your rattle and scarf and take a trip back in time...

Edward Couzens-Lake

1
YOU'VE NEVER HAD IT SO BAD

It remains, to this day, one of the more unfeasible footballing decisions to have been made by any Canary board of directors and suggests just one thing: the club were getting perilously close to being in financial trouble again.

Supporters of Norwich City had entered the sixties buoyed by a strange type of optimism for their football club's future, one that reflected the perceived uplift of spirit in a nation that was still coming to terms with the after-effects of its participation in a long and costly world conflict.

Harold Macmillan had been the first prominent figure to dare suggest to the British people that things were 'on the up' at a Conservative Party rally in Bedford in 1957 when he shook much of the nation by claiming that, 'most of our people have never had it so good'. The rights and wrongs of that famous quote and the speech that contained it have been debated, questioned and argued ever since, but, whatever the case for Macmillan's bold claim at the time, the same could certainly not be said for Norwich's football club where, even as the historic words were tumbling out of Macmillan's mouth, they had probably 'never known it so bad'.

The rot – which so nearly became terminal – began during the Canaries' 1956/57 campaign, their eleventh consecutive one in the Division Three (South), at that time as low as you could be, League-wise (along with the Division Three (North)) in the professional game in England. The club had ended the previous season in a respectable seventh place, winning nineteen of their forty-six League games and, in Ralph Hunt, having a free-scoring striker – Hunt contributed thirty-one League goals that season, including, at one point, claiming six goals in four consecutive League games.

The footballing omens, it had to be said, seemed good in and around Carrow Road, thanks to the prolific Hunt and his equally formidable partner-in-arms, Limerick-born Johnny Gavin, who had snubbed an offer from West Ham United to join the Canaries, mainly due to the fact that his close friend and Limerick teammate Kevin Holman had already agreed to join Norwich. Cometh the day, cometh the team, and, with Hunt and Gavin leading the line, Norwich were expected to make a serious bid for promotion that season; one which started promisingly enough with four wins and two draws from the club's first six League fixtures (with only one goal conceded). This form saw the Canaries make the trip to West London on 8 September 1956 to play the Queens Park Rangers, a point ahead of Southampton and Watford at the top of the Division Three (South) table. That game saw Hunt get his first goal of the season, but also saw Norwich's first defeat. The 3-1 reverse was swiftly followed by another defeat just two days later, Coventry City winning 3-2 at Highfield Road, that result sending the club down to fourth place. A thumping 3-0 (Hunt 2, Gavin 1) home win against Plymouth Argyle followed on 15 September, but the only hope that result brought was false hope, as it was the Canaries' last League win until the following March.

Quite why the club had gone into such a spectacular meltdown on the pitch (as we will discover, that meltdown was soon to be replicated off the pitch) is unclear. Perhaps complacency was playing a part? After all, player turnover had been modest over the preceding summer. Eight of the players from the team that played the last game of the previous season had been in the starting line-up for the first game of this one, and only injuries to the missing three – Ron Ashman, Billy Coxon and Hunt – prevented manager Tom Parker from naming an unchanged eleven. There were, unquestionably, some excellent footballers in the Norwich side that season, a fact that makes their near plummet into oblivion all the more baffling. Some of them – Hunt, Gavin, Ashman and half-back Roy McCrohan – remain well beloved names at the club, even today, their qualities and ability standing out and their names remembered and mentioned alongside some of the club's more contemporary heroes. Could it be, possibly, that some of their teammates were simply not good enough, were not up to the job and their collective efforts were dragging down those whose pedigree was more apparent? Norwich used thirty players during the 1956/57 season (only three fewer than had been used during the equally disastrous 2008/09 season, which saw relegation to League One as its denouement), and the reasons for the club's efforts that season were widely attributed to many of the players simply not being good enough.

Perhaps this had been exactly the case here: a squad that contained some undoubted quality (for Ashman, Gavin, Hunt and McCrohan read Ryan Bertrand, Sammy Clingan, Wes Hoolahan and David Marshall), but nowhere near enough to do anything but struggle, despite the best efforts of that particular quartet. Whatever the reasons, it was a struggle and it was terminal. In a period of twenty-five League games between 22 September 1956 and 23 February 1957, the Canaries failed to win a single match, losing sixteen of them, including a 6-3 reverse at Walsall, and a humiliating 2-5 Carrow Road defeat to Reading, a game that had seen them 0-4 down by half-time. Surprisingly, Parker remained as manager throughout this spell of games, but the day after an insipid 1-1 draw at home to Brentford, 31 March 1957, his contract was terminated.

Around three months before Parker's dismissal, the full extent of that off-field meltdown had become as well-known as the club's fall from grace on the pitch. The question of finances has always been a tricky one at Carrow Road, and the club's standing with its bankers that season was not helped when they saw fit to invest money that they didn't have by installing floodlights that season. A game was arranged against Sunderland to launch the club's floodlit era, which Norwich comfortably lost 3-0. But what was of far more pressing concern was the cost of the floodlights, which was not short of £10,000. The seriousness of the situation finally came to a head two months after the floodlights had been ceremonially switched on, when, on the morning of Wednesday 12 December 1956, the club issued a simple statement declaring that they were unable to find the cash to pay the players' wages.

The club would almost certainly have ceased to exist were it not for the timely intervention of the local media group, the Norfolk News Company, lending the club enough money for them to carry on as a going concern, at least for the remainder of that season. The long-term situation was serious and the resultant crisis was, and probably remains, the biggest one the club has ever had to face.

It took the formation of a group of local businessmen, led by the then Lord Mayor of Norwich, Arthur South, to step in and launch an appeal committee, the first meeting scheduled to be held on 7 January 1957. Their report made for grim reading. The club was in debt for £20,000 and had yet to fully pay back the loan given by the FA in order to pay for the building of Carrow Road in 1935. In addition to that, the committee estimated that the club would need an additional subsidy, from somewhere, of £300 a week just to carry on and avoid relegation. In addition to all of that, the vital revenue that came from gate receipts was down – not surprising, as spectator figures had fallen almost as dramatically as the team's form, with just 8,481 attending the Boxing Day fixture against Colchester, a year after 30,889 had shoehorned their way into Carrow Road for the game against Leyton Orient. Results, attendances, finances – the club was flat-lining.

While the newly appointed committee set about finding the money needed to ensure the club's long-term survival. Another major project was also launched that spring: to appoint a successor to the unfortunate Parker. He had been given a second chance at the club two years previously; this, no doubt partially based on the fact that he had, in his previous time at the club, won the Division Three (South) title. That had, however, been in 1934, and now, over two decades later, whatever magic touch Parker had possessed had clearly deserted him. Much to the club's surprise, the number of applicants for the post was high and included a number of high-calibre applicants, despite the very real possibility that the club would be forced out of existence before the 1957/58 season started. The board eventually decided to appoint Archie Macaulay as manager. He had enjoyed a playing career at West Ham, Brentford, Arsenal and Fulham, and represented Scotland in seven full internationals.

His appointment was an inspired choice.

For however paradoxical it may seem to commence a book that looks back at a football club's rise to prominence in the 1970s in the 1950s (regarded in the fifties and sixties as a decade that would be characterised by wondrous inventions and technologies such as personal hover cars and routine shuttle journeys to manned lunar bases), the foundations for all that Norwich City were to ultimately achieve were laid at that bleak footballing time for the club. It was the ambitions and vision of the 'three wise men' – Macaulay, South and Watling – that guided the club from a provincial lower-tier outfit to the top rank. Theirs was a vision that was, thankfully, based upon more solid and realistic foundations. In my opinion, their leadership, influence and guidance were pivotal in the club's survival pre-1970, and then into that golden era beyond.

Macaulay was a footballing force of nature. Buoyed by the full and unequivocal support of the new board and by the renewed faith shown in both himself and that board, he set about gutting the playing side of the club from top to bottom. Norwich had endured their worst-ever season, finishing bottom of the Division Three (South) in May 1957, five points adrift of the team immediately above them and an eye-watering twenty-eight points (equivalent to forty-five if three points for a win is applied) away from the team that finished champions – which just happened to be their nearest and closest rivals, Ipswich Town. The Blues had commenced on an upwardly mobile path that would culminate, just five years later, in their becoming Division One champions, and providing a World Cup-winning manager for England in the process. All that Norwich fans had to look forward to was their application to re-election to the League, the process all clubs that finished at the bottom had to go through, mindful of the ambitious and well-run non-League clubs that would only be too willing, and most certainly ready, to take their place. Luckily for the Canaries, three factors counted in their favour, primarily that the League was very much an 'old boys' network – then, as now – and were unlikely not to look after their own. Secondly, Norwich was hardly a club identified with such a footballing predicament and could fairly state that the season had been a one-off, partially down to circumstances that they had now addressed – that being the third point in their favour, the injection of finance and a new board suggesting a club that was on the up and was going to make a real go of things in the future. Thus, Norwich was re-elected to the Football League with some comfort, and the ambitions of Watling, South and Macaulay could begin to be realised. Without knowing it at the time, the club's journey to top-flight football, Wembley Cup finals and England internationals had begun.

Before we push on and look at how those foundations were laid, it is worth considering one little footnote to the club's struggle for existence that season. Macmillan's stirring speech, the one that he had hoped to united the nation in an all-consuming 'feel good' mood, had been made at that Conservative party rally in Bedford, a town that held a particular resonance for Norwich that season. A few months before those words were spoken, the Norwich team, fresh from a 4-2 home defeat to Swindon Town, had a chance to give their misfiring campaign a kick-start with an FA Cup figure against a Southern League side. Surely the Canaries' cup-fighting pedigree would shine through and they would make short work of their lowly opponents, a result and a morale-boosting performance that might not only precipitate a welcome run in the competition but also act as a catalyst to their dreadful form in the League?

As we now know, they did not. Despite being drawn at home, the Canaries capitulated to their modest opposition, losing 4-2. The opponents were Bedford Town, the team whose town Chamberlain was later to make that landmark address. Had anyone suggested to any Norwich City fan after that game that they, as supporters, had 'never had it so good', you can only conclude that the response would have been a lot more withering and dismissive than any offered to Macmillan's words a few months later!

But on to the 1960s.

From a footballing perspective, Macaulay's impact was immediate. In his first season at the club, the Canaries finished in an optimistic eighth place, with Hunt and Gavin – both retained despite fears they would be sold – scoring thirty-three of the club's seventy-five League goals that campaign. The spectre of another FA Cup upset with yet another home draw against non-League opposition was swiftly put to bed with a resounding 6-1 victory over Redhill in the first round, with Hunt contributing four of the goals. Gates were also up, a fact that would have pleased the board. Only 8,431 had bothered to attend that Boxing Day fixture against Colchester in 1956, yet, a year later, the optimism that would surge into the new decade was reflected in an attendance of 24,706 for the League game against Torquay United on 28 December, a game that Norwich won 3-1. Only a sloppy end-of-season run of three defeats and a draw in the club's last five games led to any hopes of promotion disappearing. But the disappointment was fleeting rather than set in stone, for it was clear that the combination of Macaulay and the new faces in the boardroom were getting results. And not just on the pitch, as the Canaries set their stall out for success in the last full season of the decade, the first in the 'new' Division Three, the regionalisation aspect of it having been abandoned with the creation of Division Four. Had that happened a year earlier, Norwich would have been a Fourth Division side, and you have to wonder if the club would ever have been able to progress from so low down the leagues.

Despite the steady rise in the club's fortunes, however, their inglorious past was never far from them, as typified by Macaulay's acquisition of centre-half Barry Butler from Sheffield Wednesday. Upon signing for the club, Butler was asked by Geoffrey Watling what he knew about the Canaries. Butler's reply was brief and succinct, and a surprising one for the man to make, given the club were his new employees. 'Only that they are bankrupt' was the now famous retort.

It is quite likely that the club would have secured promotion by the end of the decade had it not been for the distraction of the FA Cup. After a seventh consecutive draw against non-League opposition in the first round, one that saw Ilford defeated 3-1, the Canaries, by virtue of wins over Swindon Town, Manchester United, Cardiff City, Tottenham Hotspur and Sheffield United, found themselves playing an FA Cup semi-final in front of nearly 64,000 spectators, only two seasons after they had been knocked out of the tournament in the first round by non-League Bedford. From giant killed to giant killers, the Canaries' run to the semi-finals made household names of Macaulay and his players; in particular, forward Terry Bly, who scored seven goals in the tournament for Norwich that season, and his flying partner on the right wing, Canadian Errol Crossan, who contributed a further four. The two were even the subject of a song, 'The Ballad of Crossan and Bly', looking back in sorrow at the FA Cup final appearance that never was and the Canaries' last-gasp defeat (if not to Bedford this time, then to a team from Bedfordshire) to Luton Town after a replay.

'The Canaries have been singing ... but tonight you can hear them cry ... for what should have been the year of Crossan and Bly.'

The club could and should have combined their run to the last four of the FA Cup with a promotion to the Second Division. They had by far the strongest squad, the best players and probably the best manager as well. Plus, they had an ambitious and progressive board. In glorious hindsight it can only be concluded that the run in the cup came at the expense of their League campaign. The club played nine League and cup games in March and a staggering eleven League games in just twenty-seven days in April – or around one game every 2.4 days! The Canaries, undoubtedly disappointed by their FA Cup elimination, gave it a good shot, but it was too much to ask. Five more points from their last seventeen games would have been enough to get them up. As it is, they got twenty-five points from the thirty-four available, a wholly admirable achievement, but defeats at Bury and Swindon Town, as well as two home draws – Swindon Town again and Tranmere Rovers – sealed their fate. It was to be Division Three for another season.

That they finally made the step up to Division Two at the end of the following season was in no small way down to Macaulay resisting offers from bigger clubs, to repeat his transformations there, in order to see the job that he had started at Norwich through to a conclusion. The Canaries were among the favourites for promotion from the start and justified the faith of the bookies and hopes of their fans by finishing the season as runners-up to Southampton, seven points clear of Shrewsbury in third place, and had the Canaries not lost their home League game to the Saints on 19 December, they would have been champions.

But no matter. Job done. The Canaries would enter a new decade in a new division, a higher division, and even if some heroes – among them Terry Bly – had moved on, many had stuck around, including the inspirational Butler, the man who had admitted that all he knew about his new club upon joining was that they were 'bankrupt', as well as one half of the song's partnership, Errol Crossan – although he finally moved on in December 1960, joining Orient.

Hence the optimism as the decade progressed. Their first season back in Division Two saw Norwich finish in fourth place, with Ipswich Town again stealing the East Anglian thunder by finishing as champions (as well as beating Norwich in both League encounters). Sheffield United and Liverpool took the next two places. Progress was still being made, with every season since that disastrous one of 1956/57 being an improvement on the previous one. But, as the 1961/62 season campaign got underway, it became clear that Macaulay's head had finally been turned by the overtures of another club, and a bigger one at that. West Bromwich Albion, established in the First Division, were engaged in a somewhat indifferent start to their season, winning only three of their first thirteen League games – factors that led to their manager, Gordon Clark, leaving the Hawthorns. Macaulay had no hesitation in accepting the job when it was offered to him, announcing he was leaving following the club's 2-1 win over Swansea Town on 14 October 1961. His departure came as a bitter disappointment to all at the club who had thought, to a man – board, players and fans alike – that the club could have made it all the way to the First Division under his leadership. It was not as if money was tight, or the club's ambitions had been tempered. Shortly before he left, Macaulay signed the England under-23 winger Gerry Mannion from Wolves for £13,000, a not inconsiderable amount at the time. Mannion went on to make 119 League appearances for Norwich, scoring twenty-one goals, so Macaulay's near-to-last act as manager of the club can be considered to have been, as always, typical of the man, who knew his football and a good player when he saw one. Sadly for Macaulay, he never reached the heights expected of him at West Brom, winning only twenty-six of the sixty-seven League games the Baggies played under his stewardship before moving on to Brighton.

After some long and considered thought as to who should replace Macaulay, Norwich appointed Willie Reid his successor. Reid had previously been in charge at St Mirren, and went on to make his own little bit of history at Carrow Road by being the first Norwich manager to guide the club to success in one of the major cup tournaments – the Canaries' 4-0 aggregate win over Rochdale in the final of the 1962 League Cup coming at the end of a largely disappointing League season that had seen them finish seventeenth in the League and only six points clear of what would have been a very unexpected relegation. What was even more surprising was that Reid, barely days after that League Cup success, resigned and returned to Scotland, having been in the job for just six months.

Macaulay and, to a lesser extent, Reid, had left behind a rich legacy. The club was about to commence its third consecutive season in the second tier of English football, the first time they were set to do so since 1938, which had been the last in a brief five-season stay. The club was set to celebrate its sixtieth anniversary, and was in as good a place as regards footballing success and prosperity as it has ever been. Much of the praise should go to Macaulay, while Reid's brief stay at the club should also be acknowledged, for it was he that led the Canaries to that first elusive major trophy. It was a significant, if not spectacular return for the man from Baillieston who found the call of his Scottish homeland too irresistible to refuse, heading home almost as soon as the season had ended but, one can imagine, with a sense of satisfaction about him and a sense of a task well done.

South and Watling could also look back at their involvement at the club with some pride. The club's rapid rise, both in the League and the ability to compete and prosper financially, had been down to their involvement at the Canaries' darkest hour, that ironic time when everyone else was deemed to have never had it so good. Maybe they hadn't then, but they were surely there now? Consolidation in Division Two, plus a trophy that would keep the Norfolk & Norwich Hospital Cup company in an otherwise sparse display case in the club boardroom. But where could they go from here? The obvious answer was completely unchartered territories for the Canaries: Division One.

So, with the scene set and the characters in place, the story of the Canaries' eventful, colourful and occasionally controversial voyage into and through one of the most revered decades in the history of the English game can really begin.

The Canaries went into the 1962/63 season as League Cup holders, and among the favourites for promotion to the First Division. The second tier, was, as it has always been, a tough place to escape, and remember, at this time, there were no play-offs and only the top two clubs were promoted. The contrasting fortunes of clubs making that final leap to the land of milk and honey were perfectly demonstrated by the respective fates of the two clubs that had been promoted to the First Division in 1962. Liverpool, the champions, went on to become a dominant force in both English and European football for over two decades, while Leyton Orient endured just one season among the giants of the game, and were immediately relegated at the end of the subsequent season, eventually finding themselves fighting for scraps back in the Fourth Division. Could Norwich follow their lead and, if so, which route would they take upon promotion? The way of Liverpool seemed highly implausible while the demise of Leyton Orient was hardly desirable. There had, presumably, to be a middle way? Firstly, however, promotion had to be secured and a new manager appointed.

The man chosen by the board to move the club forward was ex-Arsenal player and manager George Swindin, a one-time colleague of Macaulay's. However, like Reid before him, his time in charge at Norwich was woefully short and unmemorable. It seems likely that Swindin, always a Gunner at heart, could not focus on the job in hand or remove the hold that Arsenal still clearly had on his heart – he'd even arrived for work at Norwich in a car that bore the number plate AFC 100. Swindin left the club after just twenty League games played under his management, with the club occupying eleventh place in the League, the position they would also be in at the end of the season. His time at the club was not without its moments – he did break the Canaries' transfer record with the £20,000 acquisition of Tommy Bryceland from St Mirren. It was a sign that, despite the managerial uncertainty at the club (City were now looking for their fourth first-team manager in just over a year) the finances were steady and, given the right man, the foundations were in place for the club to push ahead and achieve that promotion.

After two disappointing appointments at managerial level, the club knew they had to get it right the next time around and, despite a swathe of applicants, looked no further than their own dressing room, giving the job to club captain

Ron Ashman, who must have little suspected upon joining the club that he would end up, at just thirty-six, one of the youngest first-team managers in the Football League.

Ashman certainly had a large squad to choose from when he took on the job. Norwich ended up using twenty-two different players that season, six of them being players that Swindin had brought in during his spell in charge. Bryceland had been his marquee signing (and a good one, he went on to make 281 appearances for the club). However, Swindin had also spent the club's hard-earned money on Jackie Bell (Newcastle), Phil Kelly (Wolves), Alistair Murray (Wolves), Jim Oliver (Falkirk) and Barry Staton (Doncaster Rovers). All bar Murray got their chance under Ashman during the rest of the season but, once again and probably due to another change of manager and all the attendant issues that it can bring, the Canaries' season fizzled out before it had even began, although they did reach the quarter-finals of the FA Cup, with an all-time attendance record of 43,984 packing itself into Carrow Road to see Ashman's side lose 2-0 to Leicester City.

The following campaign was even more disappointing. Ashman made ten appearances as a player before focusing exclusively on his managerial duties, his place as captain being taken over by another inspirational playing figure of that time, Barry Butler. Butler had joined the club in 1957, going on to make 349 League appearances for the Canaries, as well as spending a short time as a club coach, a position that was never his to excel at fully as he unquestionably would have done. Butler being tragically lost to the club and to football in a car crash in April 1966. No book that deals with any part of the history of Norwich City would be complete without a mention and a respectful acknowledgement to Butler for who he was and what he represented – a gentleman and inspirational leader, one who could, in time, have been the Norwich City manager himself.

Butler's tragic death came at the end of yet another mediocre season for Norwich. The Canaries had followed up a lowly seventeenth-place finish in 1964, their first full campaign under Ashman, with a much more encouraging sixth-place finish in 1965. Impressive but disappointing, the club's last ten League games had seen a return of three wins, one draw and six defeats, a poor end to the campaign, which proved to be very costly. Had City won just two of those games that they lost, then they would have been promoted and Ashman would have been the man to have taken them to the summit of football for the very first time. That near miss, coupled with such poor end-of-season form, stayed with the club for the whole of the 1965/66 season, which saw Norwich finish thirteenth, scoring only fifty-two goals, the third lowest in the division. The days of free-scoring strikers like Hunt, Gavin and Bly being on the club's books and reliable for twenty-plus goals every season were long gone, with only Welshman Ron Davies scoring over ten League goals for the club that season. Indeed, without Davies there was probably every chance that Norwich would have gone down. It was a disappointing campaign that ended with the cruel loss of Butler hanging over everyone at Carrow Road. In Davies, at least, there was a glimmer of hope for the following season, one that would follow a World Cup that was being held in England. It seemed, therefore, an act of sheer folly to even consider selling Davies, but that is exactly what happened in the summer of 1966. Norwich succumbed to the advances of Southampton, selling him for just £55,000 to much rancour and criticism among the Norwich support. It remains, to this day, one of the more unfeasible footballing decisions to have been made by any Canary board of directors and suggests just one thing: the club were getting perilously close to being in financial trouble again.

By the time Davies was sold, Ashman had left the club. It was he who had signed the Welshman and he would, no doubt, have played no part in or tolerated selling him. Times were getting tough again at Carrow Road, the euphoria of a cup run, promotion and a cup win had long worn off and, far from pressing on, the Canaries now seemed as if they were set upon mid-table stagnation with the odd cup run thrown in – just as they had been for the first six decades of their history, before it nearly very abruptly ended with that bottom place in the Division Three (South) in 1957.

The club urgently needed another injection of passion, of conviction and character, such as it had been given by Macaulay when he was appointed. The decision was made, with that in mind, to appoint Lol Morgan as the new manager of Norwich City. His brief, as that of his five predecessors, was to push the club ever forward with the ultimate goal of reaching the First Division. The decision to appoint him, however, seemed a strange one. He was, at only thirty-five, a year younger than Ashman had been when he took the post and hardly had a CV that could be waved in the face of his numerous doubters, a Fourth Division runners-up spot with Darlington the previous season being his one managerial 'claim to fame'. He had a tough job on his hands: a board that expected progress and a set of loyal but questioning fans, who were not only dubious about his appointment but also furious at the decision to sell Davies. If Morgan was to get his feet under the table at Carrow Road – and remember, neither Reid nor Swindin had been able to – then he would have to act and act fast in order to impress. He did as most managers would when they want make an impression, he entered the transfer market.

Uppermost in everyone's thoughts at the club had been the need for a commanding centre-half in the shape of a Butler – missed as much for his playing ability as he was a man. Morgan's choice to fill the void was Laurie Brown, who arrived from Tottenham for £25,000, having also played for Arsenal. He was also versatile as time spent playing in attack for Northampton had shown. His stay at Norwich was a short one – signed in September 1966 and leaving for Bradford Park Avenue a little over two years later. Yet he had proved his worth in that time, making eighty-nine League appearances and contributing two goals. Morgan's other signings were Alan Black from Sunderland, Mike Kenning, who came from Charlton, and striker Laurie Sheffield, the £15,000 fee paid to Doncaster for his services having been raised and presented by the Norwich City

Supporters Club – perhaps they had concluded, in the wake of Davies' departure that, if they had a say and financial interest in his replacement, the club would not be so eager to sell?

Sheffield, as it happens, was an immediate hit at Carrow Road, making his debut in the home game against Derby County on 12 November 1966 and promptly scoring a hat-trick in the Canaries' 4-1 win. He went on to end the season with sixteen goals from twenty-five League appearances, a respectable total and enough to remove any lingering longings for Davies, now scoring on a regular basis for Southampton.

A new manager, new players, the possibility of a new hero wearing the No. 9 shirt in Sheffield, and a welcome repeat giant-killing win over Manchester United in the FA Cup as well. However, sadly for Norwich, it was a case of the more things change, the more they stay the same in the League. Their domestic campaign was, to put it mildly, woeful. The Canaries had been marooned at the foot of the table for a few worrying weeks in October 1966, and won only one of their opening twelve fixtures. Morgan shuffled his playing pack constantly – three different left-backs were used that season in Robin Gladwin, Alan Black and Joe Mullett, while again, goalscoring was a problem, with the Canaries' total of forty-nine being the club's worst over a season since 1931. Morgan was, however, given time to build a settled side (after all, he had proven promotion-winning credentials with Darlington). But, at the end of the following season, little had changed. The Canaries finished the 1967/68 season in ninth place, their end-of-season form including a 6-0 defeat at Crystal Palace. It was not a happy day for anyone but especially for second-string goalkeeper Peter Vasper, who was already finding it difficult to prove his worth and ability to fans who had attached themselves to regular custodian Kevin Keelan, who was becoming a Carrow Road favourite.

How frustrating it must have been for Arthur South and Geoffrey Watling, those two members of the triumvirate that had included Archie Macaulay some ten years earlier. Under their visionary and passionate leadership, the club's financial woes had been put to bed and, with the appointment of Macaulay, the club had really started to push on with a thrilling ride to an FA Cup semi-final, promotion and consolidation, plus success in the League Cup under Reid, but with Macaulay's players. Yet, just as everything had seemed to be in place for the club's progress to continue, and even allowing for a couple of seasons' consolidation in Division Two, this progress wasn't being made. In fact, if anything, the club was going backwards again. That promotion in 1960 and the promising first-season finish of fourth had been followed by consecutive ones of seventeenth, eleventh, seventeenth, sixth, thirteenth, eleventh and now ninth – a seven-year average of twelfth – very definitely mid-table. Four managers had come and gone since Macaulay's departure with the fourth, Morgan, being relieved of his duties shortly before the end of the season. The new man would, no doubt, be very swiftly made aware that the Canaries would need to be obviously and very quickly seen to be challenging for promotion. How much time he would get would depend on a number of factors – one of them most certainly being getting Norwich swiftly, and effectively, into the promotion-chasing pack as soon as the new season started. With Morgan having lasted three seasons, the new man would probably get that and no longer. The Carrow Road hot seat was becoming as fiery as the Coleman's mustard that was manufactured a few miles down the road.

Both South and Watling were popular figures, much respected and admired around the club and city. Indeed, it is difficult, even today, to find many people with a bad word to say about either of them, particularly Watling. The fact that, despite their struggles to see the club match their own ambitions, the two of them and the club board as a whole retained the faith of most Norwich supporters, is testament to how they were perceived at the time; even if, at times, some of their decisions – selling Davies and maybe the appointment of Morgan – had been questioned. Their stock remained high.

But, with the decade about to come to an end, their grand project seemed to have reached the buffers. US President John Kennedy had, in September 1962 in an address at Rice University, declared,

> We choose to go to the moon. We choose to go to the moon in this decade and do the other things, not because they are easy, but because they are hard, because that goal will serve to organise and measure the best of our energies and skills, because that challenge is one that we are willing to accept, one we are unwilling to postpone, and one which we intend to win, and the others, too.

It had been quite a statement to make at the time – the US had only put a man into space a year earlier, yet here they were proclaiming that they would have a man walking on the moon at the end of the same decade. South and Watling's dream at the end of the 1950s had been slightly more modest, yet no less spectacular – they chose to put their club in Division One by the end of the next decade, despite being in debt and having only just avoided expulsion from the Football League, a dream that seemed even more difficult to realise than JFK's! Yet the initial progress they had made suggested it could have just been achievable. Now that it was not, and with another new decade on the horizon, they and the club entered the 1969/70 season in a state of some uncertainty – could Norwich make the final leap forward to their own new and unexplored frontier,[1] or had the Canaries gone as far as they could?

Watling and his board were determined to get the right man this time. Possibly chastened by those previous appointments that had not worked out as planned, the club scoured the market, discussing name after name and, in many cases,

---

[1] Meanwhile, on 20 July 1969, the United States did succeed in putting a man on the moon.

disregarding them. They were focused on just one thing, getting someone who would not recoil at their demands, expectations that a lesser candidate might have deemed unrealistic. But not Geoffrey Watling.

First impressions of him may have given the casual observer the idea that this was a quiet, understated man, one who was gentle in manner and easy in the way he lived life. Far from it. He was an extraordinarily successful local businessman, one who took over the family concern when he was just sixteen and who, over the course of his life, owned over 200 other businesses, ranging from cafés and ice cream factories to ballrooms. Such was his passion for ballroom music that he became an instrumental figure in bringing some of the big US bands over to play in the UK, his friends in that business including Count Basie. Businessman and impresario, there seemed little that he would not turn his hand to. But Watling liked to play as well as work hard. He owned a fleet of fast cars, including a Buick, an Aston Martin and numerous Jaguars, as well as three speedboats that he raced at Oulton, one of the Norfolk Broads. His commitment to whatever he was involved in was total, and this now very definitely included Norwich City Football Club. For the club to succeed, he must have surmised, it needed a man similar to himself at the helm. Someone who was ambitious and focused, a disciplinarian who would stop at nothing to meet his goals, a man who would give total commitment and effort and, in turn, would expect it from the people who worked under him. Such men, particularly in football, as Watling was learning, were thin on the ground. Yet his perseverance and determination to find the right man was, finally, about to pay off and his efforts were rewarded at that footballing hotbed of Oxford United.

The man who Watling had determined would, finally, be the one to lead Norwich City to Division One was Ron Saunders. Saunders had previously been in charge at the then non-League Yeovil Town, followed by a short spell with Division Three side Oxford United. The Us were, understandably, reluctant to lose their much-thought-of young manager so soon after he had joined them, but nothing was going to stop Watling from getting his man now. Saunders was duly appointed Norwich City manager in time for the start of the 1969/70 season, Watling stating at the time of his appointment that Saunders was one of the best-paid managers in the Second Division – quite an admission for the normally parsimonious Norwich board to take and one which, in its saying, put a lot of immediate pressure onto Saunders. If he had been in any doubt as to what he was expected to achieve at his new club, that statement, publicly made by his chairman, would have underlined it. A new decade was about to dawn and a new manager was in place at Carrow Road to greet it.

New decade, new dawn, and new beginnings. The time was right. Now Saunders had to deliver.

2

SORTING THEM OUT

Some good players. Some not so good. Some good types of players, you know, as individuals, some not so good types. And obviously the problem was to sort them out.

Ron Saunders had swept into Carrow Road in the summer of 1969 with all the finesse of a wrecking ball. Yet that is not a statement designed to denigrate the man – far from it. For too long now, the men in charge at Carrow Road had delivered an open and honest intent about where they saw the club going and what their ambitions for it were. These were hopes and dreams that extended far beyond a 'plucky' cup run and the occasional day in the sun they engendered. They wanted more and in Saunders were convinced that they had found the man that could make that happen.

Watling's claim at the club's AGM that August about how the new man at the helm was one of the best paid in the division makes it sound as if the club had spared no expense in recruiting Saunders, and had made him an offer that he could not refuse. What is perhaps equally likely is that, when he was first approached for the job, Saunders had decided to call Watling's bluff and see just how serious he was about his offer, asking for a salary and, no doubt, certain guarantees, as he thought Norwich would only respond in a favourable manner if their ambition was as genuine as they claimed. If that was the case, it was the first – but most certainly not the last – time that Saunders had faced his so-called superiors full on and made it clear what he was expecting from them. Again, not for the first time, it had worked. Saunders got the package he had asked for as well as a transfer budget and full control over all aspects of the footballing side of the football club. If the buck was to stop at his door then he expected to be able to play it just as he wanted, which he then proceeded to do.

One member of the playing staff who remembers the immediate impact that the appointment of Saunders had on the club was a man who went on to become a future manager of Norwich himself, Dave Stringer. He recalls the day that the players turned up for pre-season training under him and how, right from day one, Saunders had impressed upon his charges that things were going to be different. The old way things were done at Norwich was at an end.

People speak today of the 'Costa del Colney' culture that seemed engrained at the club during some of its more fallow years in the late 1990s and the early part of the twenty-first century; an easy come, easy go time of complacency and slipping standards around the club and training ground that were only reversed when another disciplinarian, Nigel Worthington, took charge at the club. True, there was no Colney when Saunders arrived at Norwich, and the training facilities, such as they were at Trowse, were rather more basic. Nevertheless, that same atmosphere of decay, of complacency and lazy routine, had still slipped into place, typified by those disappointing League finishes as the sixties drew to a close, with Norwich remaining a club that could briefly shine and show what they might be made of, as in the FA Cup success over Manchester United in February 1967 – a 2-1 win that made the country remember the name and wonder what Norwich 'were up to these days?'. Not very much as it turned out. A week after that remarkable win, the Canaries huffed and puffed their way to a tedious 1-0 win over Bristol City in a League game at Carrow Road, before going on a run of games that saw just one victory out of six. Normal service had been resumed.

Stringer could see the new man wasn't going to have any of that. He described Saunders as being the type of man who expected nothing but hard work. If you were prepared to do that then you could stick around. If you weren't – or couldn't – then you were out of the door. The phrase 'my way or the highway' was never more apt. Stringer shared the ambitions of the club; he had joined Norwich with the idea of furthering his career and enjoying some success. The appointment of Saunders, in all likelihood, did enough to convince players like Stringer to stay. First impressions count for a lot in football; they always have and always will. Hence, on that first morning of training, Stringer was convinced, saying,

> I always remember when he first came in, the first day he stripped off – it was sunshine, pre-season and his upper body was like chipped out of bleeding marble. He was this really strong-looking fella, really solid. He sat on the ball in the middle and he said: 'Right, I want to go to the top – I want to get promotion. Anyone who doesn't want to come with me, I'll see them in the office at 12 o'clock and you can go.'[2]

The impact on Stringer was immediate. He thought, 'You'll do me!'

Saunders' tunnel vision was publicly demonstrated when he gave an interview for a local television station shortly after the Canaries had achieved that 'mission impossible' of promotion in 1972. Asked by the interviewer about his initial thoughts on the playing squad he had inherited when he took on the job as manager, Saunders, deadpan, fixed a steely eye on him and answered, 'A mixed one. Some good players, some not so good. Some good types of players, you know, as individuals, some not so good types. And, obviously ... *(telling pause)* ... the problem was to sort them out.'

---

[2] Waghorn, Rick, *12 Canary Greats* (Jarrold Publishing, 2004), p. 54.

'What was the first thing you did?' mooted the interviewer.

'I sorted them out.'

No doubts there then.

Stringer, immediately impressed with Saunders' no-nonsense attitude – and how could you argue with the methods of a man who not only looked fitter, but probably was fitter than many of the players he had inherited – talks of the new man demanding a change in his charges' mindset, as well as an improvement in their physical condition, recollecting that, 'We had more determination all round. All of the players were dedicated to one thing: promotion. Training was very painful. We had to go through a lot of hard work. It was, you know ... quite painful.' For a man as hard as Stringer to admit to feeling the pain, as well as the pressure in training, it spoke volumes of the new broom sweeping the dust and complacency of the sixties away at Carrow Road.

There is a wonderful film clip that illustrates exactly what Stringer has described. It is a brutally hot day on Mousehold Heath, an area of woodland that lies north-east to the city. Saunders has taken his men there for the day, but it is for no gentle ramble in the countryside and is certainly no picnic. He has annexed the top of one of the steep slopes that rise ever upwards near the old Britannia Barracks and is standing, stripped to his chiselled waist, astride the peak, watching, much like a warrior king of old, as his foot soldiers, grim-faced and dripping with sweat, bunny-hop their way up towards him. None of them are slacking and none of them want to be last to the top. The effort on their faces etches deep creases into them and the exertion required is palpable. Saunders observes, saying nothing. He is at the top and that is where they must join him. He doesn't shout, order, encourage or cajole. He just stands there, watching, waiting. It looks harsh. And it was, and once they had all reached him, he would then send them all down to do it again. And again. He was forging winners.

So who was this man who had made such an impact on the club, who had compelled Watling to not only personally headhunt him but agree to that wage package that not only made him one of the best-paid managers in the Second Division, but one who was probably as well paid as some of his peers in the First. What was it about Ron Saunders?

His time as a player had not suggested a career in management that would focus on defensive rigidity and on-field discipline. Far from it. Saunders had enjoyed terrorising opposing defences as a free-scoring centre-forward, enjoying a particularly productive spell at Portsmouth where, from 1958 to 1964, he scored 145 goals in 236 games – an average of around 0.62 per game, one that, were a Premier League striker to emulate it today, would yield an impressive twenty-four goals in a season. It was little wonder, therefore, that he was Portsmouth's top scorer in each of his six seasons at the club. Prior to joining Pompey in 1958, Saunders had been at Gillingham, where his free-scoring abilities had been noted at non-League Tonbridge – including one season in which Ron had contributed four hat-tricks. He didn't take long to find the net with that same chilling regularity at Gillingham either, ending the 1957/58 season with twenty-four League and cup goals, the latter of which had included a haul of five – plus a missed penalty – in a 10-1 FA Cup romp over Norfolk non-League side Gorleston, bringing his name to the attention of the football-supporting folk in the county for the first time in doing so

After his productive time on the South Coast with Portsmouth had come to an end, Saunders joined Watford, spending just one season at Vicarage Road before moving to Charlton. He retired as a player in 1967, having scored over 200 goals over thirteen years as a player, the one notable disappointment, perhaps, of his playing career being his release right at the start of it by Everton after just three appearances for the Toffees in the 1954/55 season. It would be apt, therefore, that having not been given the opportunity to establish himself as a player with the Goodison Park club, Saunders would at least get the chance to come up against them again in his first match as a top-flight manager.

His entry into football coaching, after his playing days had come to an end, was with the then non-League Yeovil Town, who he joined as player-manager in the summer of 1967, making an immediate impact at the club by signing four new players, including Ken Jones – who Saunders first met during his brief spell at Charlton – a goalkeeper renowned for his ability to kick the ball very high and very long, typically into an opposing team's penalty area; a sign, perhaps, of the tactics to come?

Initial results were impressive. By the end of September 1967, Yeovil were second in the Southern League table, their upwardly mobile progress under Saunders on the field being reflected with an average home gate of 3,000 (not that far short of their League One average for the 2011/12 season, which was 3,955) and a run to the FA Cup first-round 'proper', where, disappointingly, they lost to fellow non-League side and playing contemporaries Margate, in front of a crowd of 6,322. Their League form, which had slightly fallen away, picked up again by the New Year, and that January the club were able, thanks to the increased gates they were getting under Saunders, to make their first 'proper' transfer signing in many years, paying just under £700 for Cliff Myers, who joined from Brentford. Myers became the one lasting legacy that Saunders gave the club during his time there, going on to make 328 appearances for the club, scoring eighty-four goals in the process. As far as the here and now was concerned, however, the signing of Myers was a footballing and commercial triumph for the club – a renowned player at a higher level who had not only chosen to drop into non-League football but, in doing so, was subscribing to Saunders and his plans for the club, plans that were continuing apace as he rebuilt Yeovil from top to bottom. Myers was one of fourteen different players Saunders brought to the club in that first season!

Yeovil's on- and off-field progress soon came to the attention of several Football League sides and, in time, it was inevitable that they would lose their bright and fiercely ambitious young manager. Even so, when the time did come for him to leave Huish and its famous sloping pitch, his destination was something of a surprise, as Oxford United were then a Second Division (now Championship) club. Indeed, it was the first time that any football manager had left a non-League team to take the helm at one so loftily placed – a modern-day comparison might be to see the manager of a current non-League side like Havant and Waterlooville join Peterborough United, not completely improbable but certainly enough to raise eyebrows, especially at the new club. Nevertheless, that is exactly what happened and Saunders arrived at Manor Ground with the same determination and ambition he had taken to Yeovil, who were, it is fair to say, beginning to prosper all-round as a result of his tenure there.

But if Saunders had gone to Yeovil to rebuild and rebrand a football club, his task at Oxford was to be nothing so grandiose and long term. They had got him in, doubling his salary in the process, purely as a firefighter. When he arrived at the club in February 1969, things were looking bleak at the Manor Ground; a 2-1 defeat at Preston cementing their place in twenty-first position in the table, and with a tough fixture at Bolton Wanderers looming on the horizon. Saunders immediately battened down the hatches, his new charges earning their first away point, after six attempts, with a creditable 1-1 draw. They then followed this up with a convincing win at home against Portsmouth, the club where Saunders had made his name as a player.

Another five wins from their remaining ten League games followed, the stand-out success probably being the 1-0 win at Fulham in one of those definitive four-pointers (as they were then) that make or break a club's season at that late stage. Two consecutive home wins against Blackburn Rovers and Aston Villa followed and, suddenly and quite remarkably, the Us were safe, finishing the season in twentieth place, three points ahead of Bury. Job done and plaudits all round for Saunders. He had, however, joined the club having not signed a contract, the Us no doubt taking out a precaution against having a highly paid manager in the Third Division, should the worst have happened. It hadn't and, despite the club's management now wanting to tie him down to a long-term deal to continue what he had started, it was too late. Saunders had bigger clubs and challenges waiting for him on the horizon, with Norwich ultimately making him the offer that he couldn't refuse, one that involved getting them out of the division in the right way – promotion.

This was the man who Watling had wanted – a footballing mirror image of himself, someone who took on a challenge and made it work before moving on to the next one and doing it all over again. Saunders had started a mini footballing revolution at Yeovil, raising the club's standing and standards on and off the field before taking on a perceived mission impossible (hence the lack of a contract) at Oxford, and succeeding with room to spare. His stock in the game was high and on the rise. He was now expected to continue his rise in the managerial ranks at Carrow Road.

At least, upon his arrival at Norwich, Saunders had found a squad that, although by his public admittance it needed to be 'sorted out', had some quality in its playing ranks. Eight of the players that Lol Morgan had selected for his last game in charge featured in the first line-up of Saunders' tenure, the only notable absentee being Terry Allcock, who had retired from playing. Thus only two of Morgan's final XI missed out on the opening day of the 1969/70 season, namely Clive Payne and Trevor Howard – both of whom would still make playing contributions that campaign. Of the others that Saunders had to call upon, Stringer, whose youthful promise had included trials at Arsenal and Crystal Palace as well as an England youth cap, was a stand-out performer, as was the man who shared the distinction of playing in every one of the club's forty-four League and cup matches that season, Kevin Keelan – already a relative Canary veteran with over 200 appearances to his name. It was to be those two players, together with Stringer's comrade-in-arms in the Norwich defence, Duncan Forbes, who would become the bedrock of Saunders' Norwich side, all three players deeply in-filled with a fierce will to win. Keelan, a fitness fanatic, revelled in the demands Saunders made of his players in training, enjoying the opportunity to train, learn and improve his game, season after season, a dedication which resulted in him not only becoming Norwich City's record appearance holder but, for a number of seasons, one of the leading goalkeepers in the country. With that trio, Saunders knew that he had the beginnings of a strong side and, as the 1969/70 season progressed, he lightly tinkered with it, bringing in just two names of significance in the early weeks – striker Peter Silvester from Reading in September, and the midfield artistry of Graham Paddon, signed from Coventry City, a week later.

Silvester's arrival at the club was the beginning of the end of fellow forward Bryan Conlon's time at Carrow Road. Conlon had arrived as one of Lol Morgan's last signings, a big and physical player who had scored fourteen goals in forty-one appearances for Millwall. He started the first eight games of that season, scoring two goals – both in a 2-1 Carrow Road victory over Hull City – but found his way to the sort of first-team permanence enjoyed by the likes of Keelan, Stringer and Forbes threatened by the arrival of Silvester, as well as emergin youngster Neil O'Donnell. Indeed, Silvester went straight into the team following his arrival at the club.

The suggestion that Conlon was maybe one of those players who Saunders had described as 'not so good types' seems reasonable, especially when his performance in the game against Blackburn Rovers on 31 January 1970 is taken into consideration with Conlon reacting to being replaced in the second half by Gerry Howshall by taking off his shirt and dramatically throwing it to the ground in front of his stony-faced manager. Had Saunders had a little black book there is little doubt that, if Conlon's name was not already in it, it certainly was after that episode. He went on to play in just two more games for the club, filling in for Silvester, who was injured, before being shipped out to Blackburn Rovers; Saunders electing to bring in Malcolm Darling as part of the deal. Conlon had, as had Tommy Bryceland and Charlie Crickmore before him, been found as surplus to requirements. With the arrival of the youthful Silvester (twenty-one) and Paddon (nineteen) earlier in the season preceding the eventual departures of Crickmore (twenty-seven), Bryceland (twenty-nine) and Conlon (twenty-six), it became clear that Saunders was, just as he had at Yeovil, building a team and a squad for the long term; adding youth and potential to the core of the side he already had while shipping out those who he saw as having no real part to play in the club's future. But, unlike at Yeovil, where the arrival of fourteen new players in his first few months at the club had signalled revolution, Saunders was instigating a policy of evolution at Norwich, making the point to Watling and the club board that while promotion to the First Division was a realistic and workable target, the task in hand would take time. This meant that the chairman's long hoped-for dream of First Division football, something he had originally asked of Archie Macaulay over a decade earlier, remained on hold. In a game between two hard-nosed, ambitious, occasionally fiery characters, Saunders had won – for now. But he knew he had to deliver within the three years he had said was needed prior to his appointment.

All of this meant that, as Norwich prepared for their first fixture of the 1970s, an FA Cup third-round tie at home to Wrexham, the Canaries were not, as many would have hoped, or even expected, leading the promotion-chasing pack at the top of the table. Far from it. The Canaries headed off for FA Cup duty in sixteenth place, having lost six of their previous nine fixtures, and were now just three points off the relegation places. Unthinkable. Were there, even at this early stage, dissenting voices beginning to question the wisdom of appointing Saunders? There had, after all, been no shortage of other candidates the previous summer. Ken Furphy had been one. He'd led Sheffield United to promotion from the Division Two. The knowledgeable and respected Alec Stock had been another. Hadn't they been approached? Any doubts that may have been raised about Saunders' abilities may well have been spoken rather than whispered after the club tumbled out of the FA Cup at the first attempt, their 2-1 loss to Wrexham rather more convincing than the scoreline suggests. This defeat, coupled with an early exit from the League Cup as well as their poor form in the League, meant that Norwich entered the new decade with little or nothing to play for this state of affairs being reflected in the attendance for the following week's League game against Bristol City – only 6,523 turning up at Carrow Road for that game, the club's lowest figures of the season. This was disappointing, not for those that went who witnessed the 4-1 victory, but for the club as a whole who were investing in Saunders and backing his plans with funding as and when he had asked for it. Silvester, as exciting a prospect as had been seen at Carrow Road for many seasons, weighing in on that afternoon with two goals and a sparkling display.

That game was, however, a sign of things to come. On 4 April, Norwich travelled to Portsmouth and won by the same scoreline, Albert Bennett scoring a hat-trick. Bennett had, by this stage of his Norwich career, become something of an enigma

– a wonderfully talented player who stood out in the crowd by sporting a pair of white boots whenever he took to the field of play. Traditional black football boots are almost a rarity in the modern game, with manufacturers keen to use every colour in the rainbow to make their brand stand out. In Bennett's day, however, wearing boots that were not considered *de rigueur* tended to attract attention, and mostly from the terraces. It wasn't enough that you became an immediate focus of the opposing support (as well as their team), but you were also expected by your own fans to do something on the pitch that merited your perceived status of being a 'special one'. Bennett stood out so Bennett had to deliver.

He'd joined Norwich in February 1969 from Newcastle United, a short trip north from Chester-le-Street, the place of his birth. While at Newcastle, Albert had been given the nickname 'Ankles', in recognition of the ongoing injury and fitness concerns he had with them throughout his caree – a mighty obstacle for any aspiring footballer to overcome, much more so for one who relied upon pace and trickery, and who drew particular attention to the most vulnerable part of his body by wearing those white boots! Cynics among the Carrow Road faithful might have said that signing Bennett was a sharp piece of PR, performed in order to nullify supporter outrage at the sale of Hugh Curran to the Wolves less than a month earlier – and with some justification.

Curran had been the club's leading goalscorer in both the 1967/68 and 1968/69 seasons but, like Ron Davies three years earlier, he had been sacrificed at the altar of the club's bankers. The income and profits the Canaries could make from the sale of players was as crucial then as it would be in decades to come. Bennett was, therefore, the latest in a long line of attacking players bought by the club to replace a former favourite. It was all so familiar. Back in 1960, Terry Bly, a fan favourite if ever there was one, had been sold to Peterborough United. He had been replaced, eventually, in the affections of Norwich fans by Davies, who had himself been whitewashed over by the arrival of Curran, bought, not to play alongside him as had been first thought, but to replace him. Now Curran had gone and Bennett had arrived. These comings and goings at Carrow Road were surely not worthy of a club that pronounced itself to be ambitious and wanting to reach the top division – selling your best players and goalscorers on such a regular basis was never going to help that become a reality. In Bennett, both supporters and club hoped they finally had someone to hang the promotion hat on and who would turn out to be the player that would drive the club forward. Saunders certainly seemed to think so; he picked Bennett for every game that he was fit enough for during the 1969/70 season. Bennett repaid in kind with eight goals from twenty-six League appearances, culminating that season with three goals against Portsmouth; a game that seemed, finally, to mark Norwich out as contenders, even though they again sat in mid-table.

Was the result at Fratton Park a fluke? Not by any means. Norwich's penultimate game of the season was against Birmingham City, who had seen the Canaries off to the tune of 3-1 in the game at St Andrews. Birmingham had also endured a disappointing season and were destined to finish it in eighteenth place, a mere four points ahead of relegated Aston Villa, but even so, their determination to succeed and get promotion was as strong as it was at Norwich, and never more evident than in the appointment of Stan Cullis as their manager in 1965.

Cullis had previously led Wolves to three League championship successes and two FA Cup wins in a glittering spell of success at Molineux that has never been repeated, including, according to Cullis himself, being awarded the sobriquet 'champions of the world' after Wolves had beaten Hungarian side Honved in a friendly – then rated the world's best. Birmingham had outlined their ambition big time in appointing Cullis, and had probably strengthened it in accepting his surprise resignation without making too much of an attempt to persuade him to stay on. It was going to be interesting to track both sides' developments over the coming seasons.

Norwich certainly had the upper hand at the beginning of the decade. Saunders efforts – or rather that of his players' blood, sweat and tears – on the slopes of Mousehold Heath were beginning to bear fruit, and Norwich's 6-0 victory in front of just 12,134 fans was testimony to the resilience and all-round physical fitness that Saunders had imbued in his players. The goalscorers on the day were a spread of the old and the new. Ken Foggo had weighed in with two, while Bennett had also contributed his fifth goal in four games. Both had survived the Saunders cull the previous summer and had, to repeat the manager's lexicon, not needed to be 'sorted out'.

The other scorers, Peter Silvester and Graham Paddon, were Saunders' signings and both were rapidly making themselves key members of the side. To add insult to the away day blues of the Blues, they also conceded an own goal, the unfortunate Ray Martin getting in the way of a Paddon shot. It was Norwich's eleventh game without defeat, and their biggest League win since they had beaten Stoke City by the same score seven years earlier. The future seemed brighter for the club than it had been for many years and, with players of the obvious calibre of Bennett, Foggo, Silvester and Paddon making an impact, the morale of the club's support going into the summer of 1970 was more upbeat than it had been for a long, long time.

If the fans were optimistic that the 1970/71 season was going to be the one that finally saw the club reach the big time, Saunders had certainly not given them any fuel from which they could ignite their excitement at the season to come. He kept things ticking over during that summer with emphasis, as always, on fitness and physique at the training ground, and it is extremely likely that he was keeping things in perspective. He had arrived at the club with the intention of delivering that elusive promotion within three years, and he still had two in which to do it. But, if he was to push his intentions – and very probably the club's patience – to the limit, then this first season of the new decade was not so much about laying foundations as putting the final pieces into place for an all-out assault the following season. He certainly started as he meant to go on.

The club's pre-season tour was to be held in Yugoslavia (that part of the country which City visited is now part of modern-day Serbia), with three matches lined up in six days against opposition who, if they were not quite the giants of the Yugoslavian game – think Red Star Belgrade and Hadjuk Split – they would certainly be hard-working, hard-running, hard-tackling opponents. In other words, exactly the sort of opposition Saunders would have wanted. Just over a year earlier the team had travelled out to Benidorm for a friendly, but the trip had turned into something of a jolly, with Norwich scraping a 1-0 win. Not this time. The first game, against Radnicki, swiftly turned into a wake-up call for mind and bodies that had been softened by a few weeks' holiday, the then Yugoslavian Cup holders dispatching City 2-0 with some ease. The following game, against Vojvodina, yielded some improvement with a 1-1 draw, and was followed by a win in the last game with a 2-1 success over Bor. It was a run of results that seemed to typify Norwich as they grew under Saunders: disappointment followed by consolidation and some improvement with modest success at the end – a microcosm of the season just ended, which had started with just four wins from their opening twelve League fixtures and ended with them being undefeated in their final twelve.

The Canaries started the new campaign with a home game against Portsmouth, the team they had, with the help of Albert Bennett's superb hat-trick, seen off in such style the previous April. Saunders had shopped lightly in pre-season, the only incoming player being winger Malcolm Darling from Blackburn in a straight swap with Bryan Conlon, and even that bit of business had been carried out in May, meaning the terrors of Mousehold would have been waiting for Darling from day one.

In addition to Darling's arrival, Saunders promoted three of the club's aspiring young players into the first-team squad, with two of them, locally born Glenn Self and Steve Grapes, signing professional forms. The third, utility player Steve Goodwin, would follow later in the season. Little change therefore and, unsurprisingly, the team selected by Saunders for the Portsmouth match was exactly the same as the one that had ended the previous campaign against Watford bar one – Ken Mallender coming in for the injured Stringer. That team was as follows; Keelan, Butler, Black, Mallender, Forbes, Howard, Briggs, Bennett, Silvester, Paddon and Foggo. The result, a rather turgid 1-1 draw, enlivened only by Silvester's second-half strike, was disappointing given the pre-season optimism, as was the following game, another draw – this time a 0-0 against newly promoted Luton Town. Stringer's return at the expense of Mallender gave the side some added defensive stability in a run of six games that saw four clean sheets. Impressive stuff aided and abetted by the form and flexibility of the original goalkeeping 'cat', Kevin Keelan. Like all good managers, Saunders was building from the back, and it was starting to show.

That defensive resolution characterised Norwich for the entire season, one in which the Canaries only conceded more than two goals in a League game three times. The club's worst defeat, a 5-0 pounding at Middlesbrough on 6 February, might have suggested to Saunders that it was time to reflect on the capabilities of his back four at what is always a pivotal time of the season. However, true to form and loyal to a man, he selected the same team for the club's next game against Bristol City and was rewarded with the sort of performance that might just have given him reason to smile. For, 2-0 down and in seeming freefall at half-time at Carrow Road, Norwich rallied in the second half with goals from Bennett (injury-stricken again, it had been his first start and full game since the previous October), Silvester and Terry Anderson. Another disappointing defeat followed a week later, this time at Leicester City, who would end the season as champions. Norwich was 1-0 up at half-time, thanks to a typical opportunistic Foggo strike, but they faded in the second half, with Rodney Fern and Malcolm Partridge scoring for the Foxes. What was more disappointing for Norwich, however, was the loss, again, of Bennett to injury in that game, the third time that season he'd needed to be replaced (substitutions at that time were almost exclusively to replace injured players rather than of a tactical nature), and the sixth time in his Norwich career.

Sadly, for both club and player, this was an injury too far for Bennett. His ankles had taken too many knocks over the course of his career and this latest one was a knock of a more personal nature, convincing him that it was time to retire from the game. He was just twenty-six. It felt, with Bennett's retirement, as if the last spark had gone from Norwich's season, one that had yielded so much promise with that unbeaten run and those promising results at the end of the previous season, with Bennett one of its stars. He had ended it with six goals from nine matches, and made countless more for the likes of Foggo and Silvester. He was a popular player at the club with both his teammates and the supporters, and, notably for a player of his type, had impressed the normally dour Saunders with his natural ability to be able to pick a pass, use his pace productively and score important goals – none more so than that hat-trick at Portsmouth. It was felt, at the time, that every time the Canaries found a player who they could pin some of those considerable hopes on, he was lost to them – Bennett through injury, and Davies and Curran through transfers. Malcolm Darling filled the void left by Bennett and contributed four goals from twelve League appearances, but he was never going to be a long-term solution for the gap in the Canaries' front line. Norwich saw out the season with the occasional good result – a 3-0 win over Sunderland on 27 March stands out – however, despite the fact that win meant they were just four points adrift of second place, they were stranded in ninth place, with every team that was above them at that time having games in hand. The promotion dream was already over, as was Albert Bennett's career. It was a sad conclusion to a season that had started with such high hopes.

Yet, in among the disappointment there was still hope. Saunders was fashioning a side and a type of play that was consistent and, at least when it all came off, highly effective – those convincing wins over Portsmouth and Birmingham City at the end of the previous season had pointed to that. Equally impressive ones this time around against Charlton Athletic (2-0), Orient (4-2), Sunderland (3-0) and QPR (3-0) were again evidence of the strength and potential of Saunders' Norwich. The problem with the Canaries was that they were too inconsistent. These laudable victories would inevitably be followed by a disappointing defeat (a week after comprehensively outplaying QPR at Carrow Road, Norwich made the long but hardly fearsome trip north to play Carlisle United and lost 4-2) or a run of games without a win, including a stretch of five at one point, and three banks of four games without a victory. In addition to that, the club's away form was very poor, with only four wins from their twenty-one fixtures away from Carrow Road, including eight defeats in their last eleven away League games. The last home game of the season, against promotion-chasing Cardiff City, brought in a more than respectable attendance of 15,088 (home gates had previously dipped below 10,000 on three occasions that season), all keen to see the Canaries end their Carrow Road campaign on a high, just as they had the previous season with two consecutive victories. They were to be disappointed, however, the game ending in a 2-1 win for the (then) Bluebirds – Peter Silvester's second-half consolation effort, his fifteenth League goal of the season, the only bright moment for the Canary fans to savour.

A week later, Norwich travelled to Hull City, losing again, 1-0. Those last dozen games had seen Norwich rack up an uncomfortable-looking four defeats, the impressive victory over QPR the one spark of light Canaries fans could tether their hopes to over the summer as yet another campaign ended in mediocrity – the tenth in a row.

A decade of mid-table comfort in Division Two: that sort of respectability might have found favour with both the club hierarchy and the supporters once upon a time but that was no longer the case. Norwich had flirted with the previously outrageous notion of playing at the top level back in the 1960/61 season, when they had finished fourth in the table following promotion under Archie Macaulay the previous campaign. They'd even, through August and September of that season, flirted with topping the table, as close then as any Norwich City side had ever been to the highest echelon of English football. Their eventual failing that season was through lack of goals. Seventy goals in forty-two League games sounds a reasonable total now, yet back then it was one that was superior to only eight of their divisional rivals, seven of which had finished in the bottom eight places. Champions Ipswich Town had led the way with exactly 100 goals in their League games, with runners-up Sheffield United scoring eighty-one. Even Bristol Rovers, down in seventeenth place and only four points clear from relegation, had hit the back of the opponents' net on seventy-three occasions. Ray Crawford had led the line for Ipswich in spectacular fashion, scoring thirty-nine goals over the season; twenty-three more than Terry Allcock, who had finished with sixteen goals – the only Canary to break double figures during that campaign.

Ten years on and Norwich were still struggling to score the volume of goals that any promoted side might be expected to have. The denouement of the

1970/71 season saw them total fifty-four League goals from their forty-two League games, a total that was bettered by all but nine of their divisional peers. Ken Foggo and Peter Silvester had manfully led the line between them with fifteen League goals each, but after that, the goalscoring responsibilities had been spread very thinly, with the club's remaining goals being spread around eight different players, one of whom had been the unfortunate Albert Bennett.

If the Canaries were to push forward and make progress of any kind the following season – the last, it might reasonably be assumed, that the impatient board would have given to Saunders to deliver – then the side's penalty area frailties would have to be addressed and a new striker found in time for the following August. Norwich fans have always hung their flat caps on a bustling centre-forward (think Grant Holt, the latest in a long and respectable dynasty). So, with Silvester and Foggo clearly in need of what a future Norwich manager would memorably term 'a helping hand', they waited for developments. There were certainly options available. Middlesbrough's John Hickton had been the divisional top-scorer for the past two seasons, having ended this one with twenty-five goals. He was a powerful, hard-working and running centre-forward of the 'old school'; physical and broaching no nonsense from opponent or teammate alike – if ever there was a Saunders 'identikit' player, then surely it was Hickton. Then there was a young striker making his name on the South Coast with Bournemouth, Ted MacDougall. He'd ended the season with a staggering forty-two League goals, only a dozen shy of Norwich's total for the entire season – surely a goal-shy team like Norwich would have to be interested? It was true that MacDougall's reputation for on-field laziness and an attitude that occasionally seemed to border on surly wouldn't endear him to the disciplined and regimented regime that Saunders expected his players to buy into, but even so, if MacDougall could repeat those efforts in the yellow and green, then surely the considerable investment that would have been needed to secure his signature would have been worth it? Apparently not. The usual speculation, fuelled only by newspaper tittle-tattle at that time, came and went but no one of any significance arrived at Carrow Road that summer, and it looked for all the world as if Saunders was going to stick with his tried and trusted players as the new season approached, disregarding the very obvious weakness in the Canary ranks – the side's ability to score goals, the Achilles heel that seemed to be a permanent barrier to promotion.

But Saunders was already very well aware of his side's weaknesses. And was ready to put it right.

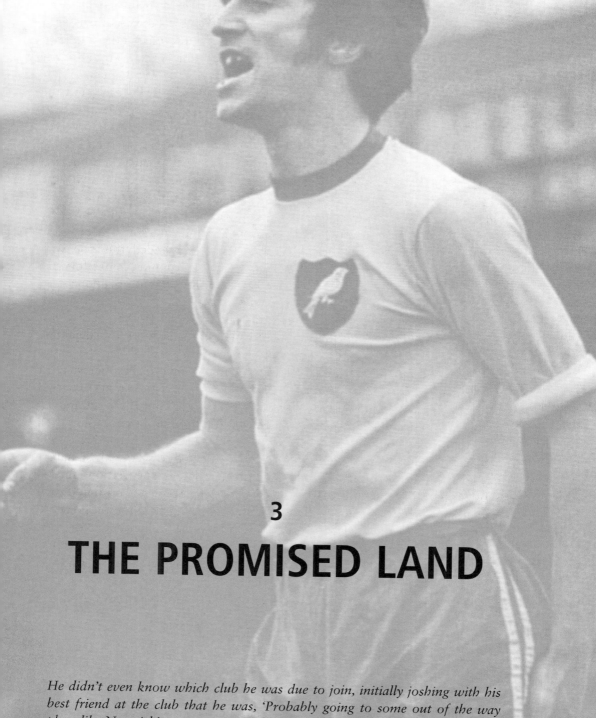

3
THE PROMISED LAND

He didn't even know which club he was due to join, initially joshing with his best friend at the club that he was, 'Probably going to some out of the way place like Norwich'.

The summer of 1970 had seen the English domestic season commence on a post-World Cup high. True, England had surrendered their crown as World Champions in the unremitting heat and humidity of Mexico, but it was generally agreed that the squad that Alf Ramsey was putting together was, potentially, going to be even better than the one that had triumphed at Wembley in 1966. And, while some of the England players that had served their nation so well in the tournaments were thought to be approaching the end of their international careers, there were very high hopes for the burgeoning crop of young players; names like Allan Clarke and Peter Osgood swiftly becoming as much household names as the two Bobbys, Moore and Charlton.

At Carrow Road there was also hope for the future in the form of the Canaries' own youngsters as the 1971/72 season approached. Some had already had their first experience of first-team football at the club. Right-sided midfielder Neil O'Donnell had been one of them; his debut had been under the tutelage of Lol Morgan in December 1967 but, even three-and-a-half years from then, the Scottish Youth International was still just twenty-one, and desperate to impress Saunders in time for the new campaign. Another who the Canaries had high hopes for was the versatile Steve Goodwin. He had made his Canaries debut while still an apprentice at the club in the defeat at Hull City on the final day of the previous season, replacing yet another youngster, Norwich-born Steve Grapes, who was just seventeen when he made his debut that March. The final member of the quartet was perhaps regarded as the most promising of them all. Govier was a centre-half by trade, not a particularly physical one as was the trend at the time, but standing at exactly 6 feet he was an early forerunner of the trend for sides to pick a more mobile, ball-playing centre-half alongside the old-fashioned 'stopper' – as was already being illustrated by Roy McFarland at Derby County and Kevin Lock at West Ham. With finances as closely managed as ever at Carrow Road, it was essential for the club to be able to develop, nurture and bring through their own young talent into the first team, especially with transfer fees now starting to rocket ever higher. Tottenham's signing of Martin Peters from West Ham for £200,000 back in March 1970 broke that particular barrier. In contrast, the most that Norwich had ever paid for a player was the £40,000 they had spent in securing the signature of Sheffield United defender Ken Mallender in October 1968, a notable investment that did not turn out for the club as they might have hoped.

That combination of economic caution plus the emergence of young talent such as O'Donnell, Goodwin, Grapes and Govier meant that there was, as was now the trend, very little transfer activity in or out of Carrow Road in the weeks leading up to the 1971/72 season. Indeed, once the previous season had finished there were rather more pressing issues for the club to deal with, not least the very future of the ground itself. The stadium and its immediate surrounds had stood on ground that belonged to the Reckitt & Coleman Food Division, the club's site taking up nearly half of the land belonging to the food company. When in May 1971 it was reported that manufacturing company Boulton & Paul had purchased the entire site, there were immediate concerns as to whether their plans for it might affect the football club in some way. As it was, the sale accelerated Geoffrey Watling's attempts to buy the part of the land that the ground stood on, with final agreement – but no actual figure – between the club and Boulton & Paul in early 1972. Watling had saved the club from an uncertain and very insecure future for a second time, and it would not be the last.

Little wonder, therefore, that purely footballing matters had been somewhat of a sideshow in the summer of 1971. The club had utilised the services of twenty-three players throughout the 1970/71 season, with all but two of them returning to Mousehold Heath for Saunders' dreaded pre-season bunny hops and other terrible deprivations the following summer. The unfortunate pair to miss out were Albert Bennett, forced to quit due to one injury too many, and the aforementioned Ken Mallender, that record signing of just under three years earlier who made just forty-eight appearances for the club, many of them as captain, before dropping down into non-League football to play for Hereford United – his long-term future at the club affected by both spells out with injury, plus the emergence of Dave Stringer and Duncan Forbes into regular first-team contention.

Two out and none in, Saunders preferring to start the new campaign 'as you were', albeit with far more focus on a strong, disciplined and physical back four. The manager's philosophy was that it was far more effective to focus on not letting goals in rather than scoring more, which might also have required some considerable expense. Having broken the club's transfer record to sign Mallender only to see him move on for nothing, it was perhaps understandable that the board was keeping what limited funds they had in the bank rather than splashing out on a Hickton or MacDougall. The onus, therefore, for goals remained on with Foggo and Silvester, but with more expected of the manager's first-choice back four to keep them out at the other end.

In the end, of a maximum total of 168 League games that the quartet might have played between them during that season, the fact that they managed 144 – with Payne and Stringer present in all forty-eight of Norwich's fixtures that season

– suggests that Saunders just might have found a back four that would perform as he expected. By the end of the campaign, Norwich's goals against column in the League table – just thirty-six in forty-two League games, as opposed to fifty-two the previous season – showed that he had got it exactly right.

One of the mainstays of Saunders' Norwich side was Kevin Keelan, a Canary veteran with 280 League and cup appearances for Norwich, and the pending 1971/72 season set to be his ninth at the club. He had shown, in a time of change and uncertainty at Carrow Road, a remarkable durability, having seen off the not inconsiderable challenge of Sandy Kennon in order to win his place in the team at the beginning of the 1963/64 season. Kennon shortly regained his place in the aftermath of a 4-2 defeat at Leeds but another thumping, 5-0 at Manchester City, saw Keelan retain the No. 1 shirt at Kennon's expense that March, a position he held until the end of that season. Although Kennon started the 1964/65 season as first choice, Keelan was always going to be the eventual winner of that particular club rivalry, his status confirmed when Kennon left the club that October, allegedly because of a disagreement with Ron Ashman. This had come about due to the fact that the no-nonsense Canary manager expected his goalkeepers to get the ball as far down the pitch as quickly as possible upon gaining possession. This was contrary to Kennon's more cerebral approach of starting a move forwards from the back, choosing to throw or pass the ball to a nearby teammate. Having disagreed with Ashman, a former teammate, there was little room for manoeuvre as far as Kennon was concerned, with Keelan the beneficiary of their falling out. Keelan went on to see off the challenge of two further potential rivals for his shirt in Geoff Barnard and Peter Vasper and, by August 1971, along with Stringer and Forbes, was a virtually automatic pick in the side for Saunders' third season at the club, just as he had been for Lol Morgan.

Stories of Keelan – man and goalkeeper – are legion and legendary. But was he the man that rumour and legend now proclaim him to be? Very probably, yes. Keelan really was a larger-than-life character, with the emphasis on character. He'd been sourced, scouted and signed by Ron Ashman in June 1963, the Norwich manager later going on to say that in signing Keelan he'd secured 'the bargain of the century'. Given Keelan's heroics during his time at Norwich, that statement doesn't seem so much hyperbole as a statement of fact.

Keelan was just twenty-two when he headed off to Norwich, a relative veteran of four clubs already. He was born in Kolkata in 1941, the son of a British soldier stationed in India. When he was seven, the young Keelan, together with his family, moved to England, settling in Kidderminster where Kevin first started playing the game, joining Kidderminster Harriers. He initially played as a midfielder before picking up the goalkeeper's gloves for the first time around his fifteenth birthday, when Kidderminster's goalkeeper failed to turn up for a game. One brilliant game later and a goalkeeper was born.

Needless to say, the young but unorthodox and occasionally spectacular Keelan wasn't going to stay unnoticed at Kidderminster for very long. In 1958, he signed for Aston Villa after having a trial for their fourth team, swiftly signing professional terms at the end of the 1958/59 season. Kevin initially understudied Nigel Sims for the Villa No. 1 shirt. Sims was something of a terrace cult figure at Villa Park. He'd been an integral member of the side that had won the FA Cup in 1957, following that up the next campaign by winning the inaugural Aston Villa Supporters Terrace Trophy, no mean feat when you consider that his peers in the Villa squad that season were players of the calibre and quality of future England international Gerry Hitchens, Peter McParland and legendary defender Jimmy 'The Laughing Cavalier' Dugdale. It was therefore clear that to usurp Sims in the team, Keelan was not only going to have to be exceptional, but have a stroke of good fortune.

As is often the case, one man's pain is another man's gain, and so it was here. Injury to Sims gained Keelan an unexpected elevation to the first team towards the end of the 1959/60 season, making his first-team debut at Ayresome Park on 5 March. Villa, then second in the Division Two table, won 1-0. It was the first of numerous clean sheets Keelan would keep in his career. He retained his place for the following two fixtures, a 3-2 win over Derby County, followed by a 2-1 win at Scunthorpe. Three games, three wins and, ultimately for Keelan and Villa, the Second Division title at the end of that season.

Keelan might have expected to get more of a chance to impress at Villa Park the following season. Sims was a popular figure but, by the beginning of that campaign, he had turned thirty, and even though goalkeepers had, as they do now, a longer 'shelf life' than outfield players, Villa manager Joe Mercer would have been more than aware of the potential and talent of the young tyro fast appearing in Sim's wing mirror. Sims started the season as first choice No. 1 but, after conceding seven goals in their first two games of the season, Keelan got another chance. Unluckily for him, Villa conceded five goals for the second game running, losing 5-3 at Blackpool. Sims retained his place for the following game, and, although Keelan made another appearance for the first team in a 1-3 home defeat to Leicester City on 1 October, his time at Villa was fast approaching its conclusion. Mercer had, by now, introduced another two 'keepers into first-team contention at the club, with Fred Potter and Geoff Sidebottom coming in. Sidebottom had joined from Wolves, where he had made thirty-five first-team appearances, including the 1960 FA Charity Shield clash with Burnley. At twenty-three, it was clear he had not been signed to make up the numbers, but as a serious rival to Sims. The fourth member of Villa's goalkeeping quartet at the time, Potter, was a year younger than Keelan, but when he got a run of six first-team matches at the end of 1960, it became clear that Keelan, who had initially impressed at his trial for the Villa fourth team, had now become the club's fourth-choice goalkeeper.

Luckily for Keelan, he had admirers. His first port of call was Fourth Division Stockport County, who he joined in April 1961. But after just three appearances for County, he was off again, briefly returning to Kidderminster before joining

Wrexham in November 1961. For the first time in his career, Keelan became undisputed first-choice 'keeper, making sixty-eight appearances for the club, and he again became a topic of interest for several more loftily placed clubs. Norwich was one of these, then two divisions higher and still looking to make an unlikely push for top-flight football, despite a disappointing 1962/63 campaign that had seen them finish in eleventh place.

The Canaries' undisputed No. 1 in the four seasons leading up to Keelan's arrival in July 1963 had been the aforementioned South African-born Neil Kennon, otherwise known as Sandy, the man who had fallen foul of Ashman for daring to throw rather than kick the ball clear whenever he took possession. Keelan duly started the 1963/64 season as the club's first-choice goalkeeper, going on to make sixteen League appearances that season. But, due to injury to Keelan, Kennon still made twenty-six League appearances. Kennon started the 1964/65 season as first choice, but he lost his place to Keelan that November. Keelan finally managed to retain the No. 1 shirt following a 0-0 draw at Northampton Town and, injury and occasional fallings out with assorted managers aside, retained it for the next seventeen years, ultimately making a club record 673 appearances for the Canaries – not bad for someone bombed out of Aston Villa at just twenty as the club's fourth-choice custodian.

Keelan was, unquestionably, at his peak for Norwich throughout the 1970s. His story and more than honourable mention could have been included in any part of this book, but he appears here because of the part he played in helping the club finally achieve that long-aspired wish of promotion to the First Division in 1972. He was an ever-present throughout the 1971/72 campaign. It was only the second time he had managed that achievement with the club, having first done so in the 1965/66 season, when Norwich's goals conceded column over the forty-two League games read just fifty-two – a total bettered by just three other clubs that season, one of whom was the runway champion, Manchester City.

His longevity at the club and reputation as a player of consummate ability – with just a little showmanship thrown in – is well documented. But what was Keelan like as a man, friend and colleague? Journalist and broadcaster Mick Dennis, a lifelong Norwich supporter who began his career with the *Eastern Daily Press* remembers Keelan, the public showman, as a consummate professional underneath that flamboyant exterior, and a player respected throughout the game for that very reason. The arrival of John Bond at Norwich in December 1973, for example, could have marked the end of Keelan's time at Carrow Road. He was into his thirties by then and had endured a tough first season with the club in Division One, avoiding an immediate relegation by just two points. When Bond arrived the following season, Norwich were bottom of the League, having won just two of their opening seventeen fixtures. If truth be told, the Canaries were in free fall, with many of the players who had contributed to their rise to the upper echelons having been 'found out' by better and more wily teams and opponents. Bond, a renowned buyer and seller of players, knew his new team needed immediate and radical surgery if it was to have any chance of surviving, and introduced a host of new players into the Canary ranks in the months that followed his appointment. Given that Bond was rather fond of bringing in players from Bournemouth, his previous club, there were those who suspected that he would bring in the Cherries' goalkeeper Fred Davies as competition for Keelan but this never materialised, although Davies did eventually end up at Carrow Road as a coach. Keelan was the established goalkeeper at Norwich, and Bond was very well aware of that fact, as Mick Dennis recalls,

> Kevin was the established goalkeeper when Bondy arrived and, to my certain knowledge, Bondy never sought a replacement nor questioned Kevin's right to the No. 1 shirt. That was its own testament to him, because Bondy was a wheeler-dealer, always looking to improve his team and squad. Roger Hansbury, who was his long-term understudy, wasn't a bad 'keeper, but Kevin was number one. The team certainly changed under Bondy. Colin Sullivan was brought in at left-back while Forbes and Stringer eventually gave way to Jones and Powell. But through all of those and the other changes, Kevin Keelan remained a consistent presence behind the defence, capable of great athleticism, yet a master of the goalkeeping basics. The 'big players' at the club – Duncan Forbes, Martin Peters, Ted MacDougall and their ilk – all treated Kevin with the respect that is obvious between the top players recognising someone who could do the job.

The ultimate respect that one professional offers another is often as simple as that: acknowledging that they can do the job needed. For Keelan to have it from someone as well versed and respected in the game as Bond was one thing, but for him to also have it from strong characters like Peters and MacDougall was something else, something special. And, like any true professional, Keelan hated to lose. Mick Dennis recalled that,

> On the way home after defeats, he was very quiet: not ranting or moaning, just an unhappy professional processing his personal disappointment. After a win or a decent draw, he was a noisy sod. He wasn't one of the card players, and there were no personal TVs or anything, so he would end up wandering up and down the coach and engaging in banter. He was good company, accepting the young reporter on the coach as just another one of the lads. There were no noticeable cliques, although some players were better friends with each other than with the rest, but Kevin was clearly well-liked by everyone. I remember that he often frequented a late night club, well, just a bar really called, I think, El Piano. And, of course, he did the seventies 'thing' of opening a boutique, which was in Anglia Square.

Keelan was a class act on and off the pitch. John Bond knew it, just as Ron Saunders had done so before him. The 1971/72 season, Saunders' third in charge at Carrow Road, was going to be a critical one admittedly, they had been for the club since Watling's involvement and avowed path towards success had commenced some fifteen years earlier. Regardless of the league they were in come August, promotion was always the sole ambition. Since the departure of MacAulay, four managers had come, failed to achieve that goal, and gone again. Ashman and Morgan had both been given three seasons to achieve what was increasingly looking to be a mission impossible for the club. Would Saunders be heading out of the exit door for the last time by May 1972 if he had followed in their footsteps and failed to deliver?

The Canaries certainly didn't set their supporters' hearts racing in the first few weeks of the season. True, they were undefeated after four games but two of those had been 0-0 draws, the second of them a dour affair against Orient at Carrow Road, a game that, in truth, you would have expected Norwich to win. Saunders certainly thought so. That game had been the second of three successive matches that had seen Malcolm Darling substituted. After a tame 1-0 win against Carlisle in front of just 10,967 at Carrow, Saunders had seen enough. Darling was gone within weeks of that game, dropping down a division to join Rochdale. In fairness to Darling, if he was being made a scapegoat for Norwich's turgid start to the season, it hardly seemed his fault. He was doomed to wear the unenviable label of 'utility player' during his time at the club, donning, and this was at a time when the number on your shirt indicated the position you played in, four different numbered shirts – No. 7, No. 8, No. 9 and No. 11, which seemed to indicate that he was, or had become, a square peg in a team of round holes. He was, without any doubt, a good footballer, shining in a struggling Rochdale side for three seasons and, after making just eight appearances for Bolton Wanderers, becoming a crowd favourite at Chesterfield, who he joined for just £10,000 in August 1974. During his time at Saltergate, Darling formed an effective striking partnership with Terry Shanahan, Spireites manager Joe Shaw giving him what Saunders had not, a first-team starting place and a settled position as one of the central strikers. He was also renowned for the number of penalties that he 'won' for the club. The Chesterfield website 'Sky Is Blue, Clouds Are White' recalled his efforts to this day, describing Darling's ability 'to turn the slightest invasion of his personal space into a spot-kick', adding that it 'puts into the new light the idea that all this modern falling down to "win" a penalty is the fault of foreigners in our game'. Malcolm Darling: penalty box predator and, by all accounts, a pioneering creative force. He is best remembered by Chesterfield fans, however, as a 'fine, mobile and quick-witted forward' – something he had never been given the chance to prove at Norwich. In all, he made 104 appearances for the club, of which only four came from the bench, scoring thirty-three goals, a more-than-respectable return for a man deemed surplus to requirements so soon into the Canaries' ultimately triumphant 1971/72 season.

Such is the fickle nature of football. Darling had arrived at Norwich in May 1970, the last of Saunders' signings of that season, or the first of the subsequent one, whichever way you want to look at it. The player he had directly replaced, Bryan Conlon, had appeared in thirty-one League games for Norwich during his time at the club, scoring eight goals – a fairly respectable figure. Conlon had been a typical old-fashioned centre-forward; 'a craggy player' according to writer Mike Davage, who went on to point out that, 'whenever he scored for City's first team, they won the match'. He might have been expected to stake a regular and long-term place in the Canaries line-up, but had spectacularly blotted his Carrow Road copybook by flinging his shirt to the ground in disgust after being hauled off by Saunders in the game against Blackburn (whose hierarchy must have seen something in his spirit to have wanted to sign him as they did at the end of that season) which Norwich lost 1-0. It was the second successive match in which Conlon had been taken off and replaced by Gerry Howshall. Such undisciplined behaviour was an act of anathema as far as Saunders was concerned and, from that moment, Conlon was on borrowed time at Norwich.

When the chance came to go to Blackburn he took it and, with Norwich having secured Darling as part of the transfer, it seemed to suit everyone. Indeed, Darling's form at Blackburn did seem to indicate that Norwich might have got the better of the deal. He'd made his debut for Rovers when he was just eighteen and played regularly in the old-fashioned inside-forward position for them, scoring goals as well as creating them, for three consecutive seasons; form which included a superb hat-trick in an FA Cup match against Portsmouth in January 1969. Darling was a player who was on the up.

Keelan had seemed to be going in the opposite direction. He'd been rejected by Aston Villa, the consequence of which saw him drop back into non-League, as well as having spells at the lower end of football's pyramid at Stockport and Wrexham. He'd gone on to join a Norwich side that were, despite their relatively lofty position in the scheme of things (Division Two), a fairly mediocre side, whose aspirations were far removed from the reality of the club's infrastructure, both on and off the pitch. Yet he went on to footballing stardom – two promotions to England's top flight, two Wembley Cup final appearances, and two-time winner of the Norwich City's prestigious Barry Butler Player of the Year Award. He would probably have had a decent chance of representing England as well, if it hadn't been for the fact that English football positively dripped with quality goalkeepers at the time Keelan was playing – Gordon Banks was coming to the end of his international career with the likes of Ray Clemence, Peter Shilton, Joe Corrigan and Phil Parkes coming through as potential successors.

Following Banks' retirement from the game, such was the dominance of Clemence and Shilton on the international scene (Ron Greenwood initially couldn't – or wouldn't – pick between the two, so they played in alternate games) that Corrigan and Parkes, who became England's unofficial third- and fourth-choice 'keepers, only managed ten England games between them, nine of which were caps for Corrigan. And then there was Manchester United's Alex Stepney, England's third-choice keeper at the 1970 World Cup finals.

For all of his successes in the game, which included a European Cup winners' medal, he only made one appearance for England. However, he still would have been considered ahead of Keelan in the international pecking order, which would have made Keelan England's sixth-choice goalkeeper, if you discounted Everton's Gordon West, who won three England caps himself from 1968 to 1969. Thus Keelan was, and always remained, in the international wilderness. But he was a footballing icon at Norwich City. He was also a goalkeeper whose outstanding all-round game and ability impressed everyone who watched him, played with him, and played against him. John Bond even had to fend off reported interest in Keelan from Manchester United. Tommy Docherty had been at the helm at Old Trafford at the time, and it was he who put in the call to Bond enquiring about Keelan's availability and what fee Norwich might have reasonably expected for him.

Bond's response had been typically honest: 'No problem Tom, I'll have a word with the lad and get back to you.' A few days passed, then a week. Eventually, Docherty was on the phone again, had Bond mentioned their interest to Keelan and what had been the response? 'Sorry Tom,' said Bond, 'I had a word with Kevin, told him about your offer. He's had a think about it, but I'll be straight with you, he says he's not interested, he's settled here and wants to see out his career with us.' Nonplussed, but accepting, Docherty hung up and went about his business. Bond, meanwhile, afforded himself one of his trademark smiles. He had no intention of selling Keelan and had not even mentioned Docherty's call or Manchester United's interest in his player. Thus Keelan stayed with Norwich, playing his final game for the club in 1980, the *Match of the Day* covered spectacular against Liverpool in which Norwich had lost 5-3, but won a lot of admirers in doing so. It was also the game that made a star out of Justin Fashanu, his eighty-first minute turn and volley winning the BBC's 'Goal of the Season award' – the first and only time the accolade has been won by a Norwich player.

Fame and relative fortune, therefore for Keelan. But for Malcolm Darling, a severe case of what might have been. He had enjoyed that productive and popular spell at Chesterfield but had never reached the heights that Keelan eventually climbed to. Teammates and equals at the start of the 1971/72 season, Keelan's career in the game was now on the launch pad, preparing for stardom. Sadly for Darling, he would not be accompanying Keelan and Norwich on the ride that was to come.

Three days after Darling made his long move north, Norwich played Sunderland at Roker Park on 9 October 1971. The 'so-so' start to the campaign that had seen three draws and a win in the first four fixtures had been much improved, the Canaries rapidly picking up speed with five League wins on the trot, a welcome run of form that elevated them to the top of the table. Among those successes had been an impressive 2-0 win at Preston, courtesy of two second-half strikes by Peter Silvester and Ken Foggo. The game at Sunderland, however, saw the debut of a new addition to the Canary ranks, David Cross. He had done the reverse journey to that of Darling, joining Norwich from Rochdale a day after Darling had gone the other way. Cross was a most welcome addition to the Norwich squad. He might not have been the biggest forward in the game, either in name or size – in fact at 5 feet 11 inches, he was the same size as Darling – but he was a far more physical player, possessing the presence and threat that Darling did not have and, as such, was a perfect complement to Foggo and his new forward partner Silvester. He signed for just £40,000, a fee that he must have repaid Norwich several times over, his two-year spell at the club eventually yielding a return of thirty goals from 106 appearances.

Cross went straight into the side at Sunderland, replacing the unfortunate Trevor Howard, another player who, like Darling, had to suffer the term 'utility player' during his time at Norwich. This is reflected in Howard's playing record at the club – he made forty-five appearances in total as a substitute, as well as having a further twenty occasions as an unused No. 12. In his favour, however, was the fact that he was a player who gave all he had in every game, an energetic and passionate performer who could always be relied upon to 'do a job' when required, usually in any one of several positions. A regular first-team place was not to be one of them and he happily yielded to Cross's arrival. Unlike the unfortunate Darling, he stayed at Carrow Road for the remainder of the season as well as the two subsequent ones.

Cross had an onerous task on his hands, he was inheriting the shirt number that had been worn, among others, by the likes of Terry Allcock, Terry Bly and Ron Davies – three Norwich legends who, between them, had scored 231 goals for Norwich. At the time the move came about, Cross has since admitted that he thought it would have been a teammate of his, Norman Whitehead, who was on the way out of Spotland, with both Everton and Manchester City rumoured to have been interested in the young winger. Even when he found out that the player due to move was himself, he remained in the dark as he didn't even know which club he was due to join, initially joshing with his best friend at the club that it was '... probably going to be some out of the way place like Norwich', and further admitting that he was hoping the buying club would be either Manchester City or Liverpool! However, when he found out that it was indeed Norwich where he was heading, he was excited about the move, saying, 'There was no way I was going to turn it down. Money wasn't a factor. I got down, met Ron Saunders, he told me what I'd be on and I just nodded.'

Deal done. And two days after his surprise move, the twenty-year-old striker was straight into the first team – from eleventh in Division Three to top of Division Two in less than forty-eight hours. He duly made a nuisance of himself at Sunderland, giving the Canaries a little bit of muscle and sinew in attack where it might have been lacking and, with that extra spark on board, Norwich got a point where before they might have got none – Peter Silvester's second-half equaliser earning the League leaders a 1-1 draw. Four days later, Cross made his home debut, his new side putting on a near virtuoso performance in ripping Burnley apart to the tune of 3-0 – Silvester and Foggo again scoring, along with Duncan Forbes. A crowd of 24,356 attended that game, quite an improvement on the 10,967 who had turned out to see the game against Carlisle a few weeks earlier. Norwich was up and running, and the fans were responding, reacting with excitement and enthusiasm to the club's first real push for Division One football since the ultimately disappointing 1960/61 season.

Three days after the Burnley mauling, Norwich was in League action again, this time welcoming Luton Town to Carrow Road. It was going to be one of those games that you needed to win to, as the press would say, 'bolster your promotion credentials'. And it wasn't a given, despite Norwich's improving form and the fact that it was at home. Luton had only lost one of their opening eleven fixtures, conceding just nine goals in the process. In addition to that, both of the games the previous season had ended in draws, with Norwich lucky to get even that from the game at Carrow Road, where a second-half Ken Foggo goal had spared Canary blushes. Not that a defeat would have been surprising, as the newly promoted Hatters had kicked off that 1970/71 season with a *joie de vivre* in their football that reflected their progressive manager, Alec Stock. They'd finished that campaign in sixth place, five points ahead of the Canaries, having scored more goals (sixty-two, compared to Norwich's fifty-four) and conceded fewer (forty-three to fifty-two). In short, they had been promoted and shown, in their first season at that level, the sort of play and form which marked them out as serious contenders for a second promotion – if not a consecutive one, then very shortly afterwards. And certainly not taking the attempts, twelve and counting, that their supposedly more illustrious neighbours to the East had so far made to get promotion.

Norwich had failed to beat Luton in any of the clubs' four last meetings at Carrow Road, which included a 0-4 capitulation in September 1961. The Hatters had also broken Canary hearts in 1959 by defeating them, in a replay, in the semi-finals of the FA Cup: difficult, nay, bogey opponents[3] to come up against, just as they had proved themselves to be in the past. But Saunders, maybe contrary to some of his predecessors, would have relished that fact and the challenge. Game on – as no one was saying in 1971.

Regardless of recent form or perceived 'bogey' team status, Luton did have a rich choice of footballing talents to pick from in their squad. Don Givens and Vic Halom were both extremely capable strikers, who would go on to further prove that fact at a higher level, while in Chris Nicholl they had one of the best centre-halves outside of the top division. Equally adept at playing a bit of football or contributing to the cause physically, when it came to Nicholl,

---

[3] A tradition that was maintained in 2013 when Luton defeated Norwich 1-0 at Carrow Road in the fourth round of the FA Cup, the first non-League team to knock a top-flight side out of the competition for nearly a quarter of a century.

both Silvester and Foggo would know they were in a game. Then there was John Ryan, a marauding full-back in the Gareth Bale mould, someone else for the Norwich defence to worry about. He'd been released by Arsenal while still a teenager and was on a mission to prove then Gunners boss Billy Wright – who you'd have thought knew a good defender when he had one – wrong.[4] This game would have been as good a chance as any. Norwich were top of the League and flying, the game was the fixture of the day in the Second Division, and there'd be a big crowd. The Hatters were ready, were more than ready in fact, to put down a marker for the rest of the season, and this game seemed an ideal opportunity to do so.

On the day it was Norwich who started a little uncertainly, a little nervously. The weather seemed to match the mood around Carrow Road for the first half – grey, dull and drizzle. Luton moved the ball around well, probing at the normally resolute City defence and asking a few questions of it with their three strikers – Halom and Givens being joined by Peter Anderson – giving Luton an ambitious-looking front three that were making people nervous, on and off the pitch, not least the usually redoubtable Forbes and Stringer in the Norwich defence. Norwich became so obsessed with those front three, they started to neglect some of their duties, and the Luton midfield, like a company of unattended bombers, were able to push forward. The inevitable goal came when Alan Slough, a midfielder with the touch of a striker, finished off a move that was made by the twin talents of midfielders Hindson and Mike Keen.

Half an hour gone then and 1-0 to the visitors. In yellow and green sympathy, the heavens duly opened. Saunders sat, his face like stone, waiting for half-time to come. You almost got the feeling that, if he could, he'd haul all of his players off and send them home. They knew what would be coming in the dressing room during the break. The Canaries manager had been awarded with his September 'Manager of the Month' award prior to the match, but it was unlikely there'd be much celebratory bonhomie in abundance at half-time. Very unlikely indeed.

Oh, to have been a fly on the wall on such occasions when the ire of Ron Saunders had been aroused. He expected 110 per cent effort from all of his players as standard – even, in all likelihood, from the substitute sat alongside him in the dugout. And he didn't as much mince his words as liquefy them. Tony Morley, a winger good enough to play for England on six occasions and the winner of a League championship medal under Saunders' stewardship at Aston Villa, admitted to the *Birmingham Post* in 2006 that, despite all that, Saunders would never be anything other than blunt with him, saying his usual greeting would be 'You're crap, Morley' but adding, 'But that was his way'. His way or the highway as they say. David Cross, still a relative new boy at Carrow

---

4 How satisfying, therefore, must have it been for Ryan to score against Arsenal for Norwich on 24 September 1977? It was one of fifteen League goals he scored for the Canaries that season, finishing it as the club's leading scorer!

Road at the time of the Luton game told Rock Waghorn in *12 Canary Greats* that Saunders was, 'big on bad people being bad footballers ... he was very hard on us if he found out we'd been out drinking.' At this time, remember, there wasn't the obsession over players' lifestyles and the need for a 'healthy mind and healthy body' that there is now. They went out for a few beers as a matter of course. No less a figure than the original 'golden boy' of English football, Bobby Moore, had, only a few years previously, appeared in a TV advertisement espousing the values of the local bar, the feature being called *Mr & Mrs Bobby Moore Look In At The Local*. In it, Moore had stood at the bar and shared some banter with the locals before joining his wife at the dartboard. Martin Peters had appeared with him. Yes, *that* Martin Peters. In the pub. It's unlikely that Saunders would ever have signed *him* for Norwich with that on his CV.

So Saunders would have made his feelings known at half-time. Luton were fast, bright and committed, whereas Norwich were slow, uncertain and nervous. Maybe he called out a few of his players, informed them they were 'crap' as well? But something must have been said, for, as Bruce Robinson noted in the *Eastern Daily Press*, 'City, who did little right before the break did little wrong afterwards.' And he was right. It was as if Saunders had made eleven changes. From kick-off, Norwich were more aggressive in their play – wanting the ball, closing down the angles, winning possession and generally putting Luton on the back foot, which had previously been the front for so much of that first period. It took ten minutes for normal service to be restored, with the marauding Butler arrowing in a fast ball across the Luton penalty area that Foggo, arriving on time and with a full head of steam, hit first time, hard and true, past Keith Barber in the Luton goal.

Carrow Road duly stirred from its rainy slumber and started to make a bit of noise.

With twenty minutes to go, Saunders had to make a change. Doug Livermore, suffering from a badly bruised thigh, came off to be replaced by Trevor Howard, the so-called 'utility player', who had still managed to carve a niche for himself at Norwich, despite being labelled with that description. He wasn't the tallest or most physical of players – at just 5 foot 7 inches, he was only an inch taller than Wes Hoolahan – but he was the epitome of what Saunders wanted in his players, he gave that 110 per cent. Busy, committed, a real 'hither and thither' player who would have been told to get among the Luton back four and bother the life out of them. It was Howard's way, and he would have relished the task in hand. Norwich had already got in front through Foggo's second goal and were hanging on in that nervous way that generations of Canary fans are only too familiar with, when Howard's angled shot rose up and just out of reach of the impressive Barber for Norwich's third, thus sealing a 3-1 win. The margin of victory was a slightly flattering one: Norwich had not been as good as it suggests, and neither had Luton been so well beaten. Yet it was a victory that demonstrated that old footballing standard, if you can still win when you are not playing particularly well, then you'll always have a chance.

As both Saunders and his players already knew, and the Norwich fans were beginning to realise, this Canaries side did have a chance. But would they take it? Norwich's next game, a trip to the Arcadian surrounds of The Den to play Millwall a week later, was a game of huge significance for both clubs. Norwich was top of the league and unbeaten, and Millwall, with only one defeat in thirteen games themselves, were just three points behind them in second place. The Lions, marshalled by one-time FA Youth Cup-winning teammate of Bobby Moore, Harry Cripps (a name that seemed more suitable for a villain in a Victorian melodrama than a footballer), were, like Norwich, enjoying an unexpectedly good season. Their League form and finishes in previous campaigns had pretty much aped Norwich's in its mid-table mediocrity. But suddenly, under Cripps and wily manager Benny Fenton who, like Cripps, had started his playing career at West Ham, they'd shot to prominence and were making a charge for the top flight that was even more improbable than that of the Canaries. They had some good players too. As well as Cripps the team also included the likes of Barry Kitchener, Keith Weller and Eamon Dunphy. Weller, of course, would later torment Norwich while playing against them for Leicester City. The sight of him, clad in black tights, gliding over the icy Carrow Road pitch on a frigid January afternoon in 1979 is more than a sore point for Norwich fans; Leicester won 3-0 on the day. Dunphy, in the meantime, became a famous media personality in Ireland, his often controversial and acerbic comments on the game a welcome change from the bland and unimaginative offerings of his British counterparts. Dunphy warmed the hearts of many a Norwich supporter in June 2013 when talking about the international pedigree of Wes Hoolahan, telling the *Irish Examiner* that, as a footballer, Hoolahan was, 'outstanding ... a leader on the field. He set[s] the tempo ... he's a bloody good footballer, he believes in himself.' Dunphy was maybe not such a 'bloody good footballer' as Hoolahan was, but back then he and his Millwall teammates had a fierce self-belief that, backed by their raucous home support, made them a formidable challenge for any team. They were, not surprisingly given that combination, unbeaten at home in the League that season, and had enough about them to send Norwich to their first League defeat of the season; Peter Silvester's first-half goal, his seventh of the season, not enough to prevent a 2-1 reverse. The Lions were now just one point behind the Canaries and on a roll. Norwich, meanwhile, after this defeat and the fortuitous win against Luton, needed to get back on one.

The Millwall game had not been a good one for David Cross. It was his fourth game for the club, a spell that had yet to yield a goal. Strikers, cliché or not, are judged on the number of goals they score, and Cross had not delivered. He had been taken off at The Den, replaced by the lively and ever-willing Howard – the man he had been brought to replace or, at the very least, send tumbling down the list of names uppermost in the manager's thoughts. And, with Saunders being the man that he was, someone who liked to 'sort people out', he must have feared for his place in the side for the Canaries' next game, a home clash against Cardiff City. Saunders did indeed spring a surprise in that game: not by dropping Cross, who found himself back in the starting XI, but by removing the popular Howard from the substitutes bench, replacing him with defender Alan Black. Vote of confidence or not, Cross responded by scoring his first goal for Norwich in their 2-1 win, the other coming from Dave Stringer. It was a welcome two points in a game that had one sour point, the loss of inspirational skipper Duncan Forbes through injury. Fortuitous indeed that Saunders had named a defender as his substitute. Black replaced Forbes in the centre of the Norwich defence and they held on. Forbes missed fifteen Norwich games during his absence, a considerable handicap for any team with their sights set on promotion, but then again one that a team with those goals in mind should be able to overcome. The No. 5 shirt was shared between three players during Forbes' absence – Steve Govier and Bobby Bell slotted in on three occasions each, with Terry Anderson, once of Arsenal and a right-winger by trade in the nine other games, with Max Briggs, a midfielder and another hard worker, filling in wherever needed in Forbes' enforced absence.

Did the Canaries miss their inspirational leader, a man so vociferous and with such a massive presence at the club, physically, personally and vocally? A famous story surrounding Forbes relates to a pre-season trip that the Canaries had taken to Portugal the previous May. Norwich had been invited, along with Scottish side Dundee to compete in the Batista Tournament,[5] alongside three Portuguese teams. Forbes, as vocal and enthusiastic as ever even in such relatively informal surrounds, had been cajoling his teammates during a gentle training session so enthusiastically that a Dundee player, who had heard his exhortations from his hotel window, leaned out of it and implored to Forbes, 'Could you please keep your voice down to a roar?' And so the Forbes legend grew. A reporter from *The Times* once commented, after covering a Norwich match that, 'Forbes got his customary booking; the referee ought to take his name in the changing room rather than on the pitch, thus saving time'. Meanwhile, respected journalist Mike Langley was typically succinct, describing Forbes as the 'Yellow Peril'. Whether or not the jibes were justified, Forbes was certainly making a name for himself, and the only thing you can be certain of in the whole debate is that there are a lot of teams who would still have found a place for him in their starting XI, despite what was being said about him.

The Canaries' record without their stentorian skipper was respectable, if not eye-watering. Of those fifteen League fixtures without him, Norwich won six,

---

5   Norwich played four games in just under a fortnight during their stay in Portugal. As well as beating Dundee 5-3, they also defeated Atletico Lisbon 2-1 and drew 1-1 with Sporting Lisbon, going on to win that game on penalties by 4-2, the club's first participation in a penalty shoot-out. But that wasn't it! Five days later, the Canaries travelled to Funchal and drew with Uniao 1-1.

drew six and lost three. One of those losses – indeed, the final game they played before he returned to the side (no doubt brandishing a claymore if it had been permitted) – was a trip to St Andrews to play Birmingham City.

The Blues hadn't had a good start to the season – they'd been as low as seventeenth in the table at the beginning of September, yet had, slowly and with some intent, begun to climb it, with a 2-2 draw at Carrow Road in what was Forbes' second game out moving them to sixth place. By the time of the Norwich game, they'd started a run of games – four wins from five leading up to it – and were enjoying the fruits of two players' labours in particular – the 'two Bobs', namely Latchford and Hatton. Throw in the emerging talents of seventeen-year-old Trevor Francis and you have a team that really is, as the well-worn saying goes, 'full of goals'. Indeed, the three of them scored sixty-four goals between them that season; the crushing 4-0 win over the Canaries providing Hatton with two of his final tally and Latchford one, with the fourth goal coming from central defender Roger Hynd. It wasn't even, in retrospect, the Blues' best performance of the season – they'd already seen off Charlton and Swindon Town 4-1, while Middlesbrough had six put past them at St Andrews. But it was, very definitely, Norwich's worst performance of the season. Birmingham's attack had torn holes at will in Norwich's brittle defence, with Bobby Bell, in particular, suffering at their expense. He had become Norwich's first-ever loan signing a few weeks earlier, borrowed from Crystal Palace to provide extra depth and experience to a defence that was clearly missing its leader. But it wasn't a happy stay. Norwich was winless during his three-game spell, conceding six goals. Bell duly returned to Selhurst Park on the following Monday, his parent club's near neighbours, Millwall, now top of the table for the first time that season after their 2-2 draw at home to Swindon Town. Norwich had been in pole position for twenty-three weeks up until then. But now, with Millwall pulling ahead of them and Birmingham making a goal-rich charge on the rails with their tails up, could Norwich stand the pressure? It was squeaky bum time, seventies style.

Forbes returned a week later for the Carrow Road encounter against Sunderland, the only change to the side from that annihilation at Birmingham. Saunders was not an impulsive manager and, far from throwing teacups around and making whole-scale team changes after heavy defeat, would merely throw the teacups around before instructing his chastened players to 'put it right'. He'd already entered the transfer market for more firepower in attack, paying an unexpected visit to Partick Thistle in order to sign the gristly striker Jimmy Bone. His debut had been in that sad melodrama at St Andrews but now, with Peter Silvester out since January with a career-threatening knee injury, Bone was ready for his Carrow Road debut, playing alongside Cross.

The 'hot Cross Bone' pairing was a far more physical and gritty attack duo than the Norwich fans were used to, but with the duo ably backed up by the midfield flair of Graham Paddon (and any opportunity I have to say he should have been the first Norwich player to have been capped by England I will take, so here it is now) plus the return of his fellow Scot in Forbes, promised a change in fortune after five games without a win. Bone, as it transpired, was exactly what Norwich needed, and an inspirational signing by Saunders.

Bone had originally made a name for himself at the Jags by scoring one of the goals in their shock 4-1 victory over Celtic in the 1971 Scottish League Cup final, one of over fifty goals he scored for the club in his four seasons at Firhill. His lifelong love of the game had come about despite the fact he had attended that sporting purgatory for any football-loving youngster, a school that played and preached nothing but the virtues of Rugby Union. The story of Jimmy Bone could therefore, have never been told, had he acquiesced to the oval ball philosophy of his school. Yet fortune particularly favours the brave-hearted of Stirling, and Bone found an outlet for his real sporting love with his local boys' brigade, from where he joined and played for prominent local junior sides Airth Castle Rovers and Bannockburn Rovers. Such was the strong reputations of these sides for producing young players of exceptional quality that Jimmy's goalscoring abilities soon attracted the attention of a number of senior Scottish sides. He went on to have trials with ten of them, including Falkirk, Hibernian and his local side, Stirling Albion, as well as being invited to one at Liverpool.

Unfortunately for Jimmy, nothing came of this effort to secure himself a contract with a bigger side, and he would have undoubtedly been considering a career outside of football when, at the age of eighteen, he was offered another trial, this time by Partick Thistle manager Willie Thornton.

Thornton had been a striker himself, enjoying a long and successful playing career with the Rangers, for whom he scored 138 goals in just 219 League appearances – a goalscoring pedigree at any level, let alone with one of the most famous clubs in football. Thornton therefore knew a decent young player when he saw one and, in the wiry form of the young Jimmy Bone, he reckoned a natural goalscoring ability in the game was a mere formality. Bone subsequently signed for the Glasgow-based Jags and proved his manager to be right in his assumptions when, in a pre-season friendly in the summer of 1968, Bone scored in a 3-3 draw at Bury. He went on to score seventeen goals in his first season at Partick, including a hat-trick in a convincing win over Hearts. Following relegation in the next campaign, Jimmy formed a formidable striking partnership with Frank Coulston. The policy of new Jags manager and veteran of over 400 League appearances for the club, Davie McPharland, to throw as many of the club's promising young players into the first team as possible clearly paid off, as they won an immediate return, as champions, to the Scottish First Division.

As a newly promoted side, Thistle were automatically made favourites for an immediate return to the Second Division the following season, but that momentum they had built up the previous campaign stayed with them and they finished in seventh place, combining that with their success in that Scottish

League Cup final where Bone had, memorably, walked the ball into the Celtic net for Partick's fourth a little before half-time.

That game and result probably remains the zenith in Partick's recent history but, for Bone, whose cheek and arrogance were shown in the manner by which he had scored that fourth goal, it was the real beginning, rather than the peak, of his career in the game. Such was his form, confidence and growing prominence in the Scottish game that he was selected to play for the Scotland under-23 side, for whom he made his second appearance in a 2-2 draw with their English counterparts at Derby County's Baseball Ground. Both of Scotland's goals had been scored by a precocious twenty-year-old striker by the name of Kenny Dalglish, but the watching scout from Carrow Road had seen enough of Dalglish's strike partner for the evening to strongly recommend him to Ron Saunders. Norwich acted quickly upon that recommendation by swiftly following up their initial enquiry with a bid, as interest in Bone was now growing. The deal was done and Jimmy headed south to Norwich.

Despite having moved from the heartlands of an industrial city of the scale and significance of Glasgow to the quieter and more rural surrounds of Norwich, Jimmy soon settled in at Carrow Road. To his teammates, however, he was a revelation, a young, confident player who was sure of both himself and his ability, cocksure qualities that, while Ron Saunders, eminently a disciplinarian, might not have approved, he quietly encouraged. The manager did have options in reserve – one of whom, Gary Sargent, was tried and swiftly rejected after just one appearance earlier that season – but had already decided that Norwich's strike force was too 'nice' and needed someone who would add a streak of mean to the ranks, to take the knocks and, if necessary, dish them out as well. This would not only give Cross a combative and willing foil, but also introduce someone who would make the most of the myriad chances that his fellow Scot, Foggo, no slouch on either wing, would create. Saunders had, in essence, been putting a promotion-winning jigsaw together at Norwich ever since his appointment back in 1969. As far as that ultimate goal was concerned – and not many people realised it at the time – the acquisition of Jimmy Bone was the final piece of that jigsaw.

Norwich drew the game against Sunderland 1-1. It was their sixth game without a win and kept them second in the table, a point behind Millwall. Birmingham had slipped back into fourth while Sunderland, by virtue of their point at Carrow Road were now in third place. It was all heading to the promotion boil very nicely. Crucially for Norwich, and despite this being the latest disappointing result in that run, there had been two positives: not only had Forbes returned to his defensive duties as if he had never been away but Bone had scored. Things were looking up, and that was not something you would normally have said of your promotion-chasing side after its sixth game without a win.

That much-needed win came against Hull City on 15 March. Fingernails were being chewed at half-time with the score at 0-0, but second-half goals from Foggo ('remember me?') and the ever-reliable twelfth man, Howard, saw Norwich take the points and return to the top of the table, where they stayed for the rest of the season with, amid occasional hiccups, some impressive form and results to call their own. Not least, a 5-1 Carrow Road win against Blackpool, captured for all eternity by Anglia TV for their *Match Of The Week* programme, a game that saw the old and the new at Carrow Road combine in their goalscoring duties, with Paddon netting two; Foggo, Cross and Bone the others. Paddon's goal was the pick of the bunch, the midfielder starting and finishing the move, his shot from well outside the penalty area easily beating John Burridge in the Blackpool goal.

The eventual denouement of that ultimately triumphant season is both well known and widely documented, so I will not dwell on it in any lengthy detail here. Norwich's penultimate League game had seen them, and what seemed like most of the population of Norfolk, travel down to East London for the game against Orient, a team who had themselves gloriously (but briefly) achieved the dream of top-flight football a decade earlier. A win would guarantee Norwich promotion and, with such massive vocal backing, how could the Canaries fail to deliver?

They certainly didn't in the first forty-five minutes. It was a dour and somewhat tame affair, played out to a carnival atmosphere of mutual delight that did not match the colour of the football on the pitch. When half-time came with the score at 0-0, Saunders scurried into the dressing room, needing to give a team talk like he had never given before. This was his moment and his team's moment; this is why he had been appointed nearly three seasons earlier. And, just as they had done in that other initially forgettable game against Luton back in October, his team came off the pitch as kittens but rejoined it as lions. Norwich began to press, with Paddon majestic in midfield, his influence and vision telling as move after move commenced at his poetic feet. Norwich had already gone a goal ahead through Foggo, but it was from Paddon's corner at sixty-seven minutes that the game was won; his long, looping delivery being inexplicably punched away by Peter Bennett, yet another West Ham old boy the Canaries had come up against that season who had played a part in their rise. It was Paddon himself, a West Ham player-to-be, who then strode up and confidently hit the penalty past Ray Goddard in the Orient goal, virtually guaranteeing Norwich the win and the promotion that came from it. It was a great moment for the fans, the players and for Saunders, but most of all, for the watching Geoffrey Watling. He had joined the club when they were in crisis and looking likely to depart – either through relegation or liquidation – the entire Football League, yet here he now sat, the chairman of a First Divison football club.

The Second Division title came, deservedly, five days later at Watford. With Norwich clad in an unfamiliar red strip and running on nearly empty, it took a goal from Dave Stringer to give them a half-time lead that was a 1-1 draw at the end. It was enough for Norwich to become champions, while for Watford, it simply completed the formalities of their season, which ended in relegation, rock-bottom on nineteen points and fifteen points adrift of Fulham, safe in twentieth position. The celebrations, when they came, were rich with relief as much as anything. *Eastern Daily Press* journalist Bruce Robinson described them in his post-match report as featuring, 'boisterous fans – and there must have been 10,000 of them – braved the dripping weather, bounded over the sodden pitch, besieged the grandstand, called for their favourites and then received them, noisily and good naturedly'.

A final word from Kenny Foggo, looking back at those moments, forever now cut into the club's history, no matter what has followed or is to come. He describes the aftermath of that win at Orient that guaranteed promotion.

> There was a little bit of champagne brought into the dressing room, but most of the lads refused it – and then, on the coach home, we just stopped on the [A]11 somewhere and just carried on. I don't think I went to bed that night.

For Saunders it had been a triumph and full vindication of the club's decision to hire him three seasons previously, as well as his to accept the offer. It had all been very tight at the end – Norwich had finished on fifty-seven points, with runners-up Birmingham on fifty-six, Millwall and QPR in third and fourth place on fifty-five and fifty-four points respectively. He now had the club's first-ever season of top-flight League football to plan for and, proving some things never change, the bookies soon had newly promoted Norwich as one of the favourites for relegation at the end of the 1972/73 season. Clearly then, as now, a promoted team would have to strengthen its ranks and bring in some experienced players, ones who had played – and competed – at that highest level. Asked, therefore, during the post-match celebrations at Watford if the club would have money for new players, he looked the reporter straight in the eye and said, 'I haven't asked yet' and then smiled.

It might have been the first time anyone had seen him smile since the previous August.

4
ALL CHANGE

Don't give them any time on the ball, don't give them any space, don't even let them have time to think.

A famous photograph taken in the aftermath of Norwich's promotion celebrations in May 1972 shows a topless and extremely sweaty Duncan Forbes assisting Canaries chairman Geoffrey Watling, smart and respectable in his three-piece suit, with the customary champagne bottle. Watling, his eyes bright with excitement and happiness, is swigging from the bottle, his presence in the victorious dressing room to share those special moments with his players a testimony to his passion and total involvement with the club that he had so willingly bought into in 1956.

One of his first acts as chairman had been to stand his ground and give good reason why the Canaries should not have been thrown out of the League, the potential fate that could have befallen them after they had finished bottom of the Division Three (South) in 1957. He was now preparing to visit grounds like Highbury, Elland Road and Old Trafford as an equal to the famous chairmen who held court in such places, men like Arsenal's Denis Hill-Wood, an Oxford Blue and member of the MCC. This was all a far cry from the usual mix of car dealership owners and local industry magnates who he would have known and socialised with during Norwich's darker days, just as playing at Highbury, famous marble halls and all, would have been from playing in front of just 4,480 fans at Accrington Stanley, as Norwich had done – winning 4-3 – in 1959. Not that Watling had delusions of grandeur. He was very much an 'of the people' person and could hold a conversation with anyone, anywhere. Yet he must have been excited at the prospect of accompanying his club to some of the greatest theatres in world football.

Norwich was about to join the elite of English football. As they had finished the 1971/72 season as Division Two champions, so Derby County had done so in the League above them, the first major title of Brian Clough's managerial career. They'd finished a point ahead of three clubs, the League runners-up, Leeds United, having eased their pain on losing a title that had been theirs to win by winning the FA Cup for the first time, beating Arsenal 1-0 in what had been a largely disappointing final. As well as games against those sides, and other giants of the game in Liverpool, Manchester United and Manchester City, Norwich also had the return of the East Anglian derby against Ipswich Town to look forward to. The two clubs had last met only a short time ago, with Ipswich securing the local bragging rights by virtue of a 4-3 win at Carrow Road on 3 February 1968. They'd then compounded Canary misery by winning the title that season, the Norwich fans' distress at that not helped by the knowledge that, had their side hung onto their 2-1 half-time lead in that game, Ipswich would have finished in third place and not gone up. It would have been a small victory, but a telling one. Instead of that, Town had taken the glory and been lording it over Norwich ever since, further backed by their unlikely Division One championship success in 1962. It was good to have a chance to slightly redress the balance, and on equal terms.

Watling's manager, Ron Saunders, had issued a rare smile when asked at the end of the previous season if he would have any money to spend in order to strengthen his side for the challenges ahead. 'I haven't asked yet' had been his answer, but then it seemed he had no intention of asking or of spending any, despite Norwich's promotion. There were no new arrivals at Carrow Road over the summer, and just one departure of any significance with forward Gary Sargent moving on to Scunthorpe United, he alone denied the chance to stake his claim in the First Division.

Norwich did, of course, have half a dozen other strikers to call upon at that time, the obvious being Bone, Cross and Foggo, as well as the ever-willing Trevor Howard. However, with the emergence of more young talent in Phil Hubbard and Cheesley, both of whom had appeared for the first team during the 1971/72 season, plus the likely return of the injured Peter Silvester to come, Sargent had become, in Saunders' eyes, his eighth-choice striker, and therefore more than surplus to requirements. He'd had his opportunity, of sorts one appearance off the bench the previous August, replacing the then soon-to-be departed Malcolm Darling at Fulham – but had Saunders any thoughts that Sargent might be a likely replacement for Darling, they came and went on that one day. That twenty-four-minute cameo appearance from the bench was the sum total of Sargent's Norwich career, one of the shortest for any first-team player in the club's history.

As the 'big kick-off' drew ever closer, the Norwich players reconvened for pre-season training, as well as the usual club trip abroad. They'd actually played two additional games before breaking up that summer, a 6-0 win over Lowestoft Town on 1 May 1972. The game that was held for the benefit of the Fishermen's Fund, followed by a game against an All-Star XI two days later, this time for the benefit of the recently retired Albert Bennett, City losing 1-0. However, there was to be no long trip abroad this summer, just work and lots of it. The Canaries had spent nearly a fortnight in Portugal the previous May, enjoyed a trip to France in 1970 (beating Rouen 4-0), Spain in 1969 (winning 1-0 against Benidorm), Czechoslovakia in 1968 (Bratlislava Slovnaft 1-0) and, with some daring originality, a tour of Iceland in June 1966. But not this time, or so it seemed. The first of the club's three pre-season games was played at the Abbey Stadium on 29 July 1972 where Cambridge United were seen off to the tune of 3-0. Three days later, Norwich were in the exotic confines of Cleethorpes, defeating Grimsby Town 1-0 and then, a week before the season started, hosted St Mirren at Carrow Road, winning that game 4-1. The Buddies were then managed by ex-Norwich favourite Tommy Bryceland, who received a warm welcome.

Saunders, impassive and taciturn throughout the pre-season matches, was finally provoked into spending some of the club's money as a result of that St Mirren game. One of their players had caught his eye, a tall and lithe forward by the name of James Blair. He had certainly made an impact in Paisley, having scored sixty-four goals for the club since his release from Hibernian. That record, in a league where defenders tended to kick first and then kick again, was enough for Saunders. By the end of September, Jim Blair was a Norwich player, an £18,000 fee having been agreed between the two clubs.

Following that game, the club put up the metaphorical shutters and got down to some serious preparation for their opening game, now just a week away. Everton were to be the guests at Carrow Road and excitement was mounting, especially as *Anglia TV*'s Gerry Harrison and the *Match of the Week*[6] team were going to be there covering the historic game. Saunders was meticulous with his preparation and it made complete and utter sense for the club to now spend the last week of pre-season not only preparing for the Everton game, but also for the tough and demanding schedule that lay ahead. The celebrations were a damp Hertfordshire memory while the memories of the pre-season tour were non-existent – unless you count Cleethorpes – as there hadn't been one. Division One started here and the Canaries were ready.

The club's matchday programme for that historic fixture bears no comparison to the glossy, digitally produced matchday magazine that Peter Rogers and the media team produce for the club's fixtures today. The Norwich programme for the Premier League game against Everton at Carrow Road on 23 February 2013 featured full-page advertising slots for world-renowned companies such as Aviva and Barclays, a full-colour, 100-page extravaganza full of information, interviews and features, including ten full colour pages dedicated to the opposition. In contrast, the programme for that opening game of the 1972 consists of just sixteen pages, with colour only available in places for text – there were, and would not be for some time, colour photographs. The advertisers are for local companies, some sadly long gone, such as Mann Egerton, while Aviva appear in the guise of the Norwich Building Society ('We are the experts when it comes to saving money').

---

[6]   Norwich's first-ever appearance on the BBC's *Match of the Day* programme had been a 1-3 Carrow Road defeat to Sheffield Wednesday in an FA Cup fifth-round tie on 11 March 1967 with Frank Bough commentating. Tommy Bryceland had scored the Canaries' consolation goal in that game, thus becoming the first-ever Norwich goalscorer on the programme. Their first appearance on the show as a First Division club was the 1-0 win over champions Derby County on 26 August 1972, with John Motson at the mike and Graham Paddon the scorer.

Everton are featured on two advertisement-heavy pages, along with photographs of their manager, Harry Catterick and Micky Bernard, the 'reported £130,000 signing from Stoke City during the summer'. The cover features a simple graphic of Duncan Forbes kissing the Second Division championship trophy and is proudly titled, *Official Match-day Programme* Volume 1 Number 1. The price? Just 7p.

Geoffrey Watling opens the programme with his own personal message. His words are optimistic but tinged with caution. However, he cannot hide the pride he has for the club he loves either, writing,

> I am proud of the achievements of Manager Ron Saunders and his players, proud of the realisation that Norwich City are now numbered among the clubs who form the greatest footballing fraternity in the world. I am sure that, as the 1972/73 season progresses we shall have no cause to lose that sense of pride. Disappointments there are bound to be, but I am confident of our team's ability to hold their own in this new company.

A chairman speaking in glowing terms of his club and manager. How sad that, a little over a year later, a fierce boardroom row between Saunders and Watling after a 3-1 defeat at Carrow Road, one that saw the Canaries slump to twentieth place in the table, was the cause of Saunders' eventual exit from the club at a time of much tension and internal upset.

The Canaries opponents on that dark day? Everton.

Perhaps the biggest disappointment on that earlier, otherwise happier day as far as the Canaries were concerned was the attendance. Amid pre-match speculation that the club would have to restrict supporter numbers to 40,000, just 25,851 turned up. A contemporary comparison would be a home game in the Premier League today where the anticipated crowd and modern-day capacity for Carrow Road is around 27,000 – ironic, isn't it, that that figure is still less than one the club considered 'disappointing'! The gate for the Everton game was, however, around 64 per cent capacity. It was a bit like Norwich kicking off the 2013/14 Premier League season (when the opponents were, ironically again, also Everton) and, amid all the expectation of getting the near-27,000 gate, a standard for the previous two seasons for even the most uninspiring of fixtures, just over 17,000 attending. People would be wondering what had gone wrong, and questions would most certainly be asked. But of who, the club or support? The support was certainly there – a midweek game against Hull City towards the end of the previous season had attracted a gate of 30,342 at Carrow Road, which was topped by another midweek League fixture; the gate at the game against Bristol City on 4 April 1972 was 34,914. So, how had Norwich managed to suddenly 'lose' so many supporters?

Keith Skipper, writing in the *Eastern Daily Press*, pulled no punches. He put the blame squarely on the club, blaming the Carrow Road hierarchy for the poor attendance, saying,

A gate of just over 26,000 for Carrow Road's history-making day made nonsense of the justified build-up. The fixing of a 40,000 limit, eve-of-match messages to fans, statistical tit-bits about big attendances – weak jokes the lot of them on the day City deserved a huge send-off. It will be remembered as the 'Glorious Twelfth' when the Canaries bagged the first point in Division One through Scottish opportunism, and the stay-at-homes caused the biggest grouse for years.

Geoffrey Watling was disappointed in the attendance as well. He had greeted his Everton counterpart John Moores and was dispensing full Carrow Road hospitality to Moores and his directors, yet the Everton man could not have failed to see the massive gaps on the terraces, and this, a club about to play its first-ever game of top-flight football. Moores may well have been a betting man – he and his family had an interest in the Littlewoods Pools Company – but he would have gambled nothing more than even odds on Carrow Road being packed to the rafters for that first game. After the game, Watling admitted, 'I think that there had probably been too much talk about numbers and too much emphasis on the worries and troubles of a big crowd.' Saunders meanwhile, said it straight, as usual, calling the attendance 'downright disgusting', the accompanying glare suggesting that he would not welcome any further comment on the matter.

Controversy or not, there was still a match to be played. Everton had completed the previous season in fifteenth place, a second successive disappointing campaign for a team who were good enough to win the League championship in 1970. Despite that, they were still a good team, albeit one that had once been a very good one. Up until the Christmas of the previous year, they had been blessed with one of the most gifted midfield trios to grace English football – the 'Holy Trinity' of Alan Ball, Colin Harvey and Howard Kendall. With the three maestros conducting the Toffee orchestra, the winning of that 1970 championship was meant to suggest a shifting of power in football and for Everton to become the dominant team in England, never mind Merseyside. But it never happened. The following two campaigns saw them finish fourteenth and then fifteenth, and Ball had had enough. With Everton once more struggling at the lower end of the table by December 1971, he signed for Arsenal, League and cup 'double' winners the previous campaign, for a then British record transfer fee of £220,000.

The aforementioned Bernard had been signed as Ball's replacement, albeit a late one, some four months after Ball's departure. Sadly for Everton, he was no Ball – a competitive and versatile player, unquestionably, but not in Ball's class. So, while Arsenal built on their success, Everton failed to do so on theirs, a decline that lasted, League championship-wise, for fifteen years. Their next title arrived in 1985 and, again, at a time when they had an exceptionally good midfield: Ball, Harvey and Kendall this time read Paul Bracewell, Peter Reid, Trevor Stephen, Kevin Sheedy. Kendall, of course, was their manager at that time. Back in 1972, however, with Kendall and Harvey now joined by Bernard and, with the precocious talent of Joe Royle in attack, they were reckoned to be in with a chance of having a good season again, and Norwich were not expected to prove too much of an obstacle in their quest to commence the season with a win and two points. So it was somewhat surprising, at least to football fans from outside of Norfolk, when Norwich started the game by far the better-looking and more accomplished team, as if it were they who were the old hands of the First Division, not their blue-shirted opponents.

The Canaries were quick to the ball, the tackle and, at times, the man – a rambunctious opening saw Bone become the first Norwich player to earn himself a booking at this level. He and Cross bothered and bullied the Toffees' back four, snappy and aggressive, and doing exactly what Saunders would have expected of them – don't give them any time on the ball, don't give them any space, don't even let them have time to think. It was working. But despite Norwich's energy and aggression, class will always show on a football pitch, even if it doesn't always come out on top, and Everton had it in abundance. A spectacular strike from Jimmy Husband looked goal-bound until Kevin Keelan managed to push it away, while Royle was a constant threat. Nip and tuck therefore; Norwich's verve and commitment against Everton's passing game. Something would have to give sooner or later in what was proving to be a fairly open and entertaining game – and it did, for Norwich and Bone. It was Bone who received Doug Livermore's pass as half-time approached, breaking away and knocking the ball past David Lawson. His wide-eyed look of excitement as he took the applause of those who were at Carrow Road is one of the iconic sights in the club's history.

It couldn't last of course. Norwich were playing with the big boys now, and they couldn't simply take charge as they had done against Blackpool the previous season and pop in another four goals at their leisure. 1-0 down, Everton continued to play as if it was still 0-0, a level of patience and self-belief the Canary players would have noticed as they, in contrast, continued to charge about the pitch at 110 mph. There was barely ten minutes left when John Connolly teased another ball into the Norwich penalty area, and Royle, who spent the twilight years of his playing career at Norwich, joyfully headed it past the otherwise imperious Keelan – the first of six goals Royle would score in seven League games.

Honours even and almost immediately the tempo of the game lessened, both clubs, it would seem, content with the draw. A late penalty appeal for Norwich when Cross was bundled over was waved away by referee Bartley Homewood and it was over.

As considerably fewer Norwich fans than usual made their way home, stopping off to get a *Pink 'Un* as well as some chips at the Kerrison Road fish and chip shop, the talk would have been largely optimistic. It was a promising start to life in Division One, if not a spectacular one, and there was much work to do. How long, most fans wondered, would Saunders retain his faith in the team that got us up (the transfer window didn't 'slam shut' until the spring back then), how long before he got some new players in? As far as that last question was concerned:

some considerable time! Impressed by his team's effort on the day, Saunders chose the same starting XI for the next game, a tantalising reboot of the East Anglian Derby at Ipswich. And again for the Canaries' third game, and their fourth. In fact, it wasn't until Norwich's ninth League game of the 1972/73 season that he made a change to the side, one forced by an injury to Dave Stringer. Terry Anderson filled in for Stringer at centre-half and Neil O'Donnell came in at right midfield. Sadly for Norwich, the gamble didn't pay off, Anderson's lack of experience and nous in that role at the highest level being ruthlessly exploited by West Ham at Upton Park, and the Hammers winning 4-0. Such was the way they dealt with Norwich on the day – or the way in which Norwich let them play – that two of the goals came from Bobby Moore crosses. Yes, Bobby Moore, the elder statesman of English football, now thirty-one, was allowed to gambol down the Norwich flanks like a fresh-faced teenager. Saunders, perhaps luckily for his charges, hadn't been at the game – he'd been at another watching a potential signing[7] – but he would have learnt enough not to gamble on square pegs in round holes again. For the Canaries' next game at home to Arsenal, Anderson was restored to his rightful place in the Norwich midfield, and twenty-year-old Steve Govier, seen as the most promising of Norwich's young players, came in to partner Forbes. The change worked perfectly. Norwich won 3-2 in front of a much more healthy gate of 32,170, Anderson scoring two goals himself, including the winner.

That game was Norwich's tenth League fixture of the campaign and the win lifted them to tenth place in the table. But better was to come. The Canaries won three of their next four League games, and a highly impressive 2-1 win at Leicester City, for whom Canary nemesis Keith Weller was on target, meant that Norwich were now sixth in Division One – an astonishing achievement for a team that had been written off as relegation fodder from almost the moment they had been promoted. They were unbeaten at home and were just four points shy of table topping Liverpool. And, just as satisfactorily, they were one place and one point ahead of their nearest rivals, Ipswich Town.

The Canaries' most impressive result of the season was against Arsenal. But it wasn't that 3-2 win in the League. It came at Highbury in a League Cup quarter-final tie on 21 November, three days after they had seen off West Brom at Carrow Road with a 2-0 win, Stringer and Paddon the scorers. That win had taken Norwich back up to sixth place in the League and, all of a sudden, everyone seemed to be a Norwich City fan. The club had adapted to life in the top flight exceptionally well, scoring goals and, crucially, winning their fair share of away games – they'd already triumphed on the road at Ipswich, Crystal Palace and Leicester City. Their points per game ration was running at a healthy 1.16 – only two points for a win remember – and had they kept that up all season, Norwich

---

7 With the signing of Jim Blair now only a week distant, it is fair to suppose that Saunders was in the company of ex-Canary and St Mirren manager Tommy Bryceland that afternoon, watching Blair play for the Buddies at home to Dunfermline Athletic.

would have finished on forty-nine points and in fourth place! It had, nonetheless, been an incredible debut season for them at the elite level, and meant they could travel to Highbury for that League Cup game in fine heart and with nothing to fear, least of all from a team that they had already beaten that season.

That they won it therefore should not be too much of a surprise. That they did so in such emphatic fashion most certainly should be. Arsenal, double winners just two seasons earlier and FA Cup finalists the season before, plus Fairs Cup (now the Europa League) winners in 1970, were then, as now, one of the powerhouse sides of English football. They were smarting from perceived 'failure' the previous campaign – fifth in the League; FA Cup finalists; European Cup quarter-finalists. They'd tumbled out of the League Cup to Sheffield United after a replay. Unlike now, this was a time when teams took the domestic cup competitions seriously; they entered strong sides, and, without question, wanted to win them. The FA Cup was, of course, the ultimate bauble to display in the boardroom, but the League Cup was not a bad consolation, and the Gunners' record in the competition was a good one – they'd reached the final in 1968 and 1969. So, make no mistake about it, they wanted to win the competition, and with a home tie against Norwich the only barrier between them and a place in the semi-finals, they'd have been itching to send the Canaries packing – as well as getting some revenge for their defeat a couple of months earlier.

They duly wheeled out the big names: the Gunners' big guns Frank McLintock, Alan Ball, John Radford and Charlie George. Plus the enigmatic Peter Marinello, an occasionally brilliant but definitely wayward forward, who had been dubbed 'the next George Best' by the British media when he'd arrived at Highbury in early 1970. The sad truth of it was of any that played on the Highbury pitch that night looked like the next George Best – and, to paraphrase Monty Python, 'there'd been a few' – he was wearing a yellow shirt and his name was Graham Paddon. Paddon even looked the part: the beard, the long, flowing hair, the popularity among the female support. He was becoming, in truth, almost too good for the effective but workmanlike Norwich side. He stood out, and in this game he shone like a beacon scoring a hat-trick. Norwich didn't just beat, they absolutely destroyed Arsenal 3-0, a result that sent shockwaves throughout the game in England, and rightly so. Norwich City had finally arrived and, tellingly, so had Paddon. He would be a wanted man from now on.

Admittedly, Norwich had always been known as a 'cup side' – it was, up until this season at least, their calling card, the way they were acknowledged by the rest of the footballing nation. Ever since their formation in 1902, the Canaries had distinguished themselves by tumbling out giants of cup competitions: Tottenham in 1914 through to Liverpool in 1937 and 1951; Arsenal in 1954; Manchester United and Tottenham in 1959; Blackpool and Manchester City in 1963; Manchester United in 1967 and Sunderland in 1968. These were all giants of the game who had been arbitrarily dismissed by Norwich in the FA Cup, their shock exits briefly but gloriously bringing the Canaries to everyone's attention. The fact that Norwich were now equals to Arsenal in the First Division seemed, for some reason, to make their firing of the Gunners in that game all the more extraordinary. From being a brief but otherwise uninteresting distraction, they had become a fixed one, a team of perceived ne'er-do-wells, led by a manager with more a reputation for being an RSM than a master tactician and, against all the odds, were succeeding in their maiden top-flight season. That game and the result, as Keith Skipper succinctly put it in the *Eastern Daily Press*, meant that the Canaries had 'thrust their top-flight calling cards under Fleet Street noses'. He was right.

Above it all stood Paddon, a man who typified the qualities of that Norwich side: flair, passion and no little skill. He glided about the Highbury pitch as if he was floating on air, his first goal coming from a Livermore pass out on the left, Paddon's low shot dribbling through and past Barnett's outstretched hands. Fluke? Maybe. But the second one wasn't. His second was fired home from a tight angle, while the third again showcased his lethal left foot, the ball being clipped rather than shot into the Arsenal goal. Cue pandemonium and a rapidly disappearing red-and-white half of the Highbury crowd. The win came at a cost – don't they always seem to when a 'smaller' club takes the glory – with Forbes, brave in defence and a born leader, had to be stretchered off and taken to hospital with a collapsed lung, an injury that would keep him out for eight League games, the very time that Norwich would have wanted to ride the very large yellow-and-green wave they were now cresting.

As for Paddon, the world seemed laid at his feet. Norwich would, and did, receive enquiries about his availability but he was a loyal player, one who had even taken some persuading to leave Coventry when Norwich had originally come calling for his services in 1969. He remained at Carrow Road despite the growing interest in him, professionally lifted, no doubt, by the words of Arsenal's double-winning skipper Frank McLintock, who said of him after that game, 'He looks a very, very good player. I liked the way that he was prepared to take on opponents, a sign of confidence. He may be all left foot but it was good enough to put three past us and not many people do that.' Indeed they don't Frank – at least not since Norwich had also put three past you, in the League, eight weeks earlier!

'All left foot' sounds a bit damning when taken into context. It implies a player is not fully rounded or developed, that he has only one trick in his armoury and, when that has been identified and dealt with, he no longer remains a threat. However, it is like saying that all Peter Lorimer could do was hit the ball hard, or that Bobby Moore could only play at centre-half – unfair on the player. His obvious ability surely meant he should have been very seriously considered by England for full international recognition that season, especially when players like Peter Storey and Alan Mullery, then into his thirties, were being considered for selection ahead of him. Perhaps McLintock's comments held Paddon back as a player. You can be certain that, if a leading club like Arsenal had been interested in buying him, then those words would have made them think twice. Paddon did eventually get international recognition in the shape of one England under-23 cap – as an over-age player – in 1976; a snub from the very top level of the game which, to my mind, was and remains a footballing disgrace.

Paddon and Norwich strode on regardless. But the more significant incident of that night was the loss of Forbes. Norwich had, the previous campaign, muddled through his enforced absence, but it was going to be more difficult this time to manage without him. They were a top-flight club coming up against class opponents and players in every game they played: they needed Forbes' presence and leadership. The Canaries played eight League games without him following their Highbury high spot, drawing two and losing six of them, conceding seventeen goals. In the preceding eight League games before that, all featuring Forbes, they had conceded seven goals, losing just two games in the process – one of those an unfortunate 1-0 defeat to Southampton at The Dell, a game Norwich had otherwise dominated.

If Paddon was the star of the show, Forbes was the side's most important player. By the time he returned to League action for the visit of Leeds United on 20 January, Norwich had been tipped from its crest and was now gasping for air from a sandy seabed. They lost 2-1 and then went on to lose against Sheffield United a week later. It made eleven League games without a win when West Ham prevailed 1-0 at Carrow Road on 10 February. That game, surprisingly, turned out to be the last in Norwich colours for talismanic striker Jimmy Bone.

Forbes' loss had not been the only downfall of that remarkable win at Highbury. The performance and influence of Paddon had made the other clubs realise that if you nullified Paddon then you nullified Norwich. Paddon needed a minder, someone to step in and put his best foot forward in defence of his silkily skilled teammate; a presence who would not only give him the time and space to play, but also, crucially, give other teams someone to worry about in the Canary ranks. And Saunders knew exactly who he wanted to fulfil that role: Sheffield United's craggy midfield enforcer Trevor Hockey.

Not surprisingly, the Blades were not too keen on the idea of parting with him. They too had an artist gracing their midfield – Tony Currie, a man who was able to play as he wanted thanks to the menacing presence of Hockey alongside him. But maybe there was a chance? The Blades had a new manager, Ken Furphy, who, like all new bosses, wanted to form a team in his own image – uncompromising, hard to beat, a touch of blood, sweat and tears about the starting XI. And, if he had not been at the club during both of their encounters with Norwich that season, there were plenty who were, one of whom was Currie. A few others, notably defenders, also had good cause to remember their bruising encounters with the team that played in yellow and green but contained one player who would have looked better in a red shirt as it was clearly the colour of the blood he was always prepared to spill for the cause. So Furphy took Saunders' call and agreed to his initial enquiry. Yes, he said. You can have Hockey. But listen, I want Jimmy Bone in part exchange.

And that was that. Furphy had never expected, not for one moment, that Saunders would agree to relinquish his hold on the tenacious Scot who had scored many of his goals through the gentle art of worrying both the ball and opposing defences half to death. But he agreed to the deal. Yes, the loss of Bone was a critical blow to a Norwich side that needed goals and wins to ensure that they didn't repeat part one of the Northampton path to oblivion straight away. But they also needed someone to rake the midfield area, picking off passes and opponents as he did so. Besides, in David Cross, Saunders felt he had sufficient attacking strength to get those goals. The equation worked. Hockey's presence would let Paddon, his passing ability blessed by telepathic play, create the chances that would be fed upon by the determined Cross, a man who was not averse to being in the thick of the action himself if necessary. Job done. Q. E. D.

Hockey duly arrived for training sessions with his new club in the days leading up to a vital League game with Newcastle United at Carrow Road. He would have presented quite a formidable sight as he arrived at Trowse on his first morning. He stood a shade under 5 feet 6 inches, yet had the look and swagger of a much bigger man, his long hair and unkempt beard giving him the look of a pirate – one who gave no quarter and expected none either. The thought of him and Duncan Forbes being introduced for the first time – craggy men, born of mountain and moor and as uncompromising as they come – is a tantalising one. With the two of them, plus the rapacious Cross in attack, Saunders didn't so much have a strong spine running through his team as a stick of dynamite.

Thus, with the new member of cast in place, the plot unfolded.

Hockey made his debut for Norwich in that game against Newcastle, donning the No. 6 shirt at the expense of the popular but occasionally inconsistent Max Briggs. Saunders selected a side and formation that would not have been too dissimilar to the 4-2-3-1 preferred by Chris Hughton today: Keelan in goal, and a back four of Payne, Stringer, Govier and Butler with Hockey and Doug Livermore providing the barrier between them, and an advanced midfield trio of Blair, Paddon and Colin Suggett, another new signing, and Cross ploughing a muddy furrow as the lone striker. Did it work? Well, to an extent. Hockey and Suggett provided the new blood, the enthusiasm and the hard work; however, the overall Norwich performance was tainted by the minds of players who had a League Cup final to think about the following weekend – for which Briggs retained his place ahead of Hockey. It was also unfortunate for Saunders that he had been without Forbes, for it was the inexperience of Govier that let the wily Malcolm McDonald sprint free and fire the only goal of the game. Norwich had now gone twelve games without a win. By the time Chelsea came to Carrow Road on 14 April, that run had stretched to nineteen. And yet, barely perceptibly, the tide that was pushing the Canaries towards the bottom of the table was beginning to turn, and Hockey's presence was very much part of that change.

His presence in the Norwich midfield in the League game against Coventry had unsettled the Sky Blue midfield so much that an uncharacteristic error from the normally reliable Willie Carr had led to Norwich opening the scoring in a 1-1 draw. Ten days later, City still started at a gallop at home to Leicester. Hockey stood at the base of the Carrow Road trenches, revolver in hand and threatening to shoot anyone who didn't advance and take the game to their opponents. It nearly worked. Paddon scored from the penalty spot and Paul Cheesley nearly added a second as Norwich looked for that elusive win. It nearly came, 1-1 again, but another point. Then Everton at Goodison and, marshalled by the superb Cross, City went 2-0 up; Hockey virtually running himself into the ground in the process and needing to be substituted, not that he would have come off that easily in the first place. He was missed; the game ended 2-2 and a precious win had escaped once again. It was, as with the games against Coventry and Leicester, becoming a case of so near yet so far.

City nearly got it at Old Trafford on 7 April. Hockey no doubt thoroughly enjoying the opportunity to imperiously stride the Mancunians' turf, effectively shackling the likes of Kidd, Charlton and Law as he did so – and so effectively that Kidd had to be taken off, battered and exhausted after as hard an afternoon's work as he would have had that season. Sadly, while Hockey minded the stars, it was left to one of the supporting cast, Mick Martin, to score United's goal, and City headed home pointless again. Nineteen League games without a win and firmly at the bottom of the table by now. It was all looking rather grim for Norwich, a far cry from those lazy, hazy, crazy days of the preceding autumn when they had lain, blinking in the fierce light of recognition, in the semi-finals of the League Cup and sixth in the table.

But the win finally came. And, when it did, it was against Chelsea, the team that Hockey would have dismissed pre-match as 'fancy dans', going on to treat them in the same dismissive manner. It's perhaps fair to say that, multi-talented as they were, the Chelsea side of Osgood and Co. didn't enjoy their afternoon in Norwich. Hockey was as belligerent as ever in midfield, causing chaos and creating space, and enabling Norwich to put in a quick passing game. They were rewarded. Mellor and Suggett combined to set up Cross, who made no mistakes. He didn't in the next game either, a rugged and bad-tempered game at West Brom that City won 1-0; the two points gained there pushing them, after weeks of doubt, into twentieth place and safety. A 2-1 win over Crystal Palace in the penultimate game of the season confirmed it. It was a game that saw Forbes and Hockey rampant, the footballing brothers-in-arms embracing the sort of atmosphere that a crowd of nearly 37,000 at Carrow Road could generate, ending it twin architects of a fight no one expected City to win.

If Paddon had been the star of the season, the far less cerebral – footballing-wise – duo of Forbes and Hockey had been its saving grace. Forbes had, for the second consecutive season, missed a large part of the Canaries' campaign and, for the second consecutive time, it coincided with a wobble in the team's form and confidence. He had, perhaps, an unfair reputation as being a 'hard man'; if that was the case, then he was far more sinned against on the pitch than the sinner. In 357 appearances for Norwich, he was never sent off once. The record of a 'hard man'? Doubtful. Indeed, proof that Forbes was more likely to have been the victim of foul play while on the pitch comes when his injury record is given the once over – cut eyes, a broken nose and a punctured lung to name but three examples. He could play, of that there is no doubt. Brave, quick to the tackle, and positionally aware in defence or at the other end of the pitch, as his twelve Canary goals illustrate. His return to the team had, slowly, brought Norwich out of their slump. Following his injury in the home win against West Brom, Norwich went without Forbes for twelve games – winning just one, with two draws and nine defeats, a run of form that took them from sixth in the League to second from the bottom. However, in the twelve games he played in following his return, the record was three wins, three draws and six defeats, enough to keep Norwich up by two points. Had Forbes been single-handedly responsible for keeping Norwich up? No, of course not. It was a team effort that featured, at one point or another, twenty different players, all of whom played some part in the League season. It seems clear, however, that the team felt more confident with him in the team than out of it, a reliable and trustworthy captain who was a born leader and had the utmost respect of everyone at the club, as well as all Norwich fans, then and now. The problem for Saunders was going to be replacing him: by the time the 1973/74 season kicked off, Forbes would be thirty-two, would his battered body stand up to another season at the top level?

Hockey, of course, should take a lot of credit for his part in the run that kept Norwich up. He made only thirteen appearances for the club, twelve of them alongside Forbes. What a combination they must have been, and a pair whose mere naming on the Norwich team sheet would have put shivers up the spine of many an opposing player. He had been brought in by Saunders to do a job and he did exactly what was asked of him. It seems strange in retrospect that the Norwich manager felt he could do without him during the next season, Hockey being sold to Aston Villa in June 1973. Compared to Forbes' longevity at the club, Hockey was there and gone in an instant, those thirteen League appearances the sum total of his Norwich record. Despite that, he is still remembered fondly in the eyes of many Norwich supporters, and it is perhaps true to say that no Norwich player has reached near legend status at the club after playing so few games.

The Canaries' ultimately successful fight against relegation was, of course, subject to a rather welcome distraction with an appearance in the League Cup final at Wembley – the first time the Canaries had appeared at the stadium, fifty years after it had been opened. Their route to the final had, of course, included the thrilling win over Arsenal at Highbury in the quarter-finals, a success that earned Norwich a two-legged tie against Chelsea in the semi-final.

If Chelsea had been favourites to reach Wembley at the Canaries' expense, then that assumption was swiftly put to rest during the first leg at Stamford Bridge on 13 December 1972. The two clubs had only met there in a League game four days earlier, one that saw the Blues prevail, winning 3-1 with some ease; goals from Bill Garner and Ian Hutchinson putting Chelsea ahead only for Bone, recalled after missing the previous game, to score a simply stunning reply with fifteen minutes left. A betting man might have put something on the Canaries at that point, but the revival was a brief one, Hutchinson getting on the end of a cross to put Chelsea 3-1 up. Given the ease of their win, and the manner in which Chelsea's two most physical players, Micky Droy in defence and striker Garner, had dominated, Chelsea boss Dave Sexton gambled on leaving both out for the first leg, preferring to bring in Gary Locke, then only eighteen, in place of Droy, and replacing Garner with Chris Garland, a striker the Blues had bought from Bristol City the previous season. Both were good players, but adequate replacements for players who had bossed Norwich for the entirety of the League game? Saunders, on the contrary, did what he always did, retaining his faith in the same line-up. It was the right decision. Bone and Cross prospered against the rejigged Chelsea, an error by the normally unflappable Houseman enabling Cross to spring free, his pass setting Bone free to score. A minute later, with the Chelsea players still pointing and making gestures to one another, Bone repaid the favour, feeding Cross who strode forward before sending a lob over Phillips to make it 2-0. There could have been another, Max Briggs hot at the post, but with Chelsea chasing shadows and Steve Govier playing magnificently in the Canaries' defence, the game was won after the second goal – on just twelve minutes – and Norwich prepared for the second leg at Carrow Road with justifiable confidence.

That second leg is now more famous for the thick blanket of fog that descended on the ground and surrounding area than the game itself. With Norwich leading the game 3-2 (and thus 5-2 ahead on aggregate), the fog swept in from the river with just five minutes of the game left, making play not only virtually invisible for spectators but for the players and referee as well. The man in charge, Gordon Hill, certainly wanted to get the game finished, with Norwich three goals ahead and just five minutes remaining, the result and conclusion of the tie was a formality. Hill initially suspended play for seventeen minutes in the vain hope that the fog would clear. However, when this proved not to be the case he had no choice but to abandon the game, much to the delight of the Chelsea players. To be fair to Hill it was his only option, and thoughts, however fleeting, that Norwich should be awarded the tie anyway, such was the magnitude of their league, were swiftly dismissed. The game *had* to be replayed. Ron Saunders was typically forthright after the game, declaring that, 'We are claiming the game. We beat them', while Doug Livermore admitted to *Eastern Daily Press* man Keith

Skipper afterwards that he was 'going to go home, have a good kip and try to forget it'. When Hill originally debated whether to try and complete the game or not, he was surrounded by Norwich players insisting that they could see perfectly and that play could continue, while the Chelsea players were adamant that it was 'impossible'.

Such is life, and football. When clear skies and perfect visibility broke over Carrow Road a little before 10 p.m., it led Peter Osgood to declare, 'Reckon we could finish it now.' If only. The Norwich chairman, Geoffrey Watling was a little more circumspect, saying, 'Naturally, we are extremely disappointed that only a few minutes separated us from our first-ever appearance at Wembley.' Watling could, after all, be fairly confident that, third game or not, Norwich's lead was strong enough to eventually reach the final. It was so proved with a Steve Govier's decisive header from a Dave Stringer corner just after half-time, sealing an on-aggregate 3-0 win for the Canaries. But it hadn't been easy. Keelan made two utterly stupendous saves from Tommy Baldwin, said player also going on to miss several other chances to make the replayed game rather more interesting than it had been, not that any of the Norwich fans were bothered about that.

It was quite a time to be a Norwich City supporter, or player. The Second Division championship the previous season had brought First Division football to Carrow Road for the first time, the opening half of that season proving to be so successful, results-wise, that the Canaries had climbed up to as high as sixth in the table that November. By the time of the win over Chelsea, however, the club had gone seven League games without a win and slid to fifteenth place. Five consecutive League defeats followed in the weeks after that game, and a week before the final, another one, this time at home to Newcastle, saw Norwich slip down to twentieth. That game had seen new signings Trevor Hockey and Colin Suggett make their debut as Saunders looked to strengthen both his side and options towards the run in; however, neither would be available for the final, as with striker Jimmy Bone, the sacrificial lamb in the deal that had seen Hockey join the club.

For the final, Saunders picked the same team that had started the season against Everton, the sole change being Jim Blair replacing Bone in attack. They were up against a Tottenham team that sported international players in abundance – Pat Jennings, Joe Kinnear, Mike England, Alan Gilzean, Martin Chivers and Martin Peters. But this had not stopped Norwich from winning against them at Carrow Road in the League back in October when two David Cross goals earned them a 2-1 win. The ingredient that had earned Norwich victory on that day had been their greater work rate, and it was expected that they would employ the same tactics again at Wembley.

The final itself, played out on about as gloomy and wet a March day as you could ask for, was a disappointment, but only in terms of the result. For Norwich acquitted themselves with the hitherto-unknown surrounds and situation well, the enjoyment the players were having on the day clearly evident. They were relaxed throughout, right from the normally nerve-inducing preliminaries before the game, pre-match pitch inspections and that long ceremonial walk onto the pitch taken in their stride, and with smiles on faces all round – more the behaviour of Wembley veterans rather than nervous first-timers. This translated into the early play, Tottenham's balance being swiftly interrupted when an injury to John Pratt after just fifteen minutes necessitated an early change, the busy Ralph Coates coming on in his place. Tottenham were then affected by another on-pitch injury, this time Mike England, and one that nearly earned Norwich the lead after half an hour. With England clearly struggling, the Norwich attack was very clearly focusing on his lack of mobility, and on a typical flank-led raid. When Terry Anderson crossed the ball over for the advancing Norwich attackers, there was no Mike England to mop up the danger. The chance and space fell to Paddon and he could, maybe he should, have scored, only for Pat Jennings, having anticipated the likely danger to snatch the ball from his feet. Later on in the half, Norwich could have scored again, a precise Briggs corner being met by Forbes, already one of the dominant players on display. His flick was meant for the waiting Cross, but again, Jennings saw the danger and gathered the ball.

More chances fell City's way in the second half. Blair and Cross combined to set up Anderson for a shot, only for it to shave the crossbar. Minutes later, the normally imperious Jennings lost both focus and concentration when Blair's challenge caused him to lose the ball, but no yellow shirt was near enough to make the most of it. Then Norwich had a free-kick; a chance for Paddon to test Jennings from distance, the colossus from Newry making amends with a timely save. Norwich continued in this manner, snapping and snarling at Tottenham's well-heeled heels, and continuing to defy the critics who had expected them to sit tight and hope to score a goal on the break. Not so, and the next chance fell to Cross. It seemed that Norwich had to score sooner or later and the yellow shirts continued to advance forward, looking for that vital opening, the one that would, in such a tight and evenly matched contest, probably win the game.

When it came of course, it was to a white-shirted player, substitute Coates, who took advantage of a deflection off England's shot, rifling home a very hard, very low shot past Keelan from 20 yards out. The goal gave both the Tottenham players and their fans some belief, and they should have gone further ahead five minutes later only for Chivers to shoot straight at Keelan.

Norwich continued to press but a lot of their early verve seemed to have been drained away, a header from Forbes that sailed over the bar in the final minute their last serious chance to score. The cup and the glory therefore went to North London, but the Norwich performance had contained much to be proud of and the Canaries headed home beaten but in good heart, content, at least, that they had made a contest on the day and that there was no reason that other ones would not be coming in the future – as indeed one would, just two years later.

Given that Wembley disappointment, and the form and results that had not only got them there but had also highlighted the first half of the season with those impressive victories against the likes of Ipswich Town, Derby County (then reigning League champions remember), Arsenal (twice) and Tottenham, it was perhaps just that Norwich did, at least, retain their First Division status at the end of the season. Relegation would have been a cruel blow to a team that had brought so much more than mere colour to the top flight. The courage that they had shown in hauling themselves away from the relegation places, including three wins from their last five games, was testimony to a club that had found their level and thoroughly deserved another chance. It had been hard, perhaps far more so than anyone had expected – except, you suspect, Ron Saunders. Whether he, a clearly ambitious manager, would want to be there to do it all over again the following season was open to question. He had, after all, delivered his remit to the board – promotion and survival. Was it time now for him to move on and for Norwich to find another young manager to continue the good work, or would Saunders, proud of his team and players, want to push on and make Norwich serious challengers? Time would tell. But as the season came to an end with Liverpool champions and Crystal Palace and West Brom promoted, most Norwich fans wanted to look back on a hectic season now passed and look forward to the next one. The logistics of it could, for the time being, wait a while.

Norwich celebrated their inaugural top-flight season by flying off to Norway a little over a week after their final League fixture, a meaningless but entertaining game at Stoke City that they lost 2-0. The one game played, against one of the country's leading sides, SK Brann, ended in a 1-0 victory. Following that little distraction, however, there was a gap of three months before the side played another game; this being the first of three pre-season friendlies played in August 1973 (a 4-2 win at Colchester United).

Saunders was, perhaps surprisingly, still at the helm. He was ambitious, that was clear. He'd said so when he arrived at the club and had repeated that mantra since. Could he achieve all of his ambitions in the game with Norwich though? That summer of 1973 drew some interesting parallels with the situation the Canaries found themselves in nearly four decades later when, after ensuring the Canaries had survived their first season back in the Premier League after a seven-year absence, another ambitious manager, Paul Lambert, was linked with perceived bigger and better things. The consensus then was that he had done all that he could ever hope to achieve at Norwich. Lambert obviously thought the same, taking the opportunity to restore the ailing fortunes of Aston Villa with some relish and not a little rancour directed at the club that had 'made him' in the process. As it was, by the summer of 1973 there was one intriguing managerial opening in the First Division, at Everton, Saunders' first club as a player.

He was born in Birkenhead, was high profile and had enjoyed an excellent two seasons with Norwich that had included an appearance at Wembley. Thus, inevitably, he was linked with the post. When it looked as if Everton were going to be successful in luring Don Revie from Leeds United as their new manager, speculation would have linked Saunders as a possible candidate to replace him there. In the end, however, Everton appointed Billy Bingham, with Revie electing to stay at Leeds. Saunders, therefore, stayed at Norwich. It may, of course, have always been his intention. My own thoughts on the matter, however, tend towards thinking he was already, much in the manner of Lambert, thinking about his next move and his next club. Time and, more crucially, the way Norwich settled into the new season would decide his fate. So for more than one reason, he would have wanted the Canaries to have another good, even a better, season.

Saunders was still in place therefore, but there was still an important and very unexpected departure from the club that season, Geoffrey Watling decided to stand down as chairman, with Arthur South taking over. South, like Saunders, was the Labour leader of Norwich City Council and a former Lord Mayor of the City. It is, perhaps, fair to say that he was a straight talker who didn't suffer fools gladly – rather like his manager, he tended to, that phrase again, 'sort them out'. Soon after his appointment he shot across the bows of Saunders, warning that there would inevitably be some sharp talking between the two of them as he, like Saunders, had a 'hard streak'.

On the footballing side, Saunders had spent the long summer break looking for reinforcements for his squad. Defender Colin Prophett arrived from Sheffield Wednesday for £40,000, while striker Billy Kellock arrived from Cardiff City on a free transfer. While neither signing was one to excite the hearts and minds of the Norwich fans, the arrival of Prophett did, at least, make some sense. The Norwich defence had been troubled by injuries the previous season, so Prophett, an accomplished and versatile player who could operate across the back four, seemed a good acquisition. He was experienced as well, having made 117 appearances for the Owls, some of which had been in the top flight. The signing of Kellock, however, was more of a mystery. The Canaries had unquestionably signed him for his potential, but in a squad that had lost Bone to Sheffield United and Foggo to Portsmouth the previous season while Peter Silvester was still out due to injury. In addition to that, Jim Blair was struggling to make an impact, so were Norwich really going to put all of their goalscoring eggs in one basket and hope that David Cross would be able to lead the line on his own that season? Norwich had other promising young players in contention – Paul Cheesley had impressed in his nine League appearances, although he had failed to score, while there was hope for Norwich-born Glenn Self: he had made his City debut in 1970 and was still described as 'promising' and 'one for the future'. Perhaps that said it all. The Canaries did, therefore, look as if they were going to go into the season with a shortage of experienced strikers, and it was deemed surprising that Norwich had not made more of an effort to improve their striking options for the new season, especially given the fact that former fan favourite and proven goalscorer Ron Davies had moved from Southampton to Portsmouth at the end of the previous season. Had Norwich been interested in bringing Davies, then still just thirty, back to Carrow Road; indeed, were they even aware of his availability? Such a move would not only have been a hugely popular one but would have presented the somewhat tantalising option of a Cross/Davies spearhead in the Canaries attack for the new season. As it was, it looked like it would be either Cross/Kellock or Cross on his own. Not a particularly appealing prospect, and not a very good start to the season either. Saunders eventually opted to play Colin Suggett in a more advanced role just behind Cross with, admittedly high quality, support coming from a midfield that included Paddon, Anderson and ex-Manchester City winger Ian Mellor, a late and fairly costly £65,000 addition to the ranks towards the end of the previous season. Providing Cross got the service, it was likely he would score the goals needed. But would he?

As it turned out, City did not have too many problems scoring goals in their opening half-dozen League games of the 1973/74 season, netting eight in total – two up on the same number of games the previous campaign. The goals were shared among five players, plus an own goal. Cross had contributed two, with another two coming from Suggett, plus one each from Mellor, Paddon and Stringer. Acceptable you would think except that, in those six games, Norwich recorded just one victory, that coming at home to Southampton in the sixth game. They therefore welcomed Arsenal to Carrow Road three days later in fine heart and voice, confident of their chances of repeating that success against a team they had beaten twice the previous season.

But not this time. Arsenal, prepared and knowledgeable of both the strengths and, crucially, weaknesses of their opponents, gave Norwich a footballing lesson, and in doing so gained some revenge for that League Cup defeat the previous November. The game ended with the Gunners winning 4-0: they were three up at half-time, and could have had more had it not been for Keelan. Also, worryingly, Stringer and Forbes had looked a little vulnerable. Much of that could have been down to the fact that Prophett was still settling into his role as right-back, concern enough for Saunders to bring in another new player: Les Wilson from Bristol City, who replaced Prophett for the game at Sheffield United. It mattered not. Norwich lost again, just as they did a week later, 1-0 at Leeds. These three consecutive defeats sunk the Canaries to twentieth in the table, and had not only seen zero points but zero goals scored as well – Cross, as expected by some, was feeling the strain of the onerous duties that had been placed upon him.

Determined to at least tighten up his defence, Saunders experimented with the back four. Stringer and Forbes were ever-present, but perming any two from Prophett, Black, Wilson and Clive Payne for the full-back positions. Geoff Butler, so consistent the previous season, was clearly missed and the side looked unsettled and lacked the confidence that had earmarked so many of their better displays the previous season, including the League Cup final defeat to Tottenham when the back four had been the very admirable Payne, Butler, Stringer and Forbes. This was perfectly illustrated on 26 October, when Norwich travelled to Stamford Bridge, only for there to be more defensive uncertainty as Chelsea won 3-0.

Norwich had now gone seven games without a win, and had only scored two goals in that time. Enough was enough as far as Saunders was concerned. Throughout his time at Norwich he had tried to stay loyal to his players, rewarding good displays with prolonged runs in the team, identifying good partnerships by making them virtually immovable, and even giving teams and players who had performed badly the ultimate vote of confidence by giving them the chance to put it right in the next game, or even the one after that, such was his faith in those players. That Chelsea game and their performance changed all that. For Norwich's next League game, a home clash with Leicester, he wielded the selection axe and made four changes to his starting XI, a move of seismic proportions for him. Out went Prophett, Black, Livermore and Mellor, and in came Payne, Wilson, Howard and O'Donnell. And it worked. Norwich won and kept a clean sheet. It had been an own goal by Leicester's Denis Rofe, but no matter, the two points took Norwich out of the relegation places (this was the first season that saw three, not two clubs go down, so twentieth place, a success the last campaign, would be disaster this time around) and gave them, hopefully, something to build on in the next few games.

It was therefore strange that three of the men (Prophett, Black and Livermore) who had borne the brunt of their manager's ire after the Chelsea game were back in for the match against Stoke on 11 November. Quite a vote of confidence in Payne, Wilson and Howard, all of whom had been drafted in and all of whom had played well in the Leicester match. However, Saunders seemed to be making more of a point to those players they had replaced, and they were duly back in the side at the Victoria Ground where Norwich's very mini-renaissance came to a halt as they lost 2-0, Stoke's overall superiority being a lot more convincing than the scoreline would suggest.

Saunders shuffled the pack yet again for the next match, a home game against Everton. Four changes again, one of those enforced by the seemingly crazy decision to sell Cross to Coventry City four days after that loss at Stoke, the considerable gap in the side being filled, and only partially, by youngster Paul Cheesley. By now, both fans, shattered at the loss of Cross, and the players were feeling dispirited, and even though Norwich went ahead through a John McLaughlin own goal, Everton hit back and scored three of their own, the third being an own goal off the unfortunate Forbes. It was all too much for the Norwich fans. Forbes had been trying, manfully and only as a captain can, to hold things together on the pitch, but even he was suffering, that own goal a comedic turn that put the seal on a woeful Norwich performance, perhaps their worst since promotion, or even since Saunders had been appointed. Large numbers of the Norwich crowd jeered at the end and cushions were, peremptorily and with some feeling, thrown onto the pitch from the crowd.

For Arthur South, witnessing those cushions sailing their rebellious arc onto the Carrow Road turf would have been a painful experience, and one he wasn't prepared to tolerate. Yes, the actions of the fans, normally among the most passive and non-demonstrative in the game, was unacceptable. As were the recent performances of the players who were, in South's mind, paid handsomely for the privilege of representing Norwich and Norfolk. He'd come into the job with the reputation of a straight-talker. Well, now it was time for some straight talking. South made his way out of the director's box and up to the boardroom, where he awaited the usual post-match arrival of his manager. Under Watling, these had been pleasant affairs, football and life in general small talk among the board and their guests, with Saunders and, occasionally, the opposing manager there as well. This wasn't going to be the case today.

What subsequently happened in the normally calm and rarefied confines of the Carrow Road boardroom shortly after the end of that match is only known to the few that witnessed it – some of whom, no doubt, would rather not have. The details behind the 'explosive row' that took place can therefore only be conjecture, at least until such times that someone who was there tells the story. But it is fair to suppose that, upset by the defeat, its manner and the reaction of the fans after the match, South challenged Saunders on all matters, asking him, perhaps reasonably (although the manner of the asking was perhaps not) what the problem was and what he proposed to do about it? South had, after all, experienced the eventual success of the club under Watling, and the popularity around the club, city and county that it had generated for Watling, both as the chairman of the football club and a man in general. Now all that seemed to be falling apart under South's tenure, and he wasn't prepared to accept that.

But neither was Saunders prepared to accept what was almost a public dressing-down by his chairman. His thoughts, like so many 'proper' football men, were that his job was to run the football side of things while the chairman looked after the finances – something he quite likely reminded South of during their brief but fierce exchange of views; one of those acts being South's decision to sanction the sale of Cross to Coventry, not one Saunders would have welcomed. With both men equally strong of character and will, there was little chance either would back down, and the damage that had been done was irreparable. For Saunders there was little option for him but to resign. He wouldn't have been prepared to back down from the points he would have been strongly making, and he most certainly would not have seen fit to apologise either – for as far as he would have been concerned, there was nothing to apologise for. It is extremely likely that, in the eyes of Ron Saunders, South was in the wrong. Unfortunately, Sir Arthur South would have felt exactly the same way about Ron Saunders. The latter promptly repeated his desire to resign and departed the room and the club, without, it is likely, even telling his players. In normal circumstances of course, such incidents are part and parcel of any business, especially football clubs when emotions can run high after a defeat. But there was no 'cooling off' period this time. Saunders had gone, and even if he went on to regret the hastiness of his decision or had second thoughts – which is unlikely – South didn't make an effort to persuade him to stay. The Ron Saunders era at Carrow Road was therefore, suddenly and with some acrimony, over.

Ron Saunders had been in charge of Norwich City for a little under four and a half years. His legacy to the club stands the test of time and will always be remembered and appreciated, He had brought some success and no little recognition to Norwich City, as well as being responsible for the purchase of several players, all of whom, like him, are now names in Canary folklore. Fifteen players joined the club during his tenure, among them names such as Graham Paddon, David Cross, Trevor Hockey and Colin Suggett, as well as the man who scored the club's first top-flight goal, Jimmy Bone. He left Carrow Road with his reputation intact and his name as an outstanding young (he was just forty-one) football manager enhanced by his achievements in Norfolk. It was clear that, despite the nature of his departure from Norwich, he wouldn't be out of work for long. This proved to be the case when an offer from Manchester City to take over as their manager came just five days later – the ambitious Saunders at last given the opportunity to prove himself with a top club, and appointed before Norwich had even started interviewing possible replacements.

South 0, Saunders 1 it seemed. The swiftness of his appointment at Maine Road did, as it does now, seem rather too sudden to have been a spontaneous one. Was, or had, Saunders always been their 'manager-in-waiting'? Tony Book, who Saunders replaced, had only been installed as the temporary man in charge following the departure of Johnny Hart a month earlier. Hart himself had only been in the job for a little over six months, having suffered a heart attack, which forced his retirement from the game – some recommendation for the top job there! But it did look as if the new man in charge at Manchester City, chairman Peter Swales, was waiting for the right time and the right opportunity to appoint a preferred man. Was that the case and was Saunders always destined for the top job at Maine Road? Again, this can only ever be conjecture. What is fairly certain is that Saunders' abrupt and abrasive manner, which met with such a favourable response at Carrow Road (remember Dave Stringer and his 'you'll do me'), did not go down quite as well with the rather more famous and high-profile (maybe even pampered) players at Maine Road, notably Francis Lee. Saunders was eventually sacked by Swales barely five months after he had been appointed, despite having reached his second successive League Cup final[8] in that time. In spite of all of this, Saunders would still have the success and recognition he knew he could achieve, given the right club, and he would cross paths with Norwich on more than one occasion on the way to doing so.

The situation Norwich found themselves in, while not exactly one of no hope, was still pretty dire. The defeat to Everton had dropped them back to twentieth place in the league and, although a 0-0 draw at Old Trafford followed, that result was not as encouraging as might have first been expected. The team from

---

[8]   It was his second successive League Cup final defeat as well, Saunders' Manchester City side losing 2-1 to Wolves in the 1974 final at Wembley. It had very nearly been a Manchester City v. Norwich final, the Canaries eventually losing to Wolves in the two-legged semi-final.

the other side of Manchester was struggling alongside Norwich and were just two places above them in the League at that time, despite the brief return to the side of the errant George Best at that time, this fixture being the only one he played against Norwich in the League. The favourite for the Norwich post at this time was reckoned to be Bournemouth manager John Bond, who, like Best, was a flamboyant and effervescent figure who liked to be entertained while watching the game. Whether this fitted in with the requirements of the chairman was initially open to debate – South was, as we have seen, a straight-talker and a relative disciplinarian. Maybe he would prefer a man made in the mould of Saunders as his replacement, someone like Jimmy Meadows for example, who had compelled Southport to an unlikely Fourth Division title the previous season against enormous odds. Then there was Alan Dicks, much respected at Bristol City, and Lawrie McMenemy, an ex-Coldstream Guardsman who had previously won titles with both Doncaster Rovers and Grimsby Town. All worthy candidates to be certain, but none ticked so many boxes as Bond did, including those of South.

5

THE ENTERTAINERS

It's perhaps fair to say that, even if the knives weren't out for Bond straight away – after all, he had played no part in the departure of Cross and would likely have wanted to keep him – then the kitchen drawer was certainly in the corner of most Norwich fans' eyes.

Ron Saunders had stood, eyeball to eyeball, with Arthur South, making a point (or three) in a heated row that he would have known, even as he was making those points, he stood no chance of winning. Those members of staff and club guests that witnessed their falling out would not have been surprised at the ferocity of both men as they put their views across; they were both known for their single-minded approach and grim determination to get what they wanted, no matter the odds against or opposition. Saunders had, after all, arrived at the club a little over three years earlier with a simple remit: get us promoted. The club had paid him the salary he had demanded as well as backing him in the transfer market. Saunders had thus delivered: a championship, survival and a League Cup final were all achievements that he could be proud of and he would, quite rightly, have reckoned they were worth perhaps just a little more respect than the tirade he was suddenly exposed to from his chairman after that defeat against Everton.

For South, it was quite probable that it wasn't so much the fact that Norwich had lost that worried him – they were, after all, still relative minnows swimming in a very big and demanding river, they were always going to lose more games than they won – but rather the manner of it and the reaction of the fans at the final whistle. Not only the jeers at the final whistle but the sight of those blue seat covers all sailing down onto the pitch in protest, a sign of discord and revolt that, if it didn't have quite the same cinematic effect as thousands of Real Madrid fans waving white hankies at an unpopular manager, it certainly would have hit home with South. His taut business mind could only have interpreted it as a message to him from the fans – sort it out. Saunders had, famously, promised to do so with the players that underperformed, now South needed to do the same with his manager.

Four decades on, and again while this is only speculation on my part, you can only wonder if either man was looking for a parting of the ways? Saunders, after all, was a Watling man, and had been his appointment. All of the good times that had followed had come under the Watling/Saunders partnership, with both men equally respectful of their opposite's ability to do the job and quite content to let them get on with it. Now that Watling had left his post as chairman and South had taken over, he was working with a manager who may not have been his choice, and after all how many successful business owners and chairmen work without having their own choice as chief executive alongside them? Equally, Saunders had lost his main and most powerful ally at the club; the man who had gone out on a limb for him, and in doing so made him one of the best-paid managers in the division. Maybe they both wanted out. The problem with that is that Norwich would never have fired Saunders; it would have been seen as a reckless act and a ridiculous one into the bargain – dispensing with the man who had done so much for them. Equally, it was unlikely that Saunders would have just decided to walk away – for him that might have been an admission that he could take the club no further, not something he would care to publicly admit, even if he might have thought it. A row seemed, bizarrely, the best way for each man to get what he wanted without too much loss of professional face. South would have been seen as the strong leader demanding answers and, in doing so, would have reminded anyone who wasn't quite aware of it just who was in charge at Carrow Road now. Saunders, on the other hand, could have played the part of the wronged innocent; the man who had dragged Norwich City up by its tatty bootlaces and into the elite, yet despite all that, someone who was very publicly castigated by his chairman. Where was the justice, the gratitude? The manner of his exit was dramatic, but he no doubt would have had the support of many. He therefore left with his head held high and his professional reputation and integrity heightened, just as South might have thought his was. It suited all parties.

As it was, Saunders made himself comfortable in the manager's office at Maine Road just five days later, determined to prove to everyone at Carrow Road, not least his erstwhile chairman, wrong – something which he would, unquestionably, do, if not in the manner he might immediately have been expecting.

With Saunders gone and team matters passed, temporarily, into the trustworthy hands of his former coaches, Terry Allcock and George Lee, the Norwich board met in order to discuss a successor. Several names were considered, their respective strengths and perceived weaknesses considered, but, time after time, whatever the criteria that they were considering at the time, one name kept appearing at the top of all their lists, the one who was ticking all of those boxes that South held so dear.

Bournemouth manager John Bond.

Young? Yes. At just forty he was four years older than Saunders had been at the time of his appointment. Ambitious? Certainly. He'd learnt the coaching ropes at Gillingham, having been rejected after he had applied for the managerial position at Torquay United. After less than a year at Gillingham he had gained such a good reputation for himself as a coach, he was appointed as manager of Bournemouth. Ever the visionary, Bond arranged, upon his appointment at Dean Court, for the club's trading name to be changed to AFC Bournemouth. Not only was it simple and easily identifiable, it also meant that the club would, forever, be the very first in the Football League, the top of the tree when all of the member clubs were listed in alphabetical order. That seems nonsense now and it probably did then, but to Bond, any psychological advantage, however slight, that gave you and your team an edge, either real or perceived, needed to be taken. It also made a few headlines at the time – all good publicity for the club and for Bond, who had been good enough in his time as a player to make nearly 400 appearances for West Ham United. During his time at Upton Park, he'd not only played under an excellent coach and mentor in Ron Greenwood, but alongside players of the calibre of Bobby Moore, Geoff Hurst and Martin Peters – two of whom he tried to get to join Norwich during his time at Carrow Road. He was a progressive coach, one who could see the changes coming to the game, not least in terms of business and commerce, and who, as a consequence, made sure he was able to get his teams to play the game as openly and freely as he was able to talk about it – and he was succeeding. His predecessor at Dean Court, Freddie Cox, had been sacked at the end of the 1969/70 season after the club had been relegated to Division Four; the first time in the Cherries' history that they had dropped to that level. Under Bond they surged to an immediate promotion the following season, narrowly missing out on a second consecutive promotion at the end of the 1971/72 campaign when they finished third in Division Three, just three points shy of promoted Brighton in second. They'd finished seventh in 1972/73 and were, again, doing well in fourth, but had been as high as second, when Norwich made their initial enquiry for him.

His managerial stock was, if not high, then certainly rising. If Norwich hesitated now, then there might not have been a second chance had a more 'traditional' appointment – and there were those who thought ex-player Allcock deserved a chance – not worked out. Thus, with the backing of his board, South invited Bond for an interview on the afternoon of 24 November 1973, hours after the 0-0 draw at Carrow Road against Manchester United.

And all seemed to be going to plan. Less than twenty-four hours later, not only had Norwich made Bond an offer but he had accepted it, celebrating, not for the first time during his tenure at Carrow Road, with a glass of champagne. Following that, Bond headed back to Bournemouth to clear up any outstanding issues at Dean Court and, in footballing parlance, to 'clear his desk'. Shortly afterwards, South announced the impending appointment, adding that Norwich had agreed a sum of £10,000 to be paid in compensation to Bournemouth as part of the recruitment process. However, it appeared that this announcement was just a little too premature for South's Bournemouth counterpart, Harold Walker, who made his own announcement to the effect that no agreement had been reached and the club were not prepared to release him from his contract – one that South, strangely for a man so determined to have what he wanted, seemed to accept, announcing that the club would now 'start looking at other names on our shortlist'.

How very close, therefore, did Norwich City come to never appointing the man who many attribute as the one who helped set the Canaries on the progressive path and good reputation that they have to this day? Very close indeed, it would seem. Indeed, it would appear that if it were not for the direct actions of Bond himself at this point, then South, so forthright and public in his reaction to the defeat at Everton, would have meekly accepted the decision of the chairman of a club two divisions below Norwich rather than fight for the man he wanted.

Bond, of course, could have taken this in two ways. First and foremost, he could have seen it as a sign of just how much the Cherries valued him and wanted him to stay put – at least for the foreseeable future, maybe, in other words, until a bigger club than Norwich came along, or maybe a club whose chairman might have a little more *cojones* about him. The other way was that his prospective new chairman wasn't all that bothered about whether he came or not. Fortunately for Norwich, Bond wasn't the type to throw a hissy fit and declare that he 'didn't want the job anyway'. Because he did. Very much. He duly arranged to meet with Walker, telling him that he wanted to leave and therefore expected the club to honour his wishes and release him from his contract. Walker did so, very reluctantly, saying soon afterwards that 'having lost the so-called pilot, we still know where we are going'. It wasn't the nicest of ways for their working relationship to have ended and seems, even now, a somewhat immature jibe at a man who was always destined to move on to bigger and better things. Not that it would have mattered a jot to Bond of course; he was now, officially, a manager in the First Division. No doubt another bottle of champagne was opened in celebration. It was certainly a case of Bond getting the job that he wanted rather than one of Arthur South getting his man, but you have to assume that he was happy with the end result. Bond duly asked his coach at Bournemouth, Ken Brown, another ex-West Ham player, to join him at Carrow Road, an offer which Brown was delighted to accept.

Bond officially took over as Norwich manager on Monday 3 December 1973, although the appointment was ratified a week earlier. As far as team selection for the side's vital home game with Birmingham City two days earlier was concerned, Bond was on a watching brief only, the onus for both team and tactics for that game remaining with Allcock and Lee. With that game falling foul of the weather, however, the new man in charge had nearly a fortnight to assess his new charges prior to the trip to Burnley on 8 December – time that wasn't wasted as he immediately set about refashioning his playing squad.

His first signing was hardly a surprise. Indeed, it had almost been 'decided' from the moment he joined the club, the *Eastern Daily Press* joining in the speculation with their headline, 'Is Supermac Canaries Top Target?' The man in question was Ted MacDougall, who had prospered as a prolific goalscorer under Bond[9] at Dean Court, so much so that he had moved on to new pastures,

---

[9]   Ted's nine goals in the Cherries' 11-0 victory over Margate in an FA Cup tie in November 1971 remains a tournament record, and the only case of a triple hat-trick in any senior League or cup game scored in England.

firstly to Manchester United and then West Ham. Bournemouth pocketed a very handy £200,000 from the deal that took Ted to Old Trafford in September 1972, then a record for a player from Division Three. Things had not worked out for Ted there and he had subsequently moved on to West Ham. But for whatever reasons, the old gunslinger's look in his eye wasn't there, and he was neither scoring goals nor enjoying his football. Despite that, Bond knew he could return Ted to his old ways and have him doing both again. Apart from anything else, the sale of Cross had left the club woefully short of any kind of proven ability in attack, so putting that right was a priority. The problem was that Ted would cost a lot of money and that, as usual, was going to be a problem for the club.

Ted certainly needed rescuing. And the thought of a reunion with his old manager, the one who had been at the helm when he had scored thirty-five times in the 1971/72 season, must have been a very appealing one. He'd signed for Manchester United while Frank O'Farrell was manager, but after O'Farrell's departure had found himself at the mercy of his replacement, Tommy Docherty, who didn't like him and said so. Docherty made it clear to Ted that he was not his type of player. The Doc's idea of a goalscorer was a nimble, fleet-of-foot striker who worked hard for both his goals and the team – think Lou Macari or Stuart Pearson, both Docherty signings. And Ted was neither. He *was* a goalscorer, of that there was no doubt. But did he put a shift in with it? Maybe not. And for that reason, his career at Old Trafford was never going to end in anything other than disappointment. Ted was a strong character, but fewer in the game at that time were as forthright or headstrong as Docherty. The big fee that United had paid for Ted and the fact he'd barely had time to settle at Old Trafford meant nothing to Docherty. Ted was excess baggage, unwanted and unproven. Someone else could have him. Norwich were, even at that stage, rumoured to be interested, but nothing came of it and Ted moved on to West Ham.

But if Ted had thought his move to Upton Park might have given him the chance to settle down and return to being a big fish in a relatively small pond again, he was mistaken. The 'Daddy' in the Upton Park dressing room was the grizzly and uncompromising Billy Bonds, who brokered no nonsense from anyone, not even a World Cup-winning captain in Bobby Moore. Ted, therefore, was meat, drink and coffee with mints to Bonds who, after a 5-1 defeat at Leeds United, took exception to some of Ted's post-match observations. A fight between the two ensued, and with Bonds unchallenged in his role at the club that meant the end for Ted, who was soon informed he would be on his way for the second time in a year.

Two high-profile moves and two equally high-profile fallings out. MacDougall was perceived as a failure, the thought being that if he had been a good player, the clubs would have retained him despite the baggage. But with neither Manchester United, a struggling team at the time who would eventually be relegated, nor West Ham – themselves mired in bottom third mediocrity – seeming to regard Ted as the answer, the question became just who would? Ted's previously explosive, brief encounters with the game at the highest level were all the evidence that his doubters, including any at Carrow Road, needed. He was a loose cannon, a maverick, an opinionated and argumentative individual who had to get his own way and who wanted to be the number one, the big name at his club. In other words, *not* the sort of player that normally showed up at Carrow Road, at least not for long. Yet it was for those reasons and those qualities that Bond eventually stepped in and signed him for Norwich – because his side needed a bully. With the departure of Cross, Norwich needed a new physical presence in attack and one thing seemed certain, the two options open to the new manager – the still raw Paul Cheesley and the keen but awkward Ian Mellor – were not the immediate answer, if at all.

MacDougall was available, but at a price. And that was a problem. Ted's last two moves had both been for around £200,000, a sum that Bond's new club would not only be unwilling but quite probably unable to pay. Despite this, however, Bond was resolute. The time to rebuild and refashion Norwich had to begin immediately, and if it meant that a sacrifice or two would have to be made for the club to get the man he wanted, then that would be the case – the sacrifice in question being the elegant, often sublime Graham Paddon, a massive fan favourite. West Ham, a club that thought itself the model of elegant, often sublime football themselves wanted Paddon in part exchange; his loss being the price the club had to pay to get their hands on MacDougall. Doubtless in response to this, more than a few Norwich fans were aggrieved at what was going on at their club. First David Cross, the club's leading goalscorer in their first and ultimately successful season in the top flight, had been sold, and now Paddon at the behest of the new manager, the Canaries' second highest goalscorer and midfield talisman. And for what? The arrival of a temperamental new striker who had flopped at both his previous clubs and, but for Bond, might already have been on his way back to Bournemouth.

It's perhaps fair to say that even if the knives weren't out for Bond straight away – after all, he had played no part in the departure of Cross, and would likely have wanted to keep him – then the kitchen drawer was certainly in the corner of most Norwich fans' eyes. Those Norfolk eyebrows were raised after Bond's first game in charge, a defeat at Burnley and one that consigned the Canaries to bottom place in the First Division. Both Bond and MacDougall, who had made his third debut at this level at Burnley, had a lot to prove.

Ted scored his first goal for the club in the Boxing Day fixture against Ipswich Town. It was a typical MacDougall goal, seizing upon a half chance before anyone else could react in order to, by whatever means, force the ball into the back of the net. Yet Norwich still lost the game. It was their third defeat in four games since Bond had taken over and a winless run of a further five fixtures was to follow; including a 4-2 reverse to West Ham at Upton Park where Paddon scored twice against his erstwhile teammates, looking the complete midfielder as he linked up with Trevor Brooking. Yet MacDougall had also scored twice, taking his tally to four goals in three games – he was, slowly but surely, beginning to look the part. Bond, meanwhile, continued to rebuild. More new players had joined the club, both former players of his at Bournemouth and both defenders, Mel Machin and John Benson, with popular right-back Clive Payne joining Bournemouth as part of the deal. Bond also took the opportunity to bring in another member of his Dean Court coaching staff, Fred Davies. Machin and Benson made their debuts in the home game against Liverpool on 15 December and, despite their somewhat modest playing CVs – neither had previously played at even Second Division level – they fitted in well and gave the Canaries' defence a robustness that the Reds failed to cope with. The eventual 1-1 draw, with Cheesley scoring after just a minute, was perhaps the Canaries' best of the season.

By the time of the return League game against Manchester United, still struggling and only one place above the Canaries in the table, Bond had given four more players their Norwich debuts. They were Billy Steele, a young winger who had been signed by Saunders and come through into the professional ranks as an apprentice; ex-West Ham midfielder Johnny Sissons, described by his former manager Ron Greenwood as having 'a left foot that was a miracle'; full-back Paul Kent, another from the youth ranks who made his debut at Old Trafford, quite a baptism for a twenty-year-old; and, most significantly of all, MacDougall's former strike partner at Bournemouth, Phil Boyer.

Bond's signing of Boyer was a masterstroke, and arguably among the three best he made for Norwich during his time at the club. Boyer had started his career at Derby County, but at just nineteen and having not made a senior appearance for the club he was, surprisingly, allowed to leave the club by Brian Clough, joining York City for £3,000. He soon hit the goal trail at York and was teamed up with Ted MacDougall for the first time, contributing thirty-four goals for the Minstermen and creating a whole lot more for Ted. A partnership was born. Ted soon moved on to Bournemouth and it wasn't that long before Phil joined him there, John Bond paying £20,000 for his signature, a handy little profit for a club like York. Boyer scored eleven goals in his first season at Dean Court, fifteen the following season, and played a major part in many of Ted's total of thirty-five.

Both Frank O'Farrell and Ron Greenwood had bought Ted in, strangely oblivious to the qualities of Boyer and his very real importance to the partnership. It wasn't as if each needed the other to become 'whole' or a better player, but they did function better as a duo than any other striker a manager could pick to play alongside them. It leaves the casual football observer wondering why, in both of his initial big moves, neither club nor manager seemed aware of Boyer's part in the proceedings. It couldn't have been because they thought Boyer would not be able to play at the higher level – had they thought that, they might not have considered Ted in the first place. Luckily for Ted, John Bond was aware of Boyer's abilities and although the usual financial constraints at Carrow Road meant he couldn't bring him in straight away – not to mention the fact that the

Cherries' hierarchy were a little bored of Norwich's repeated forays for their players and coaching staff – he got there in the end. Boyer cost the Canaries £145,000, then a club record fee.

Strangely enough, despite the duo's devastating effectiveness in front of goal, of all the games they played as a front pairing for Norwich, they only both scored on nine separate occasions – the first time being September 1974 with Norwich beating Notts County 3-0 at Carrow Road. That was, of course, a Second Division game, the arrival of Bond the previous autumn, plus all of the players that followed, not being enough to prevent the side from being relegated, and in bottom place. Norwich thus, quietly and unobtrusively, slipped out of the top division after just two campaigns, relegation being virtually assured in the home clash against Manchester United on 6 April. John Bond's pre-match comment that 'the losers will almost certainly be relegated' sadly came true. Norwich lost 2-0, thanks to second-half goals from Lou Macari and Brian Greenhoff, and their doom was confirmed four games later, despite a spirited 1-0 home win against Burnley on 20 April.

Thanks in main to Denis Law's back-heeled goal for Manchester City against their biggest rivals, one that has long been mistakenly attributed as the goal that relegated the Red Devils (nice story but not true), the headlines at the end of the season were all about United, Docherty and how they would manage in the Second Division the following season. Norwich, plus the other relegated club, Southampton, were barely given a second thought. This probably suited John Bond. He had been charged with the onerous but not impossible task of getting Norwich up at the first attempt, and despite his growing reputation, you got the feeling South would have given him just the once chance to do it. Thus, with money available 'if needed', he settled down and, lucky to be away from the fierce spotlight surrounding Docherty, started to plot for that immediate return to the top flight. One which would feature the likes of MacDougall and Boyer very heavily.

They, plus previously established players like Dave Stringer, Colin Suggett and Kevin Keelan, would all have enormous parts to play in what would be the Canaries' second serious promotion campaign in four years. And, no doubt, there would be others. Selection-wise, the 1973/74 season had been one of inconsistency. Between them, Saunders and Bond had used thirty-two different players that season, an increase of nine on the previous one and the same number as Saunders had used in the championship season. Clearly, the Canaries needed a settled side and squad, and they would be relying on those five players mentioned above to be its 'spine'. But would there really, as some expected, be a swathe of more new arrivals during the summer, or would Bond rely on who he already had, or even some of the clubs up-and-coming young players? Was it now 'the time' for youngsters like Paul Cheesley, Steve Govier and Paul Kent to make their mark and become regular first-team players, or were their careers at Carrow Road, with relegation, now as good as over?

Paul Kent now runs his own hairdressing business in Norwich where he has, like so many one-time Canaries, settled permanently since the end of his playing career. A full-back by footballing trade, Paul was born in Rotherham in 1954 and represented his school teams at all levels, as well as the local Rotherham Boys team. He signed for Norwich as an apprentice in July 1970 at just sixteen years old, thus becoming one of the early recruits to the club during the Ron Saunders era. He remembers those early days very vividly, recalling them to me one summer's evening, almost forty-three years to the day since he first arrived at the club, very young, very nervous and very unsure of himself or his place in the greater scheme of things.

> I somehow managed to work my way up to something like bathroom attendant, which was, believe me, quite a prestigious role among the apprentices. It meant that when I got in on a Monday morning, I'd have to sort out both the communal baths, jump in them and, through around 6 inches of cold, mucky water, clear the plughole of all the filthy bandages, dressings and plasters that were left there after the previous game. The players would just sit there, take them off and leave them. What water had drained away, meantime, would have done so very slowly, so there was always a load of separate tidemarks on the side of the bath; that meant, after clearing out the plughole, I had to get into action with the Ajax and a scrubbing brush. Once I'd done that, it was off to the dressing room toilets, get those cleaned. You can imagine what they were like. And no, they hadn't been touched since the previous Saturday. Just think, all those nervous players, dreading playing Norwich.
>
> But that wasn't all. I'd then have a load of boots to get clean. There might have been forty pairs in total for us to work ourselves through. We're working our nuts off and we haven't even seen a ball, let alone kicked one. The old theory was that if they starved us of the ball, then, come a match, we'd be hungry for it. But we saw so little of it, when we did see it; we wouldn't know what to do with it! Can you imagine the young lads at clubs today having to put up with all of that, the degrading work and then barely seeing a football – all we did was run. If they were treated like that now, they'd all pack up and go home.

When Paul and his colleagues were 'allowed' to play football, he learnt his trade under the watchful eye of both Ron Saunders and John Bond, two managers that were, as we have already seen, very different in both manner and approach. What were his immediate recollections of both men?

> With Ron Saunders I had, and have, great admiration for him. He had that presence about him. I used to find myself standing to attention whenever he was with or near me. His appearance was always immaculate. Cropped hair, always clean shave, collar and tie always perfect. I used to bump into him right when I didn't want to. One time I were cleaning outside the main entrance of

1. The first-team squad line-up at the beginning of the decade. Back row, from left to right: Geoff Butler, Max Briggs, Terry Anderson, Trevor Howard, Alan Black. Middle row, from left to right: Dave Stringer, Duncan Forbes (C), Mervyn Cawston, Kevin Keelan, Steve Govier, Clive Payne. Front row, from left to right: Ken Foggo, Graham Paddon, Albert Bennett, Doug Livermore, Peter Silvester. (*Courtesy of Norwich City Football Club*)

Above: 2. Kenny Foggo in typical combative action for the Canaries. (*Courtesy of Norwich City Football Club*)

Left: 3. The inspirational Duncan Forbes choosing not to keep his voice down to 'a roar'. (*Courtesy of Norwich City Football Club*)

Right: 4. Ron Saunders
– he 'sorted them out'.
(*Courtesy of Norwich
City Football Club*)

Below: 5. Kevin Keelan
repels Derek Posse
during the 2-1 defeat at
Millwall on 23 October
1971. (*Courtesy of
Millwall FC*)

6. The championship-winning 1971/72 season squad celebrate in style! From left to right: Clive Payne, Geoff Butler, Trevor Howard, Doug Livermore, Kenny Foggo, Ron Saunders*, Duncan Forbes*, Dave Stringer* (*these three seated), Alan Black, Graham Paddon, Phil Hubbard, Jimmy Bone, Kevin Keelan, Terry Anderson, Steve Govier, Peter Silvester, David Cross, Mervyn Cawston and Max Briggs. (*Courtesy of Norwich City Football Club*)

7. Duncan Forbes lifts the Second Division championship trophy on the balcony of City Hall. (*Courtesy of Norwich City Football Club*)

8. Joy after the 2-1 win against Crystal Palace on 24 April 1973 that confirmed Norwich's place in the top flight for the following season. From left to right: Duncan Forbes, Dave Stringer, Doug Livermore and Clive Payne. (*Courtesy of Norwich City Football Club*)

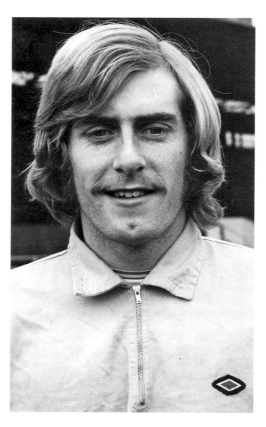

9. Graham Paddon, who should have been the first Norwich player to play for England. (*Courtesy of Norwich City Football Club*)

10. David Cross, a bargain from Rochdale at £40,000. (*Courtesy of Norwich City Football Club*)

11. Jimmy Bone, scorer of Norwich's
first-ever goal in top-flight football.
(*Courtesy of Norwich City Football Club*)

12. The Cat – Kevin Keelan, a Canary legend.
(*Courtesy of Norwich City Football Club*)

13. John Bond reshaped the club from bottom to top. (*Courtesy of Norwich City Football Club*)

14. Martin Peters, our very own World Cup winner. (*Courtesy of Norwich City Football Club*)

15. Martin Peters oozed class in whatever he did – even in those tight shorts! (*Courtesy of Norwich City Football Club*)

16. Ted MacDougall giving the camera his best mean and moody look. A laughing Keelan (red top) can be seen in the background. (*Courtesy of Norwich City Football Club*)

17. Phil Boyer, hard-working partner of MacDougall. (*Courtesy of Norwich City Football Club*)

18. Colin Suggett, an exceptional footballer, one who Bond swiftly saw as much more than 'just' a wide player. (*Courtesy of Norwich City Football Club*)

19. John Ryan – the free-scoring Gareth Bale of his day. (*Courtesy of Norwich City Football Club*)

20. Tony Powell, aggression coupled with skill. (*Courtesy of Norwich City Football Club*)

21. Colin Sullivan on near-post duty in a game against West Bromwich Albion. Dave Stringer is just behind him. (*Courtesy of Norwich City Football Club*)

22. Kevin Bond, right-back turned centre-half. (*Courtesy of Norwich City Football Club*)

23. Kevin Reeves, the Canaries' first £1-million sale. (*Courtesy of Norwich City Football Club*)

24. Justin Fashanu at the club's open day prior to the 1979/80 season. (*Courtesy of Norwich City Football Club*)

25. Fash ready to explode into action. (*Courtesy of Norwich City Football Club*)

26. The old River End being demolished in April 1979. (*Courtesy of Norwich City Football Club*)

27. A new River End takes shape. It was completed in December 1979. (*Courtesy of Norwich City Football Club*)

28. The squad line-up prior to the start of the 1979/80 season. Back row, from left to right: Martin Peters, Tony Powell, Kevin Bond, Roger Hansbury, Clive Baker, Roger Brown, Dave Bennett, Keith Robson, Duncan Forbes. Front row, from left to right: Phil Hoadley, Mark Nightingale, Peter Mendham, Doug Evans, Richard Symonds, Kevin Reeves, Mick McGuire, Graham Paddon, Justin Fashanu. (*Courtesy of Norwich City Football Club*)

the Trowse training ground and he pulls up in his car, comes walking up to me, gets right in my face. I can't help but grin, it's a nervous reaction. Is he in a good mood or a bad mood? Should I be grinning even? Then he looks me right in the eye and says, 'Son, are you laughing at me or with me?' Hell, what do I say? I mumble back, 'I'm laughing at you, boss ... laughing with you, boss ... erm' ... and I don't know what to say. And with that, he's gone. He'd do anything to wind you up, anything at all. Just to see how you'd react.

What about training and playing?

If you did well in the reserves, he'd have you join the first team for training. Like a reward. He used to love basing these on Scotland *v.* England; we had a lot of Scots at the club at the time so it fitted in well. It would be shirts versus skins. And he'd always be skins as he liked to show his muscular body off. Anyway, one game, I've cleared my lines and am making my way down the pitch. Unknown to me, Saunders is just behind me and, without me even realising he's there, he clatters me one. Down I go; I can barely breathe, let alone move. And, as I'm laying there, he leans over to me, grins, and says, 'be aware of that one son.' It was a hard lesson. But you know, I never forgot. And nobody got me like that ever again.

Bondy, he were very different. For a start, when we were at training, rather than never seeing a ball, or, at best, having about one between the lot of us, he'd bring these great sacks of balls in, so we'd have one each. It was so completely different. I could only improve under him, my game especially because of the work we did with, and on, the ball. He eventually gave me my first-team debut, which came about in a funny way. I'd been in training that week and Ted (MacDougall) had the hump. Didn't want to be there, didn't want to be training. He was irritated. So, when he challenges me for the ball, he goes in, elbow first, my eye came up like a balloon. And I thought, I don't know, but this is a bit of an injustice.

So the next time Ted got the ball I took it, took him, took everything out. He's down, moaning and grumbling away. And I get immediately sent off. This is it, I thought, the end of my career here. My last training session, last time at Trowse. Ted was the top man at the club and you didn't treat him like that. I showered, changed, left the training ground. But nothing more was said. So I kept coming in. Eventually the team sheets for the weekend games went up and I wasn't in the reserves so thought, that's it, I'm down in the A team, South East Counties League. But I weren't in that either. I'd just about given up, then I saw the team sheet for the first team. And there I am. Down as sub. Against Manchester United. Bondy must have thought that if I was prepared to kick Ted then I must have something about me. Mind you, I was risking biting the hand that fed me at the time, as I used to clean Ted's car for him and he'd pay me a fiver to do it, and that was half my weekly wage at the time.

Paul duly made his first-team debut for Norwich City in that game on 6 April 1974, replacing the injured Mel Machin. It was the game that John Bond had, in the days leading up to it, announced that would almost certainly see the losers relegated. Norwich lost and, as predicted – and not only by Bond – were indeed relegated, ending the season in bottom place, eight points adrift of safety. Kent played another two games for the club before season's end; his one start in a 0-0 draw at Newcastle, and then again as substitute in the return fixture at Carrow Road two days later, this time replacing Colin Suggett. It was his third and final appearance for the Canaries, and one made in front of both the first-team managers he played under at Carrow Road, for among the crowd that day was a certain Ron Saunders, recently sacked by Manchester City and, no doubt, keen to keep his eye in. One can only wonder what the reaction of Bond might have been had he known his predecessor was there, watching the team that he had led to promotion falter and ultimately tumble back into the Second Division under Bond. One thing is for certain, Saunders would have derived no pleasure from it at all.

Sadly for Paul Kent plus his two companions that season – Paul Cheesley and Steve Govier – the Canaries' relegation meant the end of their first-team careers at the club. Paul stayed at Carrow Road for the next two seasons but failed to make a senior first-team appearance during that time, primarily because of a long-term injury, he then joined Halifax Town in August 1976. For Govier and Cheesley, the end of their Norwich careers was rather more sudden; Govier joining Brighton a few weeks before the end of the campaign and Cheesley being shipped out to Bristol City back in December. Was it a case of none of them being good enough? Unlikely. It was more probable that Bond, even upon his appointment, had noted that his squad was lacking in all areas, in terms of both nous and experience, and actual playing ability. He was, therefore, and perhaps with some regrets, clearing the decks for what was to come; a new season in which the only thing that would keep him in the job was promotion. And he knew it – not that it would have concerned him half as much as letting some of the younger players go would have done. Their futures in the game were uncertain but Norwich's was not as far as Bond was concerned, and he would have prepared for the 1974/75 season confident of his ability to win a second promotion for the Canaries in four years; which, of course, he did, throwing in another appearance at Wembley into the bargain.

The basis for that promotion campaign began, as all good ones do, during the previous summer. With Bond confident of the proven ability and prowess of MacDougall and Boyer in attack, he set about adding to his defence and midfield; recruiting the uncompromising figure of Tony Powell from Bournemouth (his sixth signing from his former club), alongside the rather more fleet-of-foot Colin Sullivan from Plymouth Argyle – the pairing set to offer both a physical presence and attacking threat to the Canaries' midfield and defence respectively. Sullivan, in particular, was a notable signing, the full-back having already been selected by England at youth and under-23 levels. As for his midfield, Bond looked across the border to Portman Road and Ipswich's hard-working yet classy Peter Morris; a man who could pick out a 40-yard pass as easily as a 4-yard one, and someone who had seen off Norwich with two well-struck goals in the previous season's Texaco Cup final. It may have seemed unusual for any Norwich manager to downgrade by choosing to bring in a player from the self-appointed Tractor Boys, but Morris was more than ready and able to accept the challenge that lay ahead at Carrow Road, joining for a bargain £60,000.

The Norwich City side that lined up to play Blackpool at Carrow Road on the first day of the 1974/75 season contained no players that Ron Saunders had been responsible for signing and just four who had played for him during his spell at the club – Keelan, Stringer and Forbes, plus young winger Steve Grapes, who had joined the club as an apprentice in 1968. It was two of Bond's signings who scored the goals in Norwich's 2-1 victory – MacDougall and, on his debut, Powell, albeit via a panicked clearance that went in off his chest. The very fact that he had been in place for the deflection to hit him at all should, however, have spoken volumes about the way Bond was expecting his team to play – in over 200 games played for Bournemouth, Powell had only scored ten goals, despite being a box-to-box midfielder. Things were, it seemed, going to be changing, and rather quickly at that.

Norwich started the season with just four defeats in their opening twenty-one League fixtures, form that included one sequence of five consecutive wins and twelve goals scored for only one conceded. The club's form and subsequent points total at that halfway mark, reached after a disappointing defeat at Blackpool on 14 December, would normally have meant a club sitting pretty at the top of the League, or at the very least, in a very comfortable second position. But Norwich was neither. For all of that fine form, the wins and the goals scored, they were still 'only' in third place, seven points behind leaders and predictable title favourites Manchester United. In truth, the Second Division was, that year, packed to the rafters with big clubs; the proverbial sleeping giants with more than a few years of top-flight experience behind them as well as a fair share of major trophies. Norwich was, relatively speaking, one of the 'lesser' clubs in a highly competitive second flight that, along with Manchester United, contained Sunderland, Aston Villa, West Bromwich Albion, Blackpool, Bolton Wanderers, Nottingham Forest and Sheffield Wednesday – big clubs then, and big clubs, at least in the eyes of their fans, today, with all of them having more recent experience of playing in the Premier League. Expectations, therefore, were not just high at Carrow Road, they were high just about everywhere.

And yet Bond was expected to take Norwich City straight back up again. Some challenge. Some manager.

Despite the calibre of the opposition and all the pressure both board and fans would have put on the new man to succeed, Norwich were never in a lower League position than fifth for the whole of that campaign. And, even with just four League games to play and a disappointing 1-1 draw against Millwall seeing Norwich slip out of the promotion places at just the time those squeaky bums we hear so much about would have been at their shrillest, the Canaries' promotion never seemed in doubt. Even the draw at Millwall had come about because, in shades of the Paul Lambert years that lay far ahead, promotion-chasing Norwich managed to scramble a late equaliser; Geoff Butler's injury-time goal his only one for the club that season. Yet it brought about momentum and belief in abundance. Nottingham Forest, themselves a First Division side just three years earlier and under new management in Brian Clough, were seen off in masterful fashion at Carrow Road a week later. Norwich's 3-0 win was marked by a brilliant attacking performance and three goals of the highest quality – two from Boyer and one from the man whose signing by Bond just a month earlier had been, quite possibly, the best ever made by any Norwich City manager, past or present – Martin Peters.

Peters, of course, is one of only eleven Englishmen to have ever played in a World Cup final. And, if that wasn't spectacular enough in its own right, as far as his playing career is concerned, he is one of only two to have scored in the aforementioned match. He was also seconds away from scoring the winning goal, until late nerves in the England defence permitted a last-gasp equaliser for West Germany on that broiling afternoon in July 1966. Prior to that game, he had won a European Cup Winners' Cup medal at Wembley; his club at the time, West Ham, beating West German opposition 1860 Munich in the final. By the time that 1966 tournament came around, he was already being described as a complete midfielder. Two years after that, England manager Sir Alf Ramsay made the famous comment about Peters being 'ten years ahead of his time' – such was his anticipation, awareness and overall movement. He was also known in footballing circles as 'The Ghost', in tribute of his unerring ability to ghost, unnoticed and unexpectedly, into a goalscoring position. He was, undoubtedly, one of the best midfielders that English football has ever produced, or is likely to produce; a man who, were he playing today, would be regarded as an essential part of the England team, and our only true world-class player. When he left West Ham for Tottenham Hotspur in 1970, he became the first British player to move clubs for over £200,000. He had, while at West Ham, played in every position on the field, including that of goalkeeper. A complete footballer, never mind midfielder.

Despite all of this, and a successful spell at Tottenham that had seen him appear in two League Cup and two UEFA Cup finals – winning one of each, as well as winning the last of his sixty-seven England caps – Peters suddenly found himself, if not surplus to requirements at White Hart Lane, then certainly not quite as well thought of as he had been previously. A new man had taken over from the hugely respected Bill Nicholson and, as he got his feet under the table, it was clear that Terry Neill, the former Hull City and then part-time manager of Northern Ireland, was keen, as are so many new managers, to get across his own ideas and footballing philosophies. Doing that as a relatively young manager (Neill was just thirty-one when he took over) in a dressing room packed full of battle-hardened old professionals with both games and medals in their lockers can be, at the best of times, a challenge. So for

Neill, the choice was simple – make a statement, an impact. Begin as you mean to go on and make those players know that you are in charge.

Peters himself admitted that the appointment of Neill, and more tellingly his reputed dour and disciplined demeanour, didn't go down very well with those more established players, saying, 'I wasn't getting on too well with Terry Neill – I think mainly because he wasn't much older than me. I was thirty-one ... Mike England was thirty-two, Martin Chivers, thirty ... if you look at what happened to Spurs in those days, most of those players left for one reason.'[10]

The aforementioned Mike England, a veteran of nearly ten years and over 300 senior appearances for Tottenham, duly departed to play in the USA, while popular and versatile defender Phil Beal headed off to the South Coast and semi-footballing retirement with Brighton. Alan Gilzean meanwhile, perhaps sensing the end of an era at the club, announced his retirement from the game during the 1973/74 season. One of his final goals for the club had been against Norwich in the League game on 20 October. Perhaps Nicholson, much like Don Revie, the Leeds United manager who had also left his club in the summer of 1974, couldn't face breaking up his multi-talented team and was content to leave it for someone else to do, while at the same time preserving his reputation as one of the all-time legends of the game. Revie, at least, had the solace of the England job to immerse himself in while Brian Clough began to demolish his great side. For Nicholson, there was quiet retirement and reflection as Neill took on the responsibility himself. That unspoken differing of opinions between Neill and his senior pros that Peters alluded to certainly seems to have been a catalyst that led to so many of them leaving the club over the coming months, including, inevitably, Peters himself.

The end of Peters' time at Tottenham, when it did come, was surprisingly swift and simple – none of the inevitable long, drawn-out discussions featuring fleets of agents, as is so often the case in the modern game. Peters knew he wasn't part of Neill's long-term plans at Tottenham, but Norwich saw him as being exactly the opposite – someone to hold together a new team that was on the brink of a return to the top flight. Bond wanted Peters, Peters felt wanted, deal done. It was, as Peters recollects, a case of 'we had a meeting and it was done and dusted'. The fee that Norwich paid Tottenham – just £50,000 – was a derisory sum for such a proven and classy player even then. Bond had, in effect, not so much mugged Tottenham as broken into White Hart Lane in broad daylight and made off with the family silver, with neither resistance nor competition to hold him back.

Three clubs were due to go up at the end of that season, and it was generally assumed that you could perm any three from Manchester United, Aston Villa, Sunderland and Norwich for those three promotion places. They had dominated the League throughout, all of them able to put together winning runs and score plenty of goals at a whim, with the red half of Manchester enjoying one hell of

---

10 Waghorn, Rick, *12 Canary Greats* (Jarrold Publishing, 2004), p. 86.

a renaissance under a group of young and extremely talented players led by the charismatic Tommy Docherty.

Fittingly, Peters made his Norwich debut at Old Trafford on 15 March 1975 where, in front of a crowd of 56,202, the two teams played out a pulsating 1-1 draw. Stuart Pearson opened the scoring for United only for Ted MacDougall to silence the opposition boo boys and doubters after a weak kick by Stepney in the United goal gave Norwich possession and an easy goal. No wonder Docherty ended up wanting to sign Keelan who, on the day, was as masterful as ever. Peters, as you would expect, strolled through his debut with ease, his class already clear for all to see. For him, even though it was his first game at that lower level, it must have felt like he had never left the big time – a game against the league leaders at Old Trafford with a big crowd in attendance and expectation in abundance. A case of 'as you were' for The Ghost.

Peters, who had played against Norwich for Tottenham in the 1973 League Cup final, as well as the four League meetings the clubs had contested between 1972 and 1974, knew of, if not on a personal level, most of the players who were destined to become his teammates at Carrow Road. The obvious appeal for him, however, was the opportunity to play under Bond and Ken Brown, who he had known and played alongside while at West Ham – both Bond and Brown were at Upton Park when Peters had joined the ground staff there at just fifteen. The way the two had played the game, practiced what they preached and their obvious preference for playing football the 'West Ham way' – which they had taken to Bournemouth and Norwich – clearly appealed to Peters, who admitted that he probably would not have signed for Norwich had it been Ron Saunders who had wanted to sign him. Bond had learnt the game from Ron Greenwood, as had Peters, with both men treading the path of 'pass, pass, pass' as regards how they wanted to play the game, rather than Saunders' preference for 'run, run, run'. It was 'pass, pass, pass' that Bond wanted to play at Norwich, and if in the steely shape of Forbes and Stringer he had a couple of players who may not have easily adhered to changing the way they played, then there were plenty more at the club who were thriving on Bond's approach; one of whom was Colin Suggett, a player who Peters knew. Suggett had been a Saunders signing, purchased with accompanying instructions to run at opposition defences and cause the sort of chaos within that might have created chances for the likes of David Cross. But his new manager saw more in him than that.

Bond was, despite his cigar-smoking, loud-shirted and very outgoing ways, an extremely canny footballing man. He immediately recognised Suggett as a player who would be an integral member of his side. Recognising his ball skills and ability to play the killer pass, Bond brought him infield, playing him in a central midfield position. There, aided, abetted and protected by the more fundamental qualities of players like Tony Powell and Peter Morris, he became the archetypal midfield general; in modern parlance, the *trequartista*, the wearer of the No. 10 shirt whose job was to sit in that free role between midfield and attack and make the passes that mattered, passes that caused damage.

So, Suggett, once shackled as a winger with a simple brief – get the ball and run like hell – revelled in his new role, donning the yellow No. 10 shirt that had never really been filled since Graham Paddon's departure, and serving up goals on a plate for the predatory McDougall and Boyer. He also contributed a few himself, not least a stunning 30-yard effort past Aston Villa 'keeper Jim Cumbes early on in that 1974/75 promotion-winning season. Bond had, in Suggett, fashioned footballing silk from a sow's ear – Suggett was quality before that move into midfield, but Bond had given a Canary diamond an extra polish and how it was showing!

He had joined the club as an out-and-out winger. Yet, and this is without being detrimental to the exponents of that art, he was, as Bond had swiftly realised, a more complete footballer than that. Saunders had entrusted him with one brief – to run with the ball at his feet. But Bond had gone a step further, allowing him to stop and think while in possession. Why run if you can deliver a telling pass or find space for a teammate that no one else could see. Colin Suggett did all of that, finding space, moving into it, controlling the rhythm of the game and proving himself all over the pitch. He was a quality footballer who lit up the seventies at Carrow Road with his precision passing and overall presence.

This then was the mix of Bond's new Norwich side, one that featured eight of his signings for the Carrow Road clash against Portsmouth in that game's penultimate fixture; five of which – Sullivan, Morris, Powell, Peters and Mick McGuire – had been signed either before or during that season.

Peters and Suggett provided the flair and no little vision, while there was added steel in the presence of Forbes at the back, the great survivor of the previous regime. MacDougall and Boyer had already contributed thirty-nine League goals between them by that stage of the season, the time and investment made in signing both having richly paid off. Sullivan and Powell had both settled into the team as well. Both had been new boys at the start of the campaign but had adjusted to life at a higher level of competition almost immediately, Powell in particular thriving, and no doubt enjoying his personal high spot of the season – scoring the opening goal in the first leg of the League Cup semi-final at Old Trafford in front of nearly 60,000 fans. Writing in his autobiography, Peters remembers Powell as a competitive player, who, 'as you would expect, was good in the air. I used to partner him when we had head tennis competitions during training and we'd annihilate the opposition.'[11]

It says a lot for Powell that such a footballing luminary as Peters should still remember him, and in such a positive manner, given the number of players and playing colleagues that Peters would have had known throughout both his club and international career. 'Knocker', as he was known to his teammates, was the very epitome of a competitive footballer (the hint was there – he and Peters

---

[11] Peters, Martin, *The Ghost Of 66* (Orion, 2006), p. 259.

didn't just win the head tennis competitions at the club, they 'annihilated' them!), one who chased every lost cause, a player who was always, as the saying goes, quite happy to put his head where others would hesitate putting their boot. That commitment and on-field passion would be crucial in the game against Portsmouth who, among their ranks of lower-League journeymen and hardened foot soldiers, possessed the enigmatic talent of Peter Marinello; he who had been infected by the label of being 'the next George Best', as well as an ex-Canary in Kenny Foggo. He would have been particularly looking forward to welcoming some erstwhile teammates (even if it was only Keelan, Butler and Forbes) to his new home, and to his first match against his one-time employers since Saunders had bombed him out over two years previously. Despite these two talents, however, Pompey had languished in the lower regions of the League all season, and had been dispatched with consummate ease in the clash at Carrow Road, which Norwich had won 2-0. The opportunity to spoil a potential promotion party at Norwich would therefore have been an appealing one for the Portsmouth players, as well as the usual passionate and somewhat vocal Fratton Park support, who were no doubt weary of the relative success teams like Norwich were having while they, with a League championship and FA Cup success to their name, had lost their top-flight status in 1959 and been fumbling around in the lower divisions trying to retain it ever since. In an effort to try to recreate the glory days at Fratton Park, they had recently appointed ex-Liverpool centre-forward Ian St John as their manager, hoping no doubt that some of the stardust he had attracted during his playing career would follow him down to the South Coast. In all instances, that hope was a forlorn one, as Bond, who would undoubtedly have come up against St John in playing competition several times in previous years, proved to be the master of the two on this occasion. Norwich won 3-0 in a manner and comfort that belied the pressure they must have felt going into the fixture, given the implications of what defeat might have meant.

That pressure related to the tantalising fact that if Norwich won, their promotion back to the top flight after just one season out would be assured, with one game to play. However, there were conditions. If Norwich won, then for that promotion to be guaranteed, they also needed Sunderland, fellow promotion-chasers all season, to lose at Aston Villa[12] – effectively meaning the Canaries were looking to their old boss, with Saunders now in charge at Villa Park, to do them a favour. Neither

---

[12] Parallels here with Norwich's fixture at Portsmouth on 2 May 2011. On that occasion, promotion to the Premier League, this time after a seven-year absence, would have been guaranteed, providing Norwich won and their nearest rivals for promotion, in this case Cardiff City, lost at home to Middlesbrough. History duly repeated itself – Cardiff lost, Norwich won and promotion was again sealed at Fratton Park. Indeed, Norwich have not secured any of their six promotions to the top flight at Carrow Road. All have occurred away from home: Brisbane Road (1972), Fratton Park (1975 and 2011), Hillsborough (1982), The Odsal Stadium (1986), and Selhurst Park (2004), though on that occasion, Norwich had not even been playing – Sunderland's 0-3 defeat to Crystal Palace on 21 April meaning they could no longer catch Norwich for one of the promotion spots. Norwich duly clinched the title at Sunderland's home ground, the Stadium of Light. Even when Norwich were promoted from League One to the Championship in 2010, the promotion was secured at an away ground – The Valley, home of Charlton Athletic.

Ron Saunders nor the Canaries seemed to have laid their respective ghosts of his time at Carrow Road to rest. Both had moved on, but the wounds ran deep and there was still, it seemed, an element of, if not rancour then certainly rumbling discontent between both parties that time had failed to heal, despite, as far as Norwich were concerned, all that Bond had achieved in his short time at the club. Saunders, ever poker-faced and guarded, made his first return to Norwich on 29 December 1973, just six weeks after his stormy exit. On this occasion it had been as manager of Manchester City. He hadn't exactly had a storming start to his career at Maine Road, winning just two of the five games he had been in charge for, prior to his return to his old stomping (and marching, hopping, running and, quite probably, crawling) ground. For the occasion, Saunders, more a man who practiced the virtues of a footballing collective rather than indulging individual talents, chose to play all of his big names at Carrow Road, with Colin Bell, Rodney Marsh and Denis Law all starting. It made little difference. MacDougall opened the scoring after just seven minutes. If any stray eye did wander to the sight of the visiting manager sat in the opposition dugout, they would have witnessed an unhappy-looking Saunders, one who was more demonstrative than usual. His side equalised shortly before half-time via a goal from Law, and that is how the score remained. It was, undoubtedly, a better point for Saunders than it had been for Bond, yet on this occasion, it was the team in the yellow-and-green shirts, together with their fans, who felt they had secured the moral victory on the day.

Saunders was even unhappier after the League fixture between Aston Villa and Norwich early on in the following season. Following his sudden departure from Maine Road, Villa had been swift to offer him an immediate return to the game; mindful no doubt that he had driven Norwich to promotion three years earlier. The lure of repeating that achievement with a bigger club was irresistible to Saunders, who took on the task with some relish, especially given the fact that he'd be up against not only his former side but the team from the other side of Manchester who had been, at least for a short time, his biggest footballing rivals. On this occasion, the points were shared again with another 1-1 draw, Villa opening the scoring through Ray Graydon (who would prove to be more than a thorn in the side of Canary fans before the end of the season) early in the second half and, for a while, it looked as if the points were only ever going to accompany Saunders and his men on their way back to Birmingham. Norwich were not to be denied, however, and Suggett's amazing 30-yard shot sealed a draw; Villa's third consecutive one since the season had started, but the first points Norwich had dropped. A point salvaged for the Canaries but one lost for Villa, and their manager departed the scene in a fiery mood, annoyed that he had, for the second time, failed to put one over on his former employers, and Arthur South in particular.

The sides met again on 1 March, this time at Wembley. Even as early as the fourth-round stage of that season's League Cup, footballing folk in both Birmingham and Norwich said that the two sides would meet in the final, and so it proved to be the case. Norwich had a good record in the contest, winning it in 1962 as well as being losing finalists in 1973, and semi-finalists the previous season. Saunders was looking for his third consecutive final, and having lost with Norwich two years earlier and Manchester City the following year, he now wanted to return with his next club and break that losing streak – the fact he now had the chance to do so against his former club must have been, for Saunders, the icing on the cake.

The match, if you can call it that, was dire. Norwich, marginal favourites on the day and buoyed, as far as the pundits were concerned, by the knowledge and experience of what a Wembley Cup final was like through their appearance two years earlier (despite the fact that only three members of that team played in the game), froze from kick-off and failed to play or perform at anywhere near the high standards they had been showing throughout the season, despite having a host of big name players in their side: Keelan, Forbes, MacDougall, Suggett and, of course, Peters. It turned out to be a game where the winners played badly, just not as badly as the runners-up. Graydon scored the decisive goal after Keelan had initially saved his penalty and Villa fans could celebrate a cup win – Saunders' first at the third time of asking. The now iconic photograph of him hugging Graydon after the game – a rare sign of emotion – clearly showed just what it meant to Saunders. His joy and release at the win was cathartic, he could now move on and finally close the door on Norwich City. As a fan, with promotion in the offing, it was a reward that would dull the pain of this defeat, and you could only hope that Norwich City would move on as well.

With promotion won and the dust settled, that would have been the end of it, had it not been for a quirk of the fixture list that necessitated that the clubs should meet again on the very last day of the 1974/75 season at Carrow Road. How voluble would that encounter have been if Norwich had not won so impressively at Portsmouth?

Had the Canaries lost against Portsmouth game, they would have gone into this fixture level on points with Sunderland and with a inferior goal average – meaning that Saunders and his Villa side, fresh from winning the League Cup at Norwich's expense, could then have delivered the final blow and denied them promotion as well. It would have been a final-day wake at Carrow Road for the Canary faithful that would have been played out in front of the watching eyes of their ex-manager. Had the fates decreed that was to be the case, the blue cushions might once again have been sailing onto the Carrow Road pitch, and Sir Arthur South might just have been among those throwing them. Fortunately, such a possibility was only conjecture, an image from a parallel footballing universe. The atmosphere at the game, played out in front of Norwich's highest gate of the season of 35,999, was a celebratory one, and the fact that Villa won 4-1 didn't seem to matter one little bit to anyone as the yellow-and-green-clad supporters of the Canaries celebrated, regardless, into the night.

Norwich City were back.

6

ONWARDS AND UPWARDS

Imagine if you will, the opening scenes of the film Gladiator. Maximus, in the guise of Bob Paisley ruler of all Anfield, stands astride the brow of the Kop, notebook in hand and utters that immortal line, 'At my signal, unleash hell...'

It was a very different Norwich City who took their place at the elite table of English football in the summer of 1975, compared to the one that had arrived, somewhat unexpectedly – despite the ambitions of the club's board – wide-eyed and innocent for the first time just three years previously.

Much of this had been down to John Bond, who had identified areas that needed to be addressed as soon as he had joined the club. One of the most urgent had been the club's youth policy – in as much as the Canaries didn't have one. The club's training facilities were, even for that time, somewhat antiquated and in need of investment, while those young players who the club had taken on as schoolboys and apprentices did not have any properly competitive matches to play, or a league to play them in. When they did play a game, it would invariably be a hastily arranged friendly against one of the local non-League sides: Lowestoft, Gorleston, Great Yarmouth, Kings Lynn and the like. And those games would be anything but friendly, with the part-time cloggers from the county's nether regions only too keen to have the opportunity to kick their young and delicate peers in order to have something to brag about to their mates in the pub. Bond, horrified at how the club seemed to have such a blatant disregard for its young players' limbs, immediately put a stop to the practice and arranged for the club to join the South East Counties League. This was a competitive and well-managed junior league for the youth teams of clubs from all over Southern England – including Arsenal, Tottenham and Crystal Palace. This didn't seem, on reflection, too unreasonable a request. Norwich's reserve team were, after all, members of the Football Combination, whose membership included Leicester City, despite the Combination being for clubs defined as being 'from Southern England and Wales'. The club duly applied for its youth and schoolboy sides to join the South East Counties League, only to receive notification from the authorities that they couldn't join as Norwich was too far away from London. This was despite the fact that Norwich's near neighbours, Ipswich Town, *were* a member club. Clearly, in the misguided and unseeing eyes of the Football League suits, the additional 40 miles further that its coddled London brethren would have to travel in order to play Norwich was too terrible a task to impose on them. Unsurprisingly, and with no little anger in the process, Bond and Norwich appealed against the decision. And, equally unsurprisingly, the Football League upheld their decision stating, again, that Norwich could not join the league as the club was not based in the South East of England.

This was an unforeseen problem with the club's ambitions. Bond and his new coaching team wanted their younger players – the likes of Andy Rollings, Billy Steele and Steve Goodwin – to play at a higher, more professionally run level, where the opposition would not go into the game with the sole ambition of sending one of Norwich's young starlets 6 feet into the air. So he and the club got back to the Football League and again asked for admittance into the South East Counties League, stating that if they were accepted, they would be perfectly happy to play all of their games away from home. This proposal was accepted and, for two consecutive seasons, the Canaries played all of their youth team games away from Norwich. It would prove, in time, to have been an inspired move. The standard of competition and overall play improved, and so did that of some of Norwich's youngest and brightest players; proof positive coming in both the 1979/80 and 1982/83 seasons when the cream of Canary youth won the competition. Indeed, the class of 1983 – one that featured the names of Tony Spearing, Jeremy Goss and Louie Donowa – went through the entire league campaign unbeaten, as well as winning the FA Youth Cup. A fitting legacy and reward for the seeds of that Norfolk footballing youth revolution that had been sown by Bond a decade earlier, one that the latest cream of the Canary crop repeated in 2013 by winning the FA Youth Cup for the second time.

Even with a renewed emphasis and commitment on youth, Norwich still found time to reward those who had given the club a long and distinguished service. Shortly after playing in two end-of-season benefit matches for players from other clubs, Norwich took on West Ham United at Carrow Road on 9 May 1975 in a testimonial for Dave Stringer. Dave's well-earned tribute was one of fourteen matches the club played between May and August that year, a staggering number of relatively meaningless matches for a team to commit to when you would have thought the priority would have been to rest their players over the summer prior with a tough season ahead.

Stringer's game saw an entertaining 1-1 draw played out in front of just over 13,000 fans; Martin Peters scoring for Norwich against one of his former clubs. Prior to his big night, however, Dave and his teammates had been returning the favour for those opposing clubs and players. The first, played just days after that final League game against Aston Villa, was in Cambridge, an All-Star XI taking on the Canaries for the benefit of Cambridge United's Jimmy Thompson. Somewhat pleasingly, and showing no deference whatsoever to the esteemed Thompson, the Canaries won 4-2. Five days later, Norwich were on testimonial duty again, this time taking the short trip down to Layer Road to play Colchester United for the benefit of Paul Aimson, whose career at the Us had been cut short by injury. Colchester insisted on keeping to the script by winning 3-2, the right result on the day and via a dramatic last-second winner for the hosts, maybe even scored by Aimson himself? And so it went on. Two days after that game it was Dave Stringer's turn. Then, on the following Monday, Norwich were off on their charitable travels a third time, taking the short trip to Lowestoft Town for a meeting with the Trawler Boys in benefit of the Fishermans' Fund. No doubt plenty of fishermen celebrated the result in that case as Lowestoft won 1-0, a result that might have prompted cries of, 'they'll be dancing on the Waveney Road tonight'.

When it came to pre-season games, tours and tournaments in those days, the Canary hierarchy were loath to turn down any invitation, however demanding or inconvenient it might have seemed. Participation in foreign tours helped raise the Canaries' profile, and there would usually be some sort of financial incentive to visit, not something the club was in a position to turn down. The club's tour of Kenya in May and June 1975, for example, had nothing to do with getting the players fit for the coming season – as we have seen, once the regular League season was over, Norwich just carried on 'as normal'. Their first commitment after the quartet of benefit matches was a 1-1 draw at Gillingham. Then, a few days after that, the club set off on an ambitious two-week-long tour of Kenya. Their schedule included five matches, some of which were due to be played on consecutive days. Clearly, there was going to be little time for going on safari or relaxing with a few beers by the pool. As a newly promoted Division One club, the Canaries were in great demand while they were out there, with their hosts determined to make the most of their presence. Playing-wise, the club encountered few difficulties – all five matches were convincingly won with twenty-three goals scored for only four conceded, and as far as PR objectives were concerned, it was a triumph.

Yet it was not passed off without incident, albeit the incident being a locally focused issue that did not affect the club or their reputation, but did made newspaper headlines across on the other side of the world. Prior to the Canaries arriving in the country, the practice of witchcraft and its role in the game had created a stir. Kenyan soccer officials, increasingly concerned at its influence in the game and at clubs' increased use of it in order to help them win matches, threatened sanctions against any club that hired a witchdoctor, the Kenyan Soccer Federation secretary, Obare Asiko, later saying, 'Witchcraft should have no place in Kenya soccer. The practice of witchcraft is unsettling our efforts to clean up soccer.' His quote had been prompted by reports that some officials, rather than wanting to act and speak out against the use of witchcraft, were promising to not only sanction it's use but pay the salaries of any witchdoctors employed by a club that managed to beat Norwich during their tour. The story even managed to reach the esteemed pages of the *LA Times*, such was the controversy and interest generated at the time, and one can only think just how much more interest it would have caused had Norwich duly lost any of the games they played.

The success of the trip, therefore – promotions and results wise – made everyone happy, especially Kenneth Matiba, another high-ranking sporting and political figure from the Kenyan Football Federation. He was reported to have been delighted with the Canaries' performance and dominance in their 8-0 win over Champion Kenya, as it proved beyond doubt that witchcraft did not have any part to play in the Kenyan game and could not influence a result.

The Kenyan tour was one of nine different playing trips abroad that the club undertook in the 1970s. France and Yugoslavia were visited in the summer of 1970, the latter including a playing itinerary of three games played in what is now modern-day Serbia. The following summer, Norwich accepted an invitation to travel to Portugal in order to compete for the Dr Caecor Moreira Batista tournament; organised by the Portuguese Tourist Board and including a trophy – which had cost £700 – that would ultimately be presented to and kept by the tournament's winners. Norwich beat Athletico Lisbon 2-1 and Dundee 5-3 before triumphing in a penalty shoot-out against Sporting Lisbon 4-2, winning the trophy in the process. No trophy had been won in Kenya, but a lot of goodwill and mutual respect had come from the tour in terms of the club and its grateful hosts. From that moment on, John Bond was convinced of their worth, indicating to Sir Arthur South that he would be expecting another foreign trip at the end of the 1975/76 season. South, mindful of the costs involved, might have preferred a similar schedule to that the club had arranged in 1974 when the pre-season games had involved trips to Colchester, Lowestoft and Torquay. Despite this, it was agreed that upon confirmation of their First Division status at the end of the season, the Canaries would take to the skies again, hoping to repeat those happy memories and successes of past visits. With pre-season training due to resume in mid-July, however, barely a month after the club's return from Kenya, thoughts and priorities had to turn to what was, undoubtedly, going to be a challenging season ahead; the first full top-flight one for not just Bond and his coaching staff, but most of his players as well.

While the Canaries were out in Africa, Carrow Road was getting a much-needed facelift. New seats were added to the South Stand (named after the chairman rather than, as some think, the compass direction) at the end of the 1974/75 season, at a cost of £40,000. They were initially debated and even open to criticism as regards their siting and design from some fans but soon, as is usually the case, became accepted and part of the ground. In subsequent years, over £100,000 more was invested on further upgrades, including the floodlighting and on-site police and toilet facilities. Work was also taking place at the club's training ground in Trowse; the upgraded complex being officially opened by the Bishop of Kings Lynn, Aubrey Aitken, in December 1975. Bond had further strengthened the club's position in the local area by appointing a schools' relationship manager, thus ensuring that the all-new training ground had some all-new up-and-coming young stars gracing the facilities. Far too often in the past, the club had seen some of the best young talent in Norfolk head off to, of all places, Portman Road, home of their deadly Suffolk rivals, Ipswich Town. Two examples of this were players that went on to become household names in the game: Trevor Whymark and Clive Woods. Both players were born in Norwich but were completely missed by the Canaries – a fact that should, and no doubt did, cause some embarrassment to the club whose scouts could offer no excuses for missing such promising stars of the future; one of whom, the aforementioned Woods, having grown up and started playing the game within easy walking distance of Carrow Road.

Naturally, with the club committing large sums of money to improving the infrastructure at both the ground and training complex, money was a little hard to come by as far as plans for team strengthening were concerned. It wasn't as if the money had not been available to Bond. He had spent liberally during the previous campaign, as he had done since he took the job. Fifteen players had made their Canary debuts since his appointment, eight of whom had involved a transfer fee: Boyer (£145,000 – a club record); MacDougall (£140,000 – another club record); McGuire (£60,000); Morris (£60,000); Peters (£50,000); Sullivan (£50,000); Miller (£43,000); and Sissons (£30,000). Eight players costing £578,000, and all spent in a busy fifteen-month period. Add to that the expense committed to the ground and at Trowse and that all adds up to a great deal of outlay by the club with minimal return coming in through player sales. Any financial benefits from close-season tours such as the trip to Kenya were therefore extremely important and had led to an extremely busy summer; the club had – since the pre-season trip to Torquay United on 12 August 1974 to that last game in Kenya – played a total of sixty-nine matches in all. It had been somewhat quieter for the fans; they'd been sat at home scanning the back pages of the *Eastern Daily Press* for any news on a possible new signing. But it was all set to begin again with the club's participation in the Anglo-Scottish Cup at the beginning of August.

The Canaries' preparation for the new season began in earnest with the club's participation in that tournament. The Anglo-Scottish Cup was a new incarnation of the initially popular but short-lived Texaco Cup, a tournament that Norwich had previously competed in, reaching the final in 1973. On that occasion, however, the competition was played during the first part of the League season. Norwich had opened their campaign with a 3-2 aggregate victory against Dundee in September 1972, going on to have subsequent two-legged successes against Leicester City and Motherwell. This meant the Canaries had reached the final; the two games against, of all clubs, Ipswich Town due to be played at the end of the League season. Local interest was high, and nearly 36,000 eagerly attended the second-leg game at Carrow Road to see the Canaries recover a 2-1 deficit from the first leg. Alas, it was not to be. Ipswich repeated that scoreline, winning 4-2 on aggregate, meaning that Norwich had played in two cup finals that season, losing them both.

Norwich exited the tournament at the semi-final stage the following season, losing 5-2 on aggregate to Burnley. Supporter interest had dwindled by then, however, with only 11,971 bothering to attend the Carrow Road clash, which

Norwich lost 3-2. By the following season, Norwich went out at the group stage and the tournament, like the Canaries' interest in it, dwindled away to extinction. Its unsponsored relaunch the following year was, therefore, both unexpected and, in the minds of many, unnecessary. Most of all the clubs involved now regarded it as nothing more than a vehicle in order to get their players match-fit for the new season. The Canaries certainly went through the motions; losing 2-1 to Fulham – then still in the Second Division – before grabbing a fortuitous 1-1 draw at Chelsea in a game that neither club seemed particularly keen to win, as it would mean further involvement in the competition. Norwich made sure that wouldn't apply to them in their third and final group game, losing 4-1 at Bristol City, and crashing out of the tournament in the process.

So with that now out of the way and the players fit, Bond and his team could start to focus on the rather more serious matter of competitive League football and a League programme. This included fixtures against Manchester City, Leeds United, Aston Villa, Arsenal and Tottenham before the end of August – five extremely hard games in just over two weeks which would tell Bond and the club's support just how prepared they were for the new season, and whether all the hard work, preparation, and at times interminable (fourteen in fifteen weeks remember, not far short of a standard season schedule) run of summer fixtures would have been worth it.

The pivot on which the club's hopes for the new season would be rotating was clearly going to be Martin Peters. Bond had resisted the temptation to give Peters the job of captain when he had arrived, opting, very sensibly, for Duncan Forbes to retain the job. But as much as Forbes, with all of his on-field cajoling and fist pumping, was a great vocal and physical presence during games, no one was in much doubt as far as the entire football club was concerned, on and, crucially, off the pitch, Peters was the 'main man'. And no wonder. Norwich were, after all, about to commence only the third season of First Division football in their entire history, while the fast-approaching 1975/76 campaign would be Peters' fifteenth consecutive one at that level. Yet despite all of his achievements in the game, not least the fact he had scored in a World Cup final (he remains one of only four players[13] to have scored in a final who has also played League football in England) he remained a tremendously humble man; happy to be playing a part at Norwich and to be on hand to offer, if asked, any advice or encouragement to his new teammates. Speaking about his part in England's 1966 success prior to Norwich's end-of-season tour to the USA friendly fixture against the Tampa Bay Rowdies in May 1978, Peters admitted that continued selection for England always came as a surprise to him.

---

[13] In open play the other three are Peters' West Ham teammate in 1966, Geoff Hurst, plus Arsenal's Emmanuel Petit, who scored for France in the 1998 World Cup final, and Marco Materazzi, who had a short spell with Everton in the 1998/99 season, scoring for Italy in the 2006 final.

> I wasn't expecting to be on that team. I was a kid. It was a fairytale. It's every player's ambition in England to play for the national side. You're never sure until you are actually on the team. Sir Alf Ramsay pulled eleven names out of a hat. I was the last one.

Norwich had accepted the invitation to play the Rowdies as part of a trip to the USA immediately after the cessation of official football hostilities at the end of the 1977/78 season. The club stayed in America for almost a fortnight but played only two games during this time, the Tampa Bay fixture plus a game against the USA's national under-21 side. The match against Tampa Bay, then one of the leading club sides in US soccer, had come about as a gesture of thanks towards the Canaries who had 'lent' Tampa three of their players – Mick McGuire, Graham Paddon and Jim Fleeting – earlier that year. Fleeting went on to score two goals in his first two games for the club, while the signing of Paddon was regarded as so vital, and Paddon such a 'blue chip' acquisition, that he was put straight into the Rowdies side to play the New York Cosmos only two days after he had arrived in the country. The Canaries had, on this occasion, flown out to Florida with the intention of giving their players a well-earned break after a typically gruelling League season, but with Football League regulations at the time requiring clubs to play in at least one game while on such trips, they found the Rowdies more than happy to give them a game. The game, played in front of a disappointing crowd of just 2,600 spectators, ended in an 11-10 win for the Canaries – anyone thinking that means the game went to penalties needs to think again, as that was the final score after normal play! It is certainly the highest-scoring game the Canaries have ever been involved in. With just thirty seconds left, the score was 9-9 and a draw looked likely until John Ryan scored for Norwich to put the Canaries 10-9 up. That looked to be it until Tampa's Davie Robb, who would go on to sign for Norwich in September of that year, made it 10-10. But even that wasn't the final act of a truly remarkable game, and just as the game was ending the last few seconds of 'overtime', the evergreen Peters stole into space from nowhere to win the game for Norwich with his fifth goal of the night.

Neither Peters nor Norwich would have suspected that he would still have been such an important player for the Canaries three years on from that US tour. But Peters didn't need to be asked to pass on all of that knowledge – he found it came naturally to him to offer his advice and thoughts to Norwich's younger players almost as soon as he arrived at Carrow Road. He did, however, note with disappointment in his autobiography that some of them didn't seem to have the determination to succeed or the desire to improve that he had when he was a young player at West Ham.

> When I was a young player, I was interested only in improving my skills and fitness. I was devoted to my job. I wanted to be the best. At Norwich, I realised

that some of the youngsters were less interested in training and more interested in what they would be doing after training.[14]

Peters avowed himself to lead by example rather than get too involved. He knew that one of the reasons John Bond had signed him was to act as a role model for the younger players, eventually becoming involved with some of the brighter young talents at the club; a little bit of quiet advice here, some encouragement there. For players like Kevin Bond, Kevin Reeves, Greg Downs, Mark Barham and Justin Fashanu, all of whom were, at some point during Peters' time at Carrow Road,[15] fortunate enough to have the benefit of his wisdom, that must have been an invaluable time. Did it help inspire them? You'd like to think so. After all, Reeves and Barham both played for England, while Fashanu eventually became a £1-million player and a winner of the BBC's 'Goal of the Season' award. But then Norwich were like any other top-level football club at the time – of their clutch of young players, there would always be some that would make it to the top of their profession, while a lot more would fall by the wayside; Paul Wilson and Neil Davids being two examples of young players who were at the club during Peters' first full season.

Responsibilities aside, Peters settled in quickly at Norwich. He likened the way that the team played under Bond to how he had been taught to play at West Ham under Greenwood. Bond's Norwich played a fast and fluent passing game, with every player coached into being comfortable with the ball at his feet and able to run with it at his feet. Bond was a great footballing tactician who, along with his assistant Ken Brown, studied every opponent and every game in great detail, working out their respective strengths and weaknesses, and how he would expect his side to play in order to stand their best chance of winning. This naturally demanded a lot more of the Norwich players who might, either under Saunders (those few that were left) or at their respective former clubs, have been used to a more regimented and settled game plan – same old, same old every week in other words. Bond demanded more and, as a footballer, you couldn't help but improve under him because of this.

Peters was not only a pivotal figure within the club, he was one on the pitch as well. He hadn't come to Norwich for an easy life, to while away a cosy year or two before hanging up his boots – a thought he admitted that some Norwich fans might initially have had. Far from it. He became a key player and revelled in the responsibility, happy to play wherever Bond thought he would be most effective and, as a result, fitting into a number of different

---

[14] Peters, Martin, *The Ghost Of 66* (Orion, 2006), p. 255.

[15] Peters is often seen as merely 'seeing out his career' at Norwich, playing only a handful of games for the club over a short time before retirement. He did, however, end up playing more League games for the Canaries (206) than he did for Tottenham (189).

positions. This included, on one occasion, as a central attacker, alongside Ted MacDougall as the Canaries prepared for the daunting trip to Anfield to play Liverpool on 29 November 1975.

Liverpool were, at the time, fast developing into the footballing superpower that would dominate both the English and European competition over the next few years; a side packed with a frightening array of talent – Clemence, Neal, Kennedy, Keegan, Toshack and Heighway. Such would be their dominance that a well-known Norwich City fanzine was titled *Liverpool Are On The Tele Again* in mock worship of the club's overwhelming stranglehold on the game, as well as the fawning media. But not without reason. They were, especially at Anfield, a frightening proposition for any team to handle. Leeds United, champions less than eighteen months earlier and European Cup finalists, had been seen off to the tune of 3-0, as had Aston Villa. They slipped up a bit against Manchester United by conceding a goal, but the 3-1 win against Docherty's young tyros was much more convincing than the score suggests. Imagine if you will, the opening scenes of the film *Gladiator*. Maximus, in the guise of Bob Paisley, ruler of all Anfield, stands astride the brow of the Kop, notebook in hand and utters that immortal line, 'At my signal, unleash hell...'

That was pretty much what it was like to face Liverpool at Anfield in those dark and distant days, when they had aspirations of a Red Empire, and we were the fur- and woad-clad primitives who they regularly put to the slaughter en route.

But not this time.

Bond, ever canny, made a cute tactical change for the game. Peters was instructed to play in an attacking position along with MacDougall, but rather than operating as a traditional strike duo in the middle, both were told to play in wide positions. As a result of this, the Liverpool centre-halves, the normally resolute Phil Thompson and Emlyn Hughes, didn't have anyone to mark, at least not where they might have expected the Norwich players to be, and neither had they expected Peters to play so offensively. The resultant confusion in the Liverpool defence meant that Norwich were able to attack with confidence, and while there were inevitable periods during the game when Liverpool were in full flow attacking-wise (they won nineteen corners), there was always time and room for Norwich to press on the counter. With Peters and MacDougall a little wider and deeper than usual, the opportunities were there, it was just a case of could they be taken when they arose? Suggett struck first with a strike from 25 yards. Less than ten minutes later, Peters, typical Peters, ghosted into the area from nowhere to convert Sullivan's pass. Normal service did seem to resume when Hughes got one back, but Norwich were toying with their opponents by now and it was fitting that MacDougall, asked to work harder than maybe he had ever done so on a football pitch in his life, profited from a little bit of penalty box pinball to make it 3-1. It was his seventeenth goal of the season, a fitting denouement to a tactical master plan that was designed by Bond and directed, masterfully, by Peters.

Were Norwich lucky? Was it a freak result? No. They had, in their manager, a man who could, at will, outwit the opposition, whatever their status or reputation. Bond would have spent the week before the game giving his players the same message over and over and over again. You are as good as they are, if not better. We are a better team, we have the better players, we have a game plan; that means we will win. By the time the players got to Anfield, they would already have won the game in their minds. The reality of the situation mattered not one bit – if you looked at that then you might as well give up and not bother. Bond didn't accept perceived realities; he dealt in very real possibilities. He knew Liverpool could be beaten, that they could be vulnerable. The trick was to give them a situation they weren't familiar with, one they found uncomfortable. Norwich showed they were going to do just that from the moment they arrived when, against presumed formality and expectation, they warmed up directly in front of the Kop pre-match – shades of the All Blacks performing their famous Haka. This was evidence enough that the Canaries were not going to lay down and have their feathery bellies tickled.

Norwich's victory was a deserved one. This hadn't been a 'backs to the wall' type of match; they hadn't, in modern parlance, come to Anfield and 'parked the bus'. They'd arrived there as Liverpool's equals, and played the sort of game to prove a point. Writing in the *Eastern Daily Press*, Mick Dennis summed it up perfectly, arguing that luck played no part in it: 'There was no luck. Norwich City were tactically superior, had a far more inventive midfield, were sharper in attack and more solid at the back.'

This was Norwich City, after a game at Anfield. You could read it quite a few times but it never quite sank in. Yet there it was. That was the game plan of a team that was prepared, not one that was aiming to hope for the best. In Bond and Peters, the Canaries had the best of both worlds – one sat in the dugout, the other graced the pitch. The manner of the victory and the way that Norwich played genuinely made you wonder, providing that Bond was given the time and, crucially, the money, just what he was capable of achieving at the club.

Maybe the lack of money would turn out to be a problem? As we have seen, the combination of Bond's spending since his arrival at the club, together with the money that the club committed to upgrading the ground and the training complex, meant that Bond, a renowned wheeler-dealer, was unable to do much to strengthen his side during the summer of 1975. The squad had been good enough to win promotion, but could it hold up to a season of First Division football? Of the twenty players[16] who had made at least one League appearance for Norwich during the 1974/75 season, only twelve of them had played top-flight football before, and only seven of them had done so for Norwich. Top-flight priority was the priority. Undoubtedly and unequivocally

---

[16] Benson, Boyer, Butler, Forbes, Goodwin, Grapes, Hansbury, Keelan, Livermore, Machin, MacDougall, McGuire, Miller, Morris, Peters, Powell, Steele, Stringer, Suggett and Sullivan.

so. And, with both Carrow Road and the Trowse training complex having been updated and brought into line with top-flight requirements, the question everyone was asking was did the club have the players to keep the Canaries in the state they very much hoped to become accustomed to?

Norwich's first game back in the top division was a tricky tie against Manchester City. It was nip and tuck for much of the game and looked set to be ending in a 0-0 draw – not Bond's favourite scoreline, but one he would have accepted on the day – until Colin Bell fired the Manchester side ahead after an hour. Two more goals swiftly followed and Norwich was on the end of an undeserved heavy defeat. Four days later, the Canaries entertained Leeds United. The disgraced European Cup finalists from the previous season were, under the steady leadership of Jimmy Armfield, rebuilding a side and reputation that they had gathered in the mid-sixties. Some of the big names were still there – Lorimer, Bremner, Clarke – but like Norwich, Leeds was in the process of reinventing themselves and a dull 1-1 draw was the end result, one you suspect both clubs would have been delighted about. For Bond, at least, it meant that Norwich were off the mark. They'd faced a team who had only recently been League champions and European Cup finalists, and hadn't been found wanting. The players would now have some belief. The real work could now begin.

And it was led, inspired even, by Ted MacDougall.

MacDougall had been quietly,[17] at least for him, getting on with his work at Norwich. He'd been among the goals in his first full season at the club, contributing twenty-two during the 1974/75 campaign and thus easily ending it as the club's top scorer, though it hadn't been enough for him to win the club's Player of the Year award – that honour went to Colin Suggett. But with Peters swiftly becoming the headline act at Carrow Road while Suggett was establishing himself as the terrace favourite, MacDougall, ever single-minded, was as determined as ever to make a few headlines for himself. He hadn't scored for the club in open play since the previous March and was aware that there were some voices who would, just as they had during his brief spells at Manchester United and West Ham, reckon him not to be good enough to score consistently at the very highest level. The visit of Aston Villa to Carrow Road on 23 August was as good a time as any for MacDougall to remind everyone of his quality. He went on to do just that, and in emphatic fashion, scoring a hat-trick as Norwich won 5-3, more than making up for the 1-4 defeat they had endured on the last day of the previous season. True, it didn't quite make up for defeat in the League Cup final to the same side, but it was the first win in five attempts for Bond over Saunders, and one that got the season up and running on a never-to-be-forgotten gloriously sunny afternoon at Carrow Road.

---

17 Ted was a demonstrative figure at the best of times, not adverse to giving a little back to any Norwich supporters that might have questioned his on-field efforts, or offering them the V-sign in response.

It was also the start of an amazing run of goalscoring form for MacDougall. His late equaliser at White Hart Lane a week later earned Norwich a respectable 2-2 draw against Tottenham. Then, on the following Saturday, he scored another hat-trick for the Canaries, this time in a 4-2 win against Everton – though Suggett's own spectacular effort in the same match took almost as many plaudits. He followed this up with a double at Burnley in a thrilling 4-4 draw, Phil Boyer also securing a point for the Canaries with almost the last kick of the game. MacDougall then repeated the feat at Carrow Road in a 2-0 win over Leicester City, one that took the Canaries to the rarefied heights of tenth in the Division One table.

Six games, eight points and eleven goals for MacDougall: who said he couldn't score regularly at the top level? No one now, that's for certain. By the time of that famous win at Anfield, Ted had scored seventeen League and cup goals for Norwich, not a bad return in any season for any striker – but this was all a month before Christmas. He scored again in the 1-0 win against West Ham a week after the Liverpool game, repeating the feat in the club's next game; a 3-2 defeat (the last three games between the clubs had produced eighteen goals!) at Aston Villa for whom two of their goals were contributed by eighteen-year-old rookie striker John Deehan – one for the future, clearly.

That game marked the halfway point in the Canaries' first season back in Division One. Their League record of P 21 W 7 D 4 L 10 GF 30 GA 34 was maybe, at this point, not quite as healthy as Bond might have wanted – but one thing stood out, especially compared to their previous two seasons at the top level, they were scoring goals.

During the 1972/73 and 1973/74 seasons, the Canaries had only managed thirty-six and thirty-seven League goals respectively, yet here they were just halfway through the season and within striking distance of those totals already. There was room for improvement; Bond had recognised the need for some defensive strengthening and successfully persuaded the board to part with £55,000 in order to prise away centre-half David Jones from Nottingham Forest – yet another player who Bond had managed at Bournemouth, the seventh ex-Cherry to join the club since Bond's appointment.

Jones had plenty to prove upon his arrival at Carrow Road. He'd been summarily assessed and discarded by Brian Clough not long after the latter's arrival at the City Ground. Clough had picked him for Forest's League game against Norwich in April 1975, one of the few appearances that Jones made for Clough. On that day, Norwich had sauntered to a 3-0 win at Carrow Road, one of the goals coming from a Peters' header. You suspect that any central defender who lets an opponent get a header away in his own penalty area would go on to have his card marked by Clough, much more so if it was Peters, and especially if it resulted in a goal. Jones wouldn't have been the first player that Clough dismissed out of hand, neither would he be the last – it also happened to Asa Hartford, Gary Megson and John Sheridan, with the first two following Jones' route and eventually ending up at Carrow Road. Clough had been hasty and his loss turned out to be Bond's gain. Mind you, Jones' Norwich debut might have led to a triumphant 'I told you so' by Cloughie; not only was he run, harried and bullied into the ground by Newcastle's Malcolm MacDonald, he also scored a last-minute own goal, sealing United's 5-2 win at St James Park.

Welcome to Norwich. Have a nice day. Jones, patently, hadn't. But he didn't panic. Things would get better for him, just as they did for the side.

Following the defeat at Aston Villa, Norwich lost just two of their next ten League games; an impressive run of form that included victories over Leeds United (3-0), Arsenal (3-1) and Tottenham (3-1). MacDougall netted in all of those games and had now become one of the nation's most respected and feared top-flight strikers. He ended that campaign as the leading League goalscorer in the First Division; the first and, to date, only time a Norwich City player has ever achieved that accolade. His final total of twenty-three League goals from forty-two games; his nearest rivals being fellow Scot, Tottenham's John Duncan (twenty), and Newcastle's Malcolm MacDonald (nineteen), the man who many, despite Ted's obvious class, saw as the superior of the two 'Macs'.

But Ted's season had not passed without incident. He was a fiery and unpredictable character on the pitch, demanding of his teammates and hard on his opponents. You usually knew that you'd been in a match with Ted, even if you played on the same side as him! Martin Peters recalled how temperamental Ted could be, and the on-field stick he would give the Norwich wingers if they were not giving him the service he expected. Indeed, if a through ball or cross didn't meet Ted's high standards, then more often than not he would simply stand his ground and refuse to make an effort to meet it. There were times when the Norwich crowd perceived this as laziness on Ted's part, and they wouldn't be averse to giving him a little colourful advice regarding the matter. Even my own father recalls, on such an occasion, loudly imploring Ted to make an effort, to chase down the ball. Ted's reaction was simply to look my father's way, meet his eye, and without saying a single word, offer him a large, theatrical V-sign in response.

He was a curmudgeon clad in yellow and green, the Mario Balotelli of his day, but he was ours. And, as Peters went on to point out, despite the moods, the gestures, the times when he looked like he couldn't be bothered, or looked to want to kick an opposing player as much as he wanted to kick the ball, he was a natural goalscorer, one that, given even a glimmer of a chance at the near post from a Peters' pass, would immediately lose his marker and get a chance on goal – which would, more often than not, be converted.

His duels with opposing players sometimes became as much a part of the game as the football itself. On one memorable occasion, when Norwich were playing West Ham – a game that Ted found it very easy to motivate himself for – he opened the scoring at Upton Park after only sixteen minutes, volleying a fierce shot past Mervyn Day from a Suggett pass. He had already been the subject of both the home fans' and opposition players' ire before then, so with that goal and subsequent celebration, both doubled their efforts on him. Ted went on to clatter Day, as well as enjoy a flare up with Billy Bonds before the match was over; that latter one tipping the Hammers' fans over the edge to such an extent that a deluge of missiles were thrown at him from the stands. Bonds, of course, had been Ted's nemesis during his time at the club, and neither had forgotten the dressing room punch-up between them that had accelerated Ted's departure from the club, and the bad blood and rancour was obviously still there.

The Canaries played a total of eight matches in the FA and League Cup competitions that season. Such a number of games suggests a very healthy run in at least one of the cups in question, but when you consider that of those eight matches only three different clubs were involved, then a slightly different picture emerges. Norwich drew at home to Manchester City in the second round of the League Cup, a competition that they had, by now, considerable pedigree in. As well as winning it in 1962, Norwich had been finalists, semi-finalists and finalists in each of the past three seasons – might this one finally be the one that saw them win the trophy? They so very nearly put Manchester City out at the first attempt, leading at Carrow Road through the inevitable MacDougall goal, before Dave Watson scrambled an equaliser in the closing minutes; one that Bond declared post-match was not deserved, such had been the dour and unimaginative defensive play of Norwich's opponents. The two clubs duly met again a week later at Maine Road, and this time it was Norwich's turn to secure a draw in the dying minutes – MacDougall's header from a Suggett cross ensuring the game ended 2-2.

This was all at a time when neither the FA nor the Football League had even considered letting something as vulgar as a penalty shoot-out prevent two clubs from playing each other time and time again in a cup game – even if by the time the second replay came about, both fans and maybe even some of the players were beginning to lose interest. For reasons that therefore fly in the face of footballing logic, the Football League decreed that the second replay would be played at Stamford Bridge, the home of Chelsea. This meant, of course, both clubs and their supporters had to make a long trek southwards, on a Monday evening, and just two days after they had both played League fixtures – Norwich barely having time to draw breath after a long trip to Sheffield forty-eight hours earlier. It is a tribute, therefore, to the fans of both clubs that a crowd of 6,238 joined them at the Bridge; paltry by any other standards maybe, but in terms of having to be inconvenienced and travel to a neutral ground, on a Monday night, and in pouring rain, worthy of praise. Norwich had, as it turned out, nothing left to give on the night. John Bond had named an unchanged team from that which had won at Bramall Lane, and maybe that was his undoing on the night – determined to win and committed to picking his strongest side, despite the circumstances and the fact a crucial home game against Stoke City loomed large in only another five days.

Consequently, a weary Canary XI were sent packing to the tune of 6-1; their downfall on the night a calamity of defensive errors, conceded penalties and, courtesy of Geoff Butler, an own goal. A night to be forgotten therefore, the lack of interest in the game reflected in the fact that the attendance was the lowest ever recorded for a senior match at Chelsea. Maybe, just maybe, that was because neither of the teams playing was Chelsea? Common sense would suggest that after the second replay ended in another stalemate, the two captains would toss a coin to decide whose ground the second replay would be played at. Sadly for both clubs, this was not something the Football League felt necessary in order to be able to govern the game. It therefore remains a large and shameful example of the casual and almost callous disregard the footballing authorities had for its teams and, especially, their supporters at that time.

As far as the FA Cup was concerned, the draw for the third round of that competition did lead to memories of that victorious League Cup final win over Rochdale fourteen years earlier, with the two clubs being drawn to play each other – the first time they had met since that final. The match itself also provoked memories – but much more recent ones than that previous clash – of the marathon series of games against Manchester City a few months earlier as, again, Norwich took part in a cup match that needed to go to a second replay. They had, as you'd imagine, been expected to canter to a comfortable home win in the first game as they were playing, after all, a side that was then fifteenth in the old Fourth Division. That script was followed to the letter when, after just four minutes, MacDougall calmly scored from the penalty spot. Tension lifted, Carrow Road, and maybe some of the yellow-and-green-clad members of the main cast, sat back and waited for the expected goal rush. But it never came because the anticipated disintegration of Rochdale's confidence as a consequence of that early setback never came either.

They got stuck in, chasing down lost causes and winning the ball in every 50:50 challenge, so it hardly came as a surprise when, half an hour later, Phil Mullington equalised after an error by the normally peerless Suggett. Norwich huffed and puffed but never really threatened to score again, the end result being another cup replay, something they really didn't need.

Three days later, Norwich set off to Spotland for the replay – a game that Rochdale dominated and should have won. Not only did Tony Whelan's header hit the bar, the follow up from Bob Mountford clattered into exactly the same spot, Keelan well beaten on both occasions. Later on in the game, Mountford, who scored thirty-seven goals in ninety-eight League games for Rochdale, sent another header goal-bound, only for it to rebound back into play off a post. Norwich had been lucky. Very lucky.

No neutral ground for the second replay this time. Carrow Road hosted in front of a substantially bigger crowd than had turned up for the original tie, the match now unquestionably capturing the imagination – for its drama rather than the football. Mountford impressed again, his fifty-third minute header drawing

Rochdale level after MacDougall, again with a penalty, had put Norwich ahead. The game then ebbed and flowed for a quarter of an hour before Suggett put Norwich ahead from a teasing Sullivan cross; a goal that maybe had a touch of offside about it, not that it worried the Canaries. They duly held on for the win and finally a confirmed place in the fourth round where they were due to meet another old cup nemesis, Luton Town, the team that had knocked them out at the semi-finals stage in 1959. Norwich had little difficulty in winning this game, with goals from Peters and David Jones, a first in a Norwich shirt for him.

That win earned Norwich a place in the FA Cup fifth round for the first time for nine years, a disappointing run of form for a club with such a renowned FA Cup tradition. However, it hadn't just been a poor run of form for the Canaries in the competition, it was an embarrassing one. In the seven years prior to that fifth-round appearance in 1976, Norwich had tumbled out in the third round on each occasion; a dismal run that had included exits at the hands of Hull City and Wrexham. Indeed, in comparison to their stop-start progress to the last sixteen in 1976, the last time they had got to that level, in 1967, they'd got there via a famous fourth-round victory at Old Trafford, knocking out Manchester United just as they had done in 1959, only this time at their own ground. Norwich eventually succumbed to Sheffield Wednesday in the fifth round at Carrow Road in front of 41,000 spectators: the highest ever at the ground for a cup match of any kind. Indeed, the three games the Canaries had played in the competition during the 1966/67 season were played in front of an aggregate attendance of 125,718, a statistic the club would do well to emulate at any stage of the competition, even today, especially with the current Carrow Road capacity of around 27,000 falling well short of that eye-watering attendance for the Sheffield Wednesday game.

Those proverbial 'marathon ties' in the FA Cup were not unknown to Norwich fans at that time, however. In the 1972/73 season, the club had drawn Leeds United in the third round at Carrow Road, that game ending in a 1-1 draw. The replay saw the same outcome, so it was off to Villa Park on 29 January to try again, the fourth time the clubs had met in ten days; Norwich losing the League fixture at Carrow Road by two goals to one on 20 January. Sadly for the Canaries, that game went the same way, and in a convincing manner. Leeds sauntered to a 5-0 win thanks to a superb hat-trick by Allan Clarke within the first twenty minutes of the game. Leeds, of course, eventually reached the final, where they lost to Sunderland, while Norwich consoled themselves by reaching Wembley in the final of the League Cup.

Luckily for Norwich, the fifth-round draw resulted in them having as good a chance as they could ever hope to reach the quarter-finals – only the third time in the club's history. With clubs of the standing and calibre of Manchester United, Derby County (the reigning League champions), Newcastle United, Leicester City and Wolves all in the draw, Norwich got the best possible draw they could have: at home to the only Division Four side left in the competition, Bradford City.

Good times therefore at Carrow Road. They'd followed up the 2-0 win over Luton with those consecutive League successes over Leeds and Arsenal; four points out of four and six goals scored to only one conceded, taking them to fourteenth place in the table after the win over Arsenal. Norwich now sat a good eight points ahead of Wolves, in the first of the relegation places, and were only three adrift of neighbours Ipswich Town, comfortably placed in eighth. All of that plus a popular and charismatic manager, who was fast becoming a household name, and a free-scoring centre-forward and World Cup winner conducting operations on the field. Now only Bradford City stood between Norwich and a place in the last eight of the FA Cup where, as Bond would have been the first to admit, you really didn't care who you got.

The game against Bradford finally took place at Carrow Road on 23 February, just two days after both clubs had played League games. Norwich certainly seemed to have the pending cup match on their minds, as their five-match unbeaten run was brought to a sudden and emphatic end at Carrow Road by Coventry City, who stormed Carrow Road and won 3-0, ex-Canary David Cross one of their scorers. Had minds been wandering with players wanting to keep themselves fit and sharp for the Bradford game – a case of a club taking it easy in a League match in order to be best prepared for a cup game? This would be unheard of now, with clubs and players almost certain to commit to the all important games in the League before anything else, least of all the FA Cup. Or maybe Norwich had been lulled into a false sense of security? Their recent form had been among the best in the country: Arsenal and Leeds had been emphatically beaten, as had Burnley while the Canaries were unlucky not to have got both points at Everton, the game ending 1-1, although it was one they most certainly should have won. Spirits and confidence would have been riding high, the mood would have been good, the players more than capable of seeing off the Sky Blues. It was a disappointing result and one which, as Mick McGuire admitted after the game, could have seen Coventry double their winning margin. But the game was now history, and Norwich had forty-eight hours to prepare for Bradford and the victory that would take them into the last eight of the FA Cup, still at that time the honour that players in England wanted to win more than any other.

The original date for the tie to have been played had been moved twice because of an outbreak of flu at Bradford. Could Norwich have insisted the game be played regardless? It's an interesting suggestion – had Bradford had six or seven players missing with football-related injuries, there is no doubt that the game would still have gone ahead. Flu bug or not, Bradford still managed to play five games in a four-week period that included the cup game, one more than Norwich! It seems, in hindsight, they wanted to give themselves the best possible chance of winning the game, such were the potential cash bonuses on offer for reaching the quarter-finals. Finding themselves missing a few players at the time the fifth round was due to be played, they opted to use these as an excuse to get some time for those unfit or unwell players to recover in time to play the game.

It was certainly a thought that was shared in and around Carrow Road at the time, and angry words were exchanged between the clubs in the days leading up to the tie.

Conjecture or not, the wait was worth it – for the Bantams. An attendance of 27,047, higher than for the League matches against Leeds United, Derby and Arsenal, turned up at Carrow Road to witness the Yorkshire side being put in its place – or so we believed. That happy complacency was shaken when Don Hutchins gave Bradford a first-half lead, but normal service was resumed seconds later when Peters equalised. Then, as had been the case against Rochdale, the Canaries sat back and waited for the goals to come. But they didn't. Bradford, like Rochdale, was not going to sit back and accept that as inevitable. They remained focused and professional, giving as good as they got – and, ultimately, better. Their reward came with three minutes to go. A hurried Canary clearance fell at the feet of Billy McGinley and Norwich were out; for once experiencing the feeling of what it was like to be a top-flight club dumped out of the cup by a smaller team – the subjects, rather than the architects, of an FA Cup giant-killing. The Bantams and their fans duly celebrated long into the night, their long journey home all the more sweet with the taste of success. For Norwich, there was nothing more glamorous to look forward to than a trip to play Birmingham City in five days' time. The challenge for John Bond now would not be an anticipated quarter-final tie, but getting his team motivated for the more prosaic surrounds of St Andrews – not, at that time, so much a Cathedral of English soccer as a rather tatty multi-storey car park, and a long way from Wembley in May.

FA Cup lamentations aside, had anyone sidled up to John Bond at the start of that season and offered the Canaries a top-ten finish in the First Division, plus a run to the fifth round of the FA Cup, he would have taken it – taken it and, quite probably, taken even less. Mere survival would have suited the Canaries in August, and that would have included the ever-demanding Sir Arthur South. Despite that unexpected defeat to lowly opposition, the 1975/76 season was an exceptionally good one for the club, arguably the best they had yet had in their history.

That post-Bradford trip to Birmingham was a fine test of Canary mettle. With some of the players almost certainly brooding on the nature of their recent shock defeat, and morale at a long-time low among the players and the supporters, it was one of the last places you would have wanted to go if all you wanted to do was creep away and lick your wounds. The tie against Bradford had presented Norwich with a fantastic chance of reaching the last eight of the competition, and even progressing from there. Of the eight clubs that reached the quarter-finals that year, only half were from the top flight – one of those, the Wolves, were struggling and would eventually be relegated. If Norwich had prevailed against Bradford to make that total five from eight then there was every chance that they might have been drawn against Wolves, or even one of the clubs from outside of the top division. Sunderland and Southampton were both in Division Two, while Crystal Palace were in Division Three. As it was, Bradford drew Southampton at home in the quarter-final draw, while Palace went to Sunderland, meaning at least two clubs from outside the First Division would be in the semi-finals. It seemed an opportunity missed.

The trouble with hindsight, especially in football, is that when it is applied as it has been here, then at least half a dozen clubs could, feasibly or otherwise, stake their own claim as to why they could have won any particular trophy in a given year. The fact remains that they didn't, and whoever you are and whatever the circumstances, you move on, and as quickly as possible. A professional approach, and one that John Bond would have infused into his players as soon as they had arrived back in the dressing room post-Bradford and slumped dejectedly on their seats, with their heads down:

> What's done is done. We've lost; we have to deal with it. There's always next year. What's important now is Birmingham on Saturday and starting a good little run in the League again. We still need some points and I need a team on Saturday who wants to go to Birmingham and get them. Get tonight out of your systems and be ready to go again at the weekend.

Bond made two changes to his team for the Birmingham match from the side that had started against Bradford – David Jones and Mel Machin making way for Tony Powell and Billy Steele respectively. The recall for the latter was apt: Bond wanted a little more steel in his side for a game that he didn't want to lose – indeed, it was more about not losing than it was about winning. Getting into a spiral of bad results, especially at this stage of the season, could do a lot of damage to any team, especially his own. Norwich were in seventeenth place prior to the Birmingham game, five points clear of Burnley who were in twentieth with, critically, three games in hand over them. So the Canaries looked safe. But with trying fixtures coming up against sides like Derby, Manchester United, Liverpool, Ipswich Town and surprise championship contenders QPR – then fourth, third, first, ninth and second in the table respectively – it was important for Norwich to get a few more points guaranteed before those games, where doing so might not have been quite so easy.

Powell's return to the first team after a lengthy spell out injured was a particularly welcome one. He'd been taken off in the game against Newcastle back in November and his on-field presence had been missed. His great strength, aside from his willingness to work hard and win lost causes for the team, was his total and utter dependability. He hardly, if ever, had a bad game for Norwich – and in a career that spanned 275 appearances for Norwich, all but two of which were in the starting XI, that's some achievement. Such was his form, that one injury aside, and fitness that at one point in his Norwich career he played in 140 consecutive first-team matches, an achievement for an outfield player that would almost be unheard of in the modern game.

That total and utter reliability, the certainty that whatever brief he was given for the Birmingham match, together with the recall of Steele, an equally industrious midfielder but one who also had a lot of skill and ability to match that energy, meant that Norwich would have travelled to St Andrews with two confident characters in their ranks who couldn't wait to get out there and play. Their return and combined enthusiasm for the otherwise difficult task ahead would have rubbed off on the other players and, as such, was a managerial masterstroke. Bond further shuffled his pack by deploying Peters in a more defensive role than usual, thus in theory drawing whoever had been detailed to mark him away from where Norwich hoped they would be able to do the most damage.

Unfortunately for Powell, his enthusiasm at his return to the side made him overeager to impress. This was perfectly illustrated when, just over half an hour into the first half, his challenge on Trevor Francis earned the Blues a penalty, which Francis himself converted. But luckily for Norwich, Birmingham's Malcolm Page was eager to return the favour, his trip on Mick McGuire early in the second half bringing about a Norwich free-kick, which Peters powered past Peter Latchford for the equaliser.

It was a good point to get, maybe as crucial a one as the club got that season. It meant that Norwich had avoided a potentially morale-damaging defeat, and also set themselves up nicely for the game against Tottenham a week later; the first in a run of matches that saw the Canaries play Derby County, Manchester United and Liverpool. For the Tottenham game, Bond made one more change to his side, David Jones being recalled in place of Dave Stringer. It was, though few probably suspected it at the time, the beginning of the end of Stringer's long and distinguished career at Norwich, at least as a player, and explaining, as if any explanation was necessary, Bond's determination to bring Jones to the club in the first place.

The beginning of the 1976/77 season would see defensive mainstays Stringer and Duncan Forbes thirty-one and thirty-five years old respectively, and they couldn't go on forever, at least, not together. A few of the club's youngsters had tried to make an impact in the position, not least Steve Govier, of whom big things had been expected. But Govier had seen his career stall behind the imperious Forbes and therefore had leapt at the chance to kick-start his career with Brighton at the end of the 1973/74 season, clearly not fancying his long-term chances at Norwich. Others had also tried to take on the challenge of ousting Forbes and Stringer, notably Neil Davids, who Bond had signed on a free from Leeds towards the end of the previous season. Yet even for all his promise and the fact he'd come into the game training and playing alongside such greats as Jack Charlton, Norman Hunter and Gordon McQueen at Elland Road, Davids' only opportunities came at Norwich when Forbes was suspended. Like Govier, he never quite had it in him to be selected as an automatic choice when all the central defensive options were open. David Jones had broken the mould. But, because he had, it was Stringer, rather than Forbes, whose place was now seriously under threat by the emergence and development of Jones as a centre-half of some considerable promise and no little ability.

The Canaries duly delivered against Tottenham; the 3-1 win engineered, with some relish, by Peters, who ran the show. Norwich, playing with confidence, even gave their opponents the opportunity to take the lead, Ralph Coates winning a eminently debatable free-kick, which Chivers, not a player you would normally have associated with set-piece finesse, scored from via a post. But Norwich held firm. Suggett scored the equaliser, MacDougall added a second from the penalty spot after Keith Jones had punched an effort from the impressive Jones off the line, and then Boyer capped off a fabulous team performance with the third. The win lifted Norwich to thirteenth in the Division One table. The Canaries were now seven points ahead of the ultimately doomed Burnley, with three games still in hand on them. They were, to all intents and purposes, safe from the fear of relegation, going on to guarantee their top-flight status with a run of five wins and two draws in their remaining eleven League games, one of which was a much-enjoyed win over Ipswich in the East Anglian Derby on 31 March; Peters the scorer in a 1-0 win.

Despite the joy of that win, however – and any win over Ipswich is a good one – the most significant game, as far as the division was concerned, that the Canaries would play that season was yet to come. When it did, it was a classic, and made Norwich the club that legions of supporters of a certain West London club would hate forevermore. The team in question was the Queens Park Rangers who, much to the collective astonishment of the footballing cognoscenti that season, made a prolonged and very real challenge for the First Division title, which, rather than falling away over the closing weeks as many in the past from similarly small and relatively undistinguished clubs had done, just kept on going, and was now going to go to the wire.

The man at the helm at Loftus Road was Dave Sexton. Character and personality-wise, he and Bond were chalk and cheese. Bond was avuncular, charismatic and media friendly, whereas Sexton was quiet, thoughtful and relatively insular, choosing a few well-spoken and considered words here and there, compared to Bond and his ever-ready list of sound bites. However, the one thing that the two men did have in common was their belief and their passion for playing good football; attractive and entertaining football, a game based on passing, pace and speed of thought rather than the still-prevalent game of power and all things physical. Sexton didn't like his teams to push and bully the opposition out of the game. He preferred to play and pass them out of it. He had been, during that 1975/76 season, captured in a lightning-in-a-jar moment; that time when everything in and around a football team comes together at just the right time to create something special. It couldn't have happened before then and couldn't immediately afterwards. It was a one-off, a time when you had to grasp the moment and hold it close, for it would never come your way again. Therefore, as far as QPR were concerned, that season was win or bust. There wouldn't be any second chances.

Sexton, like Bond, had gathered together a team of mixed talents and qualities, players young and old. His captain, Frank McLintock, a recent double winner at Arsenal, was to QPR what Peters was to Norwich – experience and expertise personified, a man who was a class act, both as captain and as a rarely ruffled and confident defender who led by example, and his presence had been the catalyst to QPR's remarkable season under Sexton. He certainly had some good players around him. Goalkeeper Phil Parkes was good enough to be considered as England's third choice in that position at that time, behind only the dominant Ray Clemence and Peter Shilton – not too bad a claim to fame when you consider the abundance of high-quality English goalkeepers around at the time, Kevin Keelan for one. In front of him, Parkes had two full-backs who also played for England – Dave Clement and Ian Gillard – while in the team's midfield Gerry Francis was good enough to captain England, a sure sign of your quality as a player when you have that job yet play for one of the smaller sides. Then there was the attack featuring the one and only Stan Bowles, a footballing maverick among mavericks, as likely to score a hat-trick against you as have a fit of the sulks and be as anonymous on the field as if he weren't playing. Norwich had to hope, as so many other teams did, that this game was going to see him have one of those off days.

So Sexton's side were good. Very good. And with just three League games of their season left, they had a very real chance of winning the title. QPR's current form was just about as good as it could get: eleven wins and one draw in their last twelve games, a run that included seven clean sheets and twenty-seven goals scored, including four against Wolves, Coventry and Middlesbrough. That run and their timing had been perfect; they'd gone to the top of the table following the 4-1 win over Coventry on 3 March, and now had their fate in their own hands. A win at Norwich and wins in their last two games, both at home where they were undefeated (Norwich had been seen off to the tune of 2-0 on Boxing Day), would see them Champions of England. An unlikely but nevertheless remarkable achievement, it would also secure a second title in five years for McLintock. The game at Carrow Road against a Norwich side whose season was all but over was hardly going to provide them much of a challenge, was it?

The West London club's supporters certainly felt it was a game that would go a long way to sealing the title for them. Norwich's best home attendance of the season, 31,231, was greatly boosted by the near 11,000 noisily chanting blue-and-white-clad hoards that packed the trains from Liverpool Street and turned the then relatively quiet roads heading north from London into a sea of noise – the title was theirs as far as they were concerned, and Carrow Road was simply a late-season party stop en route. Broadcasting the game was a no-brainer of course, and the BBC duly pitched up late the previous evening to screen the festivities for *Match of the Day*. When the day dawned it was warm and sunny, blue skies interrupted by a few high-flying fluffy white clouds. An omen, of course.

It suited Norwich that everyone was talking about, and talking up their opposition. From the way people were, it was as if their part in things was to do nothing more than lie down and make a gift of the points. Certainly the London-based media saw things that way, but that attitude put all of the pressure onto Sexton's side, meaning Norwich could just turn up and play. And play is something they could do just as well as their opponents. After all, weren't there some decent players in the Norwich line-up as well? A World Cup winner for a start, as well as two men who had already scored thirty-six goals between them that season. Norwich wasn't the type of team, nor were these the type of players, that you underestimated. If you did, the trip back would seem a lot longer than the one that got them there.

QPR, playing with a confidence that occasionally bordered on abandon, had arrived to win, to win well and to do so by attacking the game and Norwich. What they hadn't anticipated was that Norwich would, far from sitting back and absorbing their inevitable pressure, be only too willing to have a go themselves. Which they did. For those following the game from the main stands it must have been like watching a game of tennis as the game ebbed one way then the other, each side taking it in turn to mount an attack. Suggett and Peters drove Norwich forward, then Dave Thomas and Don Givens responded for QPR. While these craftsmen went about their work, each side's ball winners, their warriors, also settled into their own. Forbes, now nearing thirty-six but relishing the younger, quicker legs of Powell, McGuire and Jones around him, set up a base camp at the edge of the Norwich penalty area, snarling and growling at any unfortunate opponent that came too close, those more youthful colleagues of his making the most of QPR's resultant indecision by whipping in and stealing the ball away. Forbes was a great player to have in such games; it was like going for a walk with a lion tethered to a long lead – people gave you a wide berth – and the opposing players tried to go anywhere but where he was or where he might be. Because of that, Norwich began to edge possession and get more and more into the game.

For a game that featured so many skilful players, it was perhaps a surprise that the decisive area of the pitch was the midfield, and the amount of work that each team's ball winners were putting into it. For Norwich, this was one of the roles of Mick McGuire, and the ex-Coventry man was loving it. For each crunching tackle his more illustrious peer, Dave Webb, once of Chelsea, put in, McGuire got one in back, and should the two of them end up going for the same ball, the resultant impact could be felt at Norwich Castle over a mile away. Both wanted to win. No quarter was asked and none was expected, although it is perhaps fair to say that the sheer ferocity and shared determination that Norwich had on the day surprised some of their opponents and certainly their supporters, who were to be silenced further when Norwich went ahead. The architect? Not Peters and not Suggett but McGuire, winning yet another tackle and striding away from it with the ball at his feet, riding a further challenge, then another and then, almost comically, beating Boyer, a teammate. But there was method in McGuire's madness. Suggett was found on the left-hand side; he looked up and teased the ball into the opposition area where the QPR defenders proceed to treat it like a stick of dynamite, backing off else half-heartedly making a challenge, going through the motions in the vain hope that someone else would clear up the mess. Such indecision was meat, drink and even a light dessert to MacDougall who pounced on Clement's apologetic header, steering the ball past Parkes to give Norwich an unexpected but fully deserved lead.

Sexton's side were pricked and they duly bled, throwing themselves back into the game with a renewed fervour that woke up their support, slumbering as one in the sun. Thomas was, by then, their most dominant player, taking on that responsibility in place of Bowles who didn't want to play. Sexton didn't indulge him and Bowles remained on the pitch, simmering, scowling, swearing, and for the most part ineffective. This didn't stop Thomas who eventually got the reward his play had been asking for with a superb equaliser just before half-time. Game on.

More cut and thrust ensued in the second half but the goals wouldn't come. When one did it was with just over twenty minutes to go and an uncharacteristic goal from a player who was as unfamiliar to troubling the opposing goalkeeper as MacDougall was to goal-line clearances. Morris was the scorer; his 20-yard shot Parkes all ended up for pace and power despite his getting his hands to it. Recalling the goal in a Norwich City match programme a quarter of a century later, Morris recalls the moment with still amused clarity, saying,

> I can still see people like Ted MacDougall, Colin Suggett and Charlie Boyer dancing around me calling it a fluke! But I'd been looking at it for eighteen months – it wasn't a fluke! Forbesey was jumping around saying 'You've come good!' It pleased my manager, Bondy – he's had faith in me since I'd joined the club.'[18]

It was Morris's first goal for Norwich in eighty-four games and could, in its scoring, thwart QPR's dream of a first League championship in their ninety-four-year history. Could they respond?

No! Because Norwich scored again. And this time it was Boyer. Making the most of the space an increasingly desperate opposition were giving him, and meeting the ball as it was headed across the goal by Jones, Boyer looped it past the despairing Parkes and some frantically scrambling, scrabbling QPR defenders to make it 3-1. Agony for QPR, and further agony for those listening to their transistor radios (no *Twitter* in those dim and distant days!) who learned that Liverpool are winning at Stoke – if things remained as they were then the title would be in the hands of the men from Anfield, the sort of advantage they don't yield easily once it is theirs to own. QPR pressed forward again, more and more,

---

[18] OTBC, Norwich City matchday programme *v.* Coventry City, 7 May 2011. Peter Morris was talking to Trevor Burton.

throwing caution to the wind and were rewarded when Powell, under pressure from the eternally running Givens, put the ball into his own net. But it was too little too late and Norwich held on to win.

For Sexton and his team it was their first defeat since January, and the first time all season they had conceded three goals. And what a time to experience it. The League table now told a very different story to what it had two hours earlier. Liverpool were now top and a point ahead of QPR. They just needed to win their last two games to take the championship, which not surprisingly they did. Agonisingly for Sexton's team, they also won their last two League games, meaning that, had they won this game, they would have ended the season as First Division Champions.

Which is why QPR fans of a certain age will always have a certain amount of antipathy in their hearts for Norwich City.

When the dust had settled on that match and the season in general, the BBC's John Motson looked back at it, talking about how close QPR had come to winning English football's greatest prize, only to have it snatched from their grasp at the last moment by the team from Norfolk. He described it as 'cruel luck on a sparkling team'. That QPR had brought some sparkle to that season there is no doubt, but so had Norwich, who ended it in a best-ever tenth place after a campaign that had included famous wins at Leeds United and Liverpool.

Norwich also ended the season impressively with five wins from their last eight games, the only disappointment being defeats by Sheffield United and Wolves in games that the Canaries might reasonable have been expected to win. Had they done so, their finishing place would have been seventh, immediately below and level on points with Ipswich Town. But tenth would do. In fact it would do very nicely.

Because it meant that Norwich City had arrived.

7

BOND AND SON

Charlie would run all day. He would chase lost causes. He could hold it up and bring people into play. He would also run the channels. Defenders got fed up of going with him. Ted wasn't interested in doing that.

The summer of 1976 went down in history as one of the sunniest, driest and hottest in British history, with average temperatures reaching record highs; a daytime peak of 37 °C being recorded in one part of the country. Lazy, hazy, crazy days of summer.

And lazy, hazy, crazy and very happy days for supporters of Norwich City.

The 1975/76 campaign had turned out to be the most successful in the club's history. True, there was no famous cup run to boast of as there had been in 1959. Indeed, Norwich had been on the receiving end of a giant killing for once at the hands of Bradford City. But that was ultimately inconsequential compared to what had been achieved at the club, which was very real and positive progress.

Tenth place in Division One. League victories over Everton, Liverpool (and at Anfield), Leeds United, Arsenal, Tottenham and season-long championship contenders Queens Park Rangers had shot Norwich to a position of footballing prominence in England that never even come close to being achieved before. The good results and publicity must have given Sir Arthur South and his board of directors immense, if unexpected, pleasure. And in players like Ted MacDougall, Phil Boyer, Colin Suggett and the timeless Kevin Keelan, Norwich had players who were fast becoming household names, featuring widely on TV and in the printed media and becoming as well known in the wider footballing world as they were in East Anglia. Then, of course, there was Martin Peters.

Tottenham's decision to sell Peters to Norwich nearly eighteen months earlier must have, by the summer of 1976, looked more and more careless by the day. Peters had, in his first full season in a Norwich shirt, been beyond imperious. He'd played in every minute of all of the club's fifty League and cup games, scoring thirteen goals in the process and winning, at a canter, the club's Player of the Season accolade in the process. There had also been, quietly at first as that season wore on and the following one commenced, very serious talk surrounding the possibility of him getting an international recall. The England side was certainly already beginning to show signs of a lack of direction under the leadership of the somewhat ill-fitting international figure of Don Revie. The clarion call for an experienced, popular and influential figure like Peters was understandable.

His influence on the Norwich side, as well as his stand-out ability as one of the best players in the country during those 1975/76 and 1976/77 seasons, however, raised not one iota of interest from Revie who, amazingly, preferred to select or, at the very least scout, players who were nowhere near Peters in terms of ability or how they could influence a game.

These unlikely names included Willie Maddren, Colin Viljoen, Tony Towers, and the Bolton pairing of Paul Jones and Sam Allardyce. The clamours of 'Peters for England' (which were most certainly not restricted to the confines of Carrow Road) continued throughout the rest of his time at Norwich, not least when Ron Greenwood, his old manager at West Ham, took over the national team role, with suggestions that if England were to qualify for the 1980 European Championships, then Peters should be considered. Alas, despite proving his class again and again and again for Norwich in his five-year spell at the club, the recall never happened. Interestingly, when rumours did begin to circulate as to why Peters' claims had been ignored, it was suggested that both Greenwood and the FA felt Peters' age (he turned thirty-six in November 1979) counted against him. This did not stop Liverpool's Ian Callaghan, a player who operated in the same position as Peters, being picked by England for a World Cup qualifying game against Luxembourg in October 1977. That shock call-up was only Callaghan's third for England and came over a decade since his last appearance for the country. He was thirty-five at the time, and nearly a year older than Peters. His selection proved one thing and raised suspicions about another in the process. Firstly that as far as international selection was concerned, age was no barrier. And, secondly, that if age was not one then the club that you played for may well have been, for Callaghan certainly would not have been considered if, like Peters, he played for Norwich rather than Liverpool.

Not that Peters seemed bothered at his continual omission from the England side. Indeed, despite the fact that England and Revie were due to spend the summer of 1976 touring North America in the USA Bicentennial Cup Tournament, Peters was more concerned about throwing a good party for his teammates in celebration of the season they had just all enjoyed. This particular end-of-season 'jolly', one which didn't make the tabloids, saw Sir Arthur South join John Bond, Ken Brown and all the players and their respective wives at his new Norwich home, dancing to a succession of Abba records that played over and over again on the jukebox he had hired for the occasion. Good times, and rightly so.

You can be certain that, even as he joined in the celebrations and let his hair down as much as anyone else who was there, John Bond would still have been plotting for the season ahead. It would be a misnomer to suggest that it was going to be a difficult one for the club – it would be of course, but no more and no less than any the Canaries have had at that level, before or since. The Canaries would, inevitably, go into it as one of the bookies' favourites for relegation, along with newly promoted Bristol City and Birmingham. Due to certain circumstances, the summer of 1975 had seen Bond unable to bring in as many new players to the club as he might have wanted, but the squad that he had started the season with had more than proved its mettle, with David Jones being the only significant addition during that campaign.

Jones was one of only four players who made their senior Canaries debut during the 1975/76 season, as opposed to seven the previous time around, six of whom had been transfer signings. In sharp contrast to that, the three players who made their Norwich bows along with Jones during the Canaries' successful return to the top flight had all come through the ranks, making their way to the first team by that most testing and difficult of routes. For two of the three, their time as a first-team player was fleeting and over before it had really begun. Neil Davids, unwanted at Leeds, had been picked up on a free in April 1975. He eventually got his chance for Norwich in, of all games, the home clash against Ipswich Town a year later. That debut only came about because of injuries to Stringer and Jones, with Forbes also missing out due to suspension. Despite his late and unexpected inclusion, he acquitted himself well and was duly marked down as one for the future – a future that, unfortunately for Davids, was not going to be at Norwich. He managed to retain his place for the Canaries' next game, a disappointing 3-1 home reverse against Sheffield United, but once those senior players were available again, he found it very difficult to break back into the first team, with Bond more than happy to let him out on loan to Northampton earlier the following season. Davids eventually moved to Swansea in the summer of 1977, those two appearances being the sum total of his efforts during his two-year stay at Norwich.

Paul Wilson, the second of the three youngsters that Bond trusted with their first-team debuts during the 1975/76, had an even shorter Norwich career than Davids. His big moment came as a substitute in the 2-1 Carrow Road loss to Newcastle on 22 November, his thirty-five-minute second-half cameo in place of the injured Tony Powell making his senior Norwich career one of the shortest on record.

The third and final name in this hopeful trio is a slightly more well-known one; a player who not only went on to make 161 first-team appearances for the club but also enjoyed a very good career in the game after he left Norwich. This included playing spells at Manchester City and Southampton, time spent in the managerial hot seat at Bournemouth and time spent as a coach at clubs like Newcastle United, Tottenham Hotspur and Queens Park Rangers. You can only wonder if quite such a wide and varied career in the game, one that has now spanned nearly four decades, had ever crossed the mind of the then eighteen-year-old Kevin Bond as he made his way onto the pitch as a replacement for Billy Steele in the 0-0 draw at Leicester City on 10 April 1976.

Kevin, of course, was John Bond's son and had come to the club as an amateur from Bournemouth in June 1974, signing professional forms for Norwich a week before he made that first-team debut – one in which he distinguished himself by not touching the ball once! Bigger and better things were to come for Bond however. His hugely respectable career in the game since then was a testament to his determination to succeed and to prove himself, often in the face of overwhelming odds. One early critic was Kevin's own father, John admitting that when he was a young boy, he'd felt Kevin had been too small and weak to make it as a professional footballer – paternal criticism being quite an obstacle for anyone to overcome, no matter what their chosen profession. Yet he did, and it is a fair bet that no one would have been more pleased or proud than his dad. Managers often regale a willing audience of the times when they have had the thoroughly unenviable job of having to tell a young player that they do not think they are going to make it in the game, and the club is going to have to release them. In his own managerial career, John Bond must have done it on dozens of separate occasions. There is, however, normally a caveat attached, the instruction to the soon-to-be departed youngster to 'prove me wrong' – and many have. Maybe this was Bond's own challenge to his son; his thought that he was too small and weak all that Kevin needed to spite him and succeed regardless. If that was the case, and I think it may well have been, then it worked!

I met with Kevin Bond in his adopted home city of Southampton to find out more about his time at the club, as well as his memories and thoughts of his much-missed father. He was an engaging and fascinating person to be with.

My time at Norwich was the most enjoyable of my career. Without question. As a group of players we gelled, we fed off each other – in training or when playing matches. There were so many young players at the club at the same time as me, that helped; we all got on, looked out for each other. And some quality players as well: Kevin Reeves, Justin Fashanu, Peter Mendham. We had a great time and really enjoyed our football, we all got a chance to play, we all got games.

Not, I suggested, something that Kevin and his peers might have enjoyed at other, perhaps bigger clubs?

No. We wanted to progress, the club wanted us to progress. There was so much encouragement there. Like I said, everyone got on, everyone wanted to work together, to do well. And Dad loved it. He regretted leaving Norwich, he wished he hadn't done so. It was his happiest time in the game as well. The club wanted him to stay. Sir Arthur South offered him a ten-year contract. Unheard of – then or now. Dad said, 'That's great, but what about Ken Brown, I want him here with me so he should have a ten-year contract as well, we're a team.' Sir Arthur South thought about it and said, 'No, we're not offering Ken a ten-year contract as well.' So Dad said, 'Right, if you're not offering it to Ken, then I'm not signing mine, forget it.' So Sir Arthur South comes back to Dad a second time: 'OK,' he says, 'We'll offer a ten-year contract to Ken as well.'

I liked Sir Arthur South. He was a very firm man, very firm, but he was also a very fair one, he'd listen to you. A proper 'old school' football chairman and a really great man. I'm still in touch with the South family. But he made it a family club. And it was. You hear that about football clubs, even today, but Norwich *were* a family club. When the club went out to China on tour [in 1980] all the directors came along as well, even my Mum came! But that's how it was at Norwich. Real togetherness.

Who were, I wondered, the big characters at the club as far as the players were concerned?

Kevin Keelan. He was fantastic, a fantastic man. The way he held himself up, presented himself; he was immaculate. You knew when he walked into a room. And what a goalkeeper! He never seemed as if he was going to stop. Every summer you'd think, is this Roger's (Hansbury) season, is he finally going to come out of the shadows as Kevin's understudy? But no, Kevin would start the season in great form, maintain it and just keep his place throughout. Poor old Roger! Kevin's still coaching goalkeepers, even now. My wife and I have been out to stay with him and his wife in Florida. He still loves the game.

Martin Peters for me was a bit of a Pied Piper character. I found myself just watching him, observing what he did in training, and how he conducted himself at training and at the ground, before matches, during them and afterwards. Whatever he did you couldn't help but follow. He was such a classy individual and a fantastic player, easily the best I've ever played with. During training we used to play eight-a-side and Martin would always play at the back in those games. He was never what you would call quick, energetic or powerful, far from it. But he was elegant; he had all the time in the world – on or off the ball. He seemed to be in all areas of the pitch all of the time. Such class. It was the same if the lads went out for a drink after the game, else had a little get together. We'd all be at the bar having pints but Martin would be stood at the corner of the bar just quietly sipping half a lager. It looks better than drinking a pint doesn't it? He may well have ended up having more than any of us, but it never looked like he was drinking.

Clearly the influence of Peters on Kevin and his teammates had been enormous, and has lasted. Kevin is recollecting a time in his career and a teammate who he would have last played with well over three decades ago – yet those memories are still told with a sparkle in his eye and smile on his face.

He was a great influence on me, and he didn't even have to try. It was never about, 'you must do it this way' or 'this is how you should play', far from it. It was just the way, as I said earlier, that he behaved, did things, how he composed himself. He did everything properly. Take when he moved to Norwich. He and his family were settled in Essex. Today if a player moves, they'll keep their main home and just rent or buy a flat or something near their new club, and for as long as they need it. Martin sold his house and bought a new one near Norwich. Uprooted himself, his wife and children because of his move. But they found a lovely new home and settled in very quickly. He was committed, when he did something, whatever it was, he did it properly and he did it with a touch of class. A terrific person and a terrific player.

Kevin had talked about the eight-a-side games that he and his teammates had taken part in as part of their training at Norwich. What was training like in general at the club, and what did he remember of the sessions that his dad would have led there?

It didn't matter who we were or what position we played in, Dad always encouraged us to get forward, to play the ball forward and to put the emphasis on attack. It worked very well for me – I got a few goals in my time at the club coming forward from defence. My best season was 1979/80 when I got eleven, although a few of those were penalties (six in total of those eleven goals were penalties). It was a new way of playing for Norwich though, Dad had changed things around a bit from the Ron Saunders era, there was more emphasis on going forward when he took over. And everything in training was about going forward as well. In fact, just about everything we did focused on the final third of the field. Now, today, in the modern game, it's very much about coaching the team as separate units. The back four. The midfield four. When they move up, when they support each other. But you coach them separately as much as you do as a team – look at how disciplined the Arsenal back four were under George Graham, now that was a defensive unit and was coached as one.

I worked with Dad as my coach for seven, maybe eight years. During all of that time and especially at Norwich, we never did one session on coaching the back four as a separate unit. Not one. He might have done some individual stuff, some one and ones and so on, but never a straight session on the defence and the defence as a working unit. His beliefs about how to coach and play the game came from Ron Greenwood at West Ham. When Dad left West Ham for Torquay, all set to start making his way in coaching and management, one of the last things Ron said to him was, 'I hope you've got a good memory.' Well, he did. So much of what he did, how he coached and wanted to see the game played, came from Ron Greenwood, he was passing on what he had been taught himself. And he was a good coach. And that's not just me saying that, that's what so many people have said to me who have been in the game and were coached by him. A very good coach indeed.

Kevin entered the coaching side of the game himself with Manchester City in 1996, and has been involved in the game ever since, a near eighteen-year period that has

included two years as manager at Bournemouth, who John also managed. What
has he taken into his coaching career that his dad might have approved of?

> Well, there are big differences in the game today. You can't not work on your
> back four as a single unit, likewise the midfield. The modern game demands
> that they know how to work as such and that is always something I've done
> at my clubs. And you have to. You ask anyone in the game today what the
> definition of a good coach is, they'll always say one who can organise the team
> well, make the different parts of that team work together well as that single
> unit. Now, Dad would argue against that. He'd say, and he did, whenever we
> talked about the game, that what was good for Ron Greenwood and what was
> good for him and how he wanted his teams to play would work now and that's
> how he would coach now. Me? I get by. I'm nowhere near as good a coach as
> my Dad was, nowhere near. But I'm a different person.

Did Kevin think that the 'John Bond' way really could be effective in the modern
game?

> Well, to a certain extent, it's how Harry Redknapp likes to play the game now.
> Like Dad, he doesn't like to see gifted players held back, he wants them to be
> able to go out and play; to have a certain amount of freedom. The fans, of
> course, love that. But the funny thing is, if things aren't going your way then
> they don't like it, and you hear the moans about how the side isn't organised
> or disciplined enough. It's about taking your chances, taking a risk. With so
> many teams now, possession is everything. And I mean everything. So much
> so, in some cases, that it comes with the possibility that, having strung twenty
> to thirty passes together, a team will find itself on the edge of their opponent's
> penalty area and rather than take a chance, a risk and trying to get something,
> the ball will get knocked back to the midfielder on the halfway line who'll then
> pass it back to the 'keeper, and they'll start that all over again. Sometimes a
> team will do that for eighty-odd minutes, just to wear their opponents down,
> finally break through and score and take the 1-0 win. Do you want to watch
> that? Keeping possession like that might look good, it might appeal, but is
> it entertaining? We are in the entertainment business. I think people have
> forgotten that. At Norwich if we had the same situation, if we'd kept hold of
> the ball and were in a good position offensively, let's just say, for example, that
> Jimmy Neighbour would be somewhat discouraged to pass the ball back else
> try to keep possession. If we, if he had the ball on the edge of the opposition's
> penalty area, we'd be expected to try to create a chance, to take the risk and
> risk losing the ball in doing so? Maybe, yes. But it's worth it if you score a
> goal. If you lose the ball? Then win it back again. It comes back, again, to the
> entertainment business. We were expected to entertain. The fans expected it.
> And Dad wanted the game played accordingly.

How can you hope to entertain and create chances, score goals with just one player up front? I went to a game last season, one of the teams was playing 4-5-1. The striker they played was completely isolated in attack, on his own, no support. When his teammates got the ball they'd hit it to him but he had no one there to pass it to, nothing. So back it came again. It was mediocre. Can you imagine the Norwich side back then just playing Ted MacDougall on his own in attack? It wouldn't have worked. Ted needed Phil Boyer alongside him. And what a player Charlie (Boyer) was. He was brilliant, a great player. He was the perfect foil for Ted; he did all of Ted's running for him. Because Ted could be a little bit lazy, though he came alive in the penalty area. But Charlie would run all day. He would chase lost causes. He could hold it up and bring people into play. He would also run the channels. Defenders got fed up of going with him. Ted wasn't interested in doing that. Phil was like another player we had, Kevin Reeves. He was just the same. They worked their socks off. But could either Ted or Charlie play alone, without the other in a 4-5-1? I don't think they could have, in fact, it wouldn't even have been considered. All teams played two in attack then. That's very different to today. What, for example, would Liverpool do today if they had Kenny Dalglish and Ian Rush? Would they just play one up front and stick the other on the bench?

The obvious question to ask Kevin was the sort of treatment he received from his manager – his Dad and his boss. How did he find it and was it easy to adapt and fit in regardless of his unusual status, player-wise?

I probably had it harder than anyone else. Dad treated me like any other youngster at the club, but he was tough. I was a late developer, so he pushed me. He had faith that I'd eventually make it. But I had to work hard. Physically when I was an apprentice, at Bournemouth then at Norwich I was quite small and not very strong. So I found it very hard. And anyone who was around or with Dad at the time, they didn't hold back. They'd say to him that I had no chance; that I wouldn't progress in the game. But Dad saw something in me, something he thought worth pursuing. He gave me a chance and stuck with me, he didn't care what anyone else said or did. So yes, he was tough with me but that's because he could see I'd make it in the game if only I stuck at it and worked hard. And I did. I'd initially signed on for three years as an apprentice at Bournemouth. After I'd done two years, Dad left for Norwich. He contacted Bournemouth soon after he took over at Carrow Road and asked about me, what was my position at the club? They said they were happy for me to leave and would pay up my contract. I'd earned £6 a week in my first year as an apprentice, £7 in my second, and was due to earn £8 in the third. But they arranged to pay it off so I got about £250 and joined Norwich.

When I got there, the club were in the process of applying to play in the South East Counties League. Up to that time, the young players were competing alongside Eastern Counties League players; so Yarmouth Town, Lowestoft, clubs like that. Full-grown men. Big blokes, very strong, very physical. It was tough and you got kicked. George Lee, a lovely man, was looking after us at the time. He'd meet with my Dad on Mondays after these games, go through them, how the team played, individuals played. Dad would ask George, 'How did Kevin play?' 'Didn't get a kick,' George would say. The opposition were too big, strong, fast – and I hadn't developed. But then, just as Dad knew I would, at eighteen, I started to develop. I went from being around 5 feet 8 inches and around 117 pounds, to 6 feet 2 inches and 173 pounds. It helped me compete, gave me confidence, I could deal with the physical demands of the game. I grew so quickly that new clothes would only be good for a few months! But the fact that I got there, that I developed that way and was able to compete and play was all down to my Dad. He had that patience with me. I would not have been a professional footballer if anyone else had been my manager, no one else would have had that faith and patience. He'd take me to one side, have a little word: 'You've got time. Don't worry. It'll come and you'll get there.' I found it difficult at times, of course I did, there were as many downs as there were ups. But he had unwavering faith in me. And I'd like to think I paid him back, got a decent career out of the game.

Something no one could dispute. But being the son of the manager, did Kevin ever find himself getting criticism or stick from the fans at any of his clubs, or even his teammates?

It probably got as bad as it could get at Manchester City. When I went there the player who was their regular right-back was a bloke called Nicky Reid. Manchester-born, a huge fan favourite. He went off to spend the summer playing in the US soon after I arrived, just as I had done the previous year [Kevin spent the summer of 1981 with Seattle Sounders in the NASL, Nicky joined them the following summer]. He was due to come back of course, but the Man City fans didn't think that, they thought I'd come to take his place. So there I was, the manager's son and brought in to replace the fan favourite – that's how they saw it. Anyway, the last home game of that season, we played Coventry City. We kick off and straight away the ball is passed back to me. And as soon as I take a touch, all of the home fans started booing me – all of Maine Road it seemed. And these are my own fans! Yet, at the end of the 1982/83 season, those same fans voted me as their player of the season. So I won them over in the end.

The Norwich fans weren't like that; they never seemed critical. Norwich fans have always had time for younger players getting into the team; they like to see it, doesn't matter who you are. And the club were doing well at the time. We had some good players, playing good football. It was a lot more relaxed; there wasn't so much pressure. So I never felt any pressure or experienced any stick or abuse from the Norwich fans. If I played well, great. If I didn't, well, Dad would drop me, just as he would any player. The pressure never came from the Norwich fans, it was always the people around Dad. They'd be saying, 'What's he doing, picking his son. He'll never make it.' All that went over my head, I never knew about it. I just got on with playing.

Kevin's career developed at Norwich with him initially playing at right-back before he switched to playing as centre-half. How did that come about?

It was down to John Benson, who was coaching at Norwich at the time. He said to Dad, 'Why don't you give young Kevin a couple of games at centre-half, see how he gets on there.' So I played there for the reserves and it went well, eventually becoming my favoured and my best position. John Benson had played there so he knew a centre-half when he saw one. He also worked with Dad at Man City.

Did Kevin keep in touch with any of his old Norwich teammates?

Yes, I see quite a few of them else have kept in touch. John Ryan is a very good friend of mine. He lives in Spain now. Good player, very strong. He played in defence and midfield, scored a lot of goals one season.[19] Mel Machin. Mel, again, was a very good player. Hugely underrated. Very cultured on the ball. And a tough coach, you didn't mess with Mel. Tony Powell, he's in the States. So is Ted, still coaching. Colin Sullivan, he's a market gardener now I think. And Mick McGuire. Mick did a lot of work for the PFA, he's a good bloke is Mick. Kevin Reeves is up at Everton now, I still see him. Peter Morris as well – he still does a bit of scouting I believe. I see Martin Peters at Spurs occasionally. Billy Steele, I've only just got back in contact with him. He's now living in Canada. So yes, lots of them. And so many are still involved in the game, one way or the other. Peter Morris got that great goal for Norwich against QPR when they nearly won the title – Norwich won and that put an end to their chances. There is a big picture of that team at Loftus Road even now.

So many memories, Ed. Justin and his goal of the season against Liverpool; that made his name, the club sold him and rebuilt the River End with the money from the transfer. Peter Mendham, good player. And Graham Paddon, bless his heart. Wonderful times and a really fantastic club to be part of.

Did he have any favourite stories from his time at the club?

Yes. I remember we were playing Nottingham Forest, at their place. They were doing well, winning something like six games from their first eight, and John

---

[19] John Ryan scored sixteen goals for the Canaries in the 1977/78 season, ending it as the club's top scorer for that campaign.

Robertson was on fire for them. What a player he was. Very special, he could be unplayable. He'd run at you, drop his shoulder; you didn't know where he was going. Anyway, Dad wasn't having any of this. Before the game he took me and John Ryan to one side and said, 'Look, I want you both to mark Robertson. Keep him quiet. Kevin, you from right-back and John just ahead on that right-hand side.' So we did, we stick to him throughout the match.[20] Anyway, we're about midway through the second half and John Ryan and I are stuck to Robertson, as usual, on their left. He hasn't said a word up until now, but at this moment, he looked up at us and just said, 'Why don't you two piss off?' So we must have been doing our job properly.

Ken Brown was good for my Dad at that time; they worked really well together. A lovely man Ken, a great player in his day and a good coach. They complemented each other very well. But that's how it was at Norwich at that time; a group of people who wanted to do well, who worked well together and got on as a group. I really enjoyed my time there. I haven't had the chance to go back to the club in any kind of formal capacity since I left in 1981, but football is a funny game and is always teaching you to never be surprised as anything can happen. Norwich City was a fantastic club to be at during my time there.

I'm led to believe nothing has changed.

At the time of our meeting Kevin was working alongside Harry Redknapp and the rest of the Queens Park Rangers' coaching staff in preparation for the pending 2013/14 League season, his thirty-ninth successive campaign as either a player or coach in the English game – an admirable and impressive record. In total, he made 161 senior appearances for Norwich, 156 of which were starts, scoring fourteen goals. His ability as a player is best recognised by the fact that he won Player of the Year Awards at both Norwich City (1980) and Manchester City (1983). His popularity within the game and standing as a good coach will be something that his father, the late and much missed John Bond, would be very proud of.

---

[20] It must have worked to a certain extent! The game in question was played on 1 October 1977 and ended in a 1-1 draw, Martin Peters scoring for Norwich. Forest ended that season as champions, drawing both their League games against the Canaries.

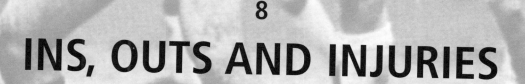

8
INS, OUTS AND INJURIES

He'd bossed the Norwich defence that afternoon, giving the then still imperious
Stringer and Forbes as hard a physical battle as they would have all that season, as
well as terrorising debutant Norwich 'keeper Roger Hansbury at every set piece,
jumping for him as much as he did the ball at every opportunity. It was a classic
centre-forward performance, one that the Norwich manager had not forgotten.

With that record-breaking tenth place secured at the end of the 1975/76 season, the Norwich City management and team had good reason to spend the summer in a celebratory mood – the proceedings launched by that Abba-rich party at the home of Martin Peters. The former Tottenham man and World Cup winner had taken the club into his heart, and the feeling was mutual with Peters seen as the catalyst for the good times the club were now enjoying. The respect that he had at the club was inevitably acknowledged by Bond when, following an early-season injury to Duncan Forbes, Peters was appointed as the team captain, a position he proudly held for the rest of his Norwich career. He'd already had experience of being the captain at West Ham and Tottenham as well as England, who he led on six occasions. Despite all of that, he did not immediately inherit the position when he joined Norwich; the redoubtable Forbes retained the armband and with it the right to give Peters on-field orders, as well as the odd telling-off if he had thought it justified!

Forbes' injury in the game against Coventry on 11 September 1976 kept him out of the team until the following January, and even then he was in and out of the side, ending that season with just twelve League appearances to his name. Injuries had always been part of Duncan's game – he was the type of player who would put his head in places that other players might hesitate before putting their boot in, such was his characteristic bravery. That unfortunately meant there were often spells in a season when Duncan's presence would be missing from the team, either due to injury or because of suspension. Indeed, of the eleven seasons that saw Duncan serve the Canaries, he was only ever-present on one occasion, that being the 1969/70 season.

Bond had been incredibly loyal to Forbes since his arrival at the club. But this was not, nor ever was, down to sentiment. Bond deserved his reputation in the game as a manager who preferred to surround himself with players that were made of that similar West Ham mould that he had been cast in – clever players, ones who were eager to learn, to absorb new information and tactical advice, ball players who had flair, imagination, who could play. Forbes' didn't fit into that template. He was by no means a limited footballer, but if you were to choose a few words to describe his character and manner of play then those words would be ones like rugged, tough, no nonsense and physical. In other words, the archetypal centre-half of *Boys Own* fame: uncompromising and ready to make his presence felt. Yet these were qualities that Bond loved. Yes, of course he wanted to make Norwich a team known for playing good football, for having players that were permitted to express themselves, to entertain. Yet those players would always need a minder, an on-field presence who would, when the going got tough, be able to grab the game by the scruff of its neck and shake the life out of it. Forbes was a warrior, a leader of men and a captain who led by example – he ran the walk. And because of this he was, for Bond, even in the presence of Martin Peters, someone who would, fitness and availability pending, always be in his team. However, the commencement of the 1976/77 season saw Forbes, at thirty-five, need a little longer to get over the myriad knocks and sprains that he would have felt after matches or training. The intent was still there, as was the roar, but the body – one that seemed to stand 7 feet tall during matches but which was, in reality, just 5 feet and 11 inches – was beginning to hint that it might soon be time to retire from active service.

Forbes' professional career had started in 1961 at Colchester United, making his US debut in the club's Division Four game at Crewe on 14 April 1962. It was not the best of debuts for a twenty-year-old centre-back looking to impress and make his way in the game, as Colchester lost 4-0. Nevertheless, he had more than enough about him to impress both Benny Fenton and his successor, Neil Franklin, going on to make a total of 296 games for the club – a run in which, remarkably, he was only booked on one occasion; a sign, you suspect, of a somewhat more liberal attitude of the referees at the time rather than any caution on the part of Forbes. Franklin in particular rated him, and he would know a decent defender when he saw one, being an ex-centre-half himself who had not only played for England on twenty-seven occasions, but also spent a short spell playing for Independiente Santa Fe in Chile.

Despite the imposing form of Forbes in their defence however, Colchester struggled to make any real impact, and just two years after winning promotion from the Fourth Division, found themselves back there at the end of the 1967/68 season. They had, upon winning promotion, boasted the best defensive record in the League. Relegation inevitably meant that the club had to make cuts, as well as look to raise some money by selling some of its prime assets, one of whom, of course, was Forbes.

Norwich signed him for £10,000 in September 1968. It was a large fee for Norwich to commit to at the time, especially for a player from the Fourth Division, but the club were impressed enough by his showings for Colchester to take the plunge. Forbes officially joined the Canaries on 12 September 1968, making his debut a month later in a 3-1 defeat at Fulham. That game saw Forbes become the fourth Norwich player to wear the No. 5 shirt in only fourteen games; the role having previously been filled by Laurie Brown, Dave Stringer and Trevor Howard. He went on to make twenty-two League appearances that season, scoring his first goal for the Canaries in a 2-1 defeat at Aston Villa, while wearing the No. 11 shirt! Duncan was no winger, that was for certain and he reverted back to the centre of defence for the last three games of that season before making that No. 5 shirt his personal property at the start of the next campaign, the one that ultimately saw him replace Ken Mallender as the Canaries' captain.

His Norwich career had seen some highlights: a promotion-winning captain in 1972 for one thing, as well as having the honour of being the first Norwich player to lead his side out at Wembley, something he did twice and a feat that it is unlikely to be repeated by any future Canary. As was the case of so many of his equally deserving Norwich teammates when he, and they, were at their pomp from the early seventies onwards, he did not get any international recognition, that strange bias against Norwich players once again rearing its familiar head. Given the fact that, among those Forbes was in competition with for a place at the heart of the Scotland defence were players like Jim Holton, John Blackley and Eddie Colquhoun, it seems even more a mystery. These were competent enough players but ones who were so much more so than Forbes that they continually prevented him from a chance to pull on a Scotland shirt. Like Kevin Keelan, Forbes can rightly feel aggrieved at his lack of opportunity at international level, especially after he had so impressed at the top level throughout the 1975/76 season. Norwich were traditionally seen as quite generous defensively, but they had reversed that trend, conceding just fifty-eight goals in their forty-two League fixtures – an average of 1.3 per game and a total equal to Derby County's and better than, among others, the illustrious back fours of Tottenham, Everton and West Ham, all of which included international players.

Yet now, a season later, time was catching up with him. Bond would, of course, give Forbes every opportunity to regain his fitness and win back his place in the side, but the fact remained that he was approaching the end of his top-flight career. Bond had already identified the need for new personnel among the back four with the signing of David Jones, and it was Jones who slotted seamlessly into Forbes' place for much of that season, ending it with thirty-five League appearances, as well as international appearances for Wales, despite the fact (and despite his name!) that he was born in Portsmouth.

With Jones' rise to prominence, the Carrow Road times they were indeed a changin' and Forbes was not the only Canary institution who was coming to the end of his career at the club at this time. Dave Stringer, his long-time partner in central defence, was also struggling with injury. He'd made just fourteen League appearances during the 1975/76 season, and then only as a replacement for the injured Tony Powell. As soon as Powell was fit again he was back in the side and Stringer was out. Even a year beforehand, this would have been an unthinkable scenario, yet here it was. The long and famous partnership of Forbes and Stringer in the centre of the Norwich defence took its final bow on the opening day of the 1976/77 campaign, Norwich losing 1-0 at Liverpool 21 on August. A little over a month later, Stringer joined Cambridge United. At least he had gone out on a high, and would, in time, return to take the club to hitherto unknown heights in an extraordinarily successful spell as manager – preceded, of course, by his success in charge of the Youth Team and culminating in the Canaries' success in the 1983 FA Youth Cup final.

But Dave Stringer was not the only famous name to leave Carrow Road in the opening weeks of the 1976/77 season. A bigger name, and a far greater shock, was to follow.

Ted MacDougall, plunderer of twenty-eight League and cup goals the previous season, was missing from the Norwich side for their first two fixtures of that campaign. Ever competitive, Ted had been sent off in one of the club's end-of-season matches during a tour of Norway. Friendly or not, Ted was served notice that he would have to sit out a two-game ban for his on-field misdemeanour; a ridiculous decision by any stretch of the imagination. Norwich were on a goodwill visit, fitting in three games against modest opposition, one of which, Larvik Turn, were a sports club (they also fielded teams in athletics, gymnastics, handball and wrestling) rather than a football club. Ted's dismissal, astonishingly, was included in the FA's disciplinary totting-up procedure that they operated during a League campaign, and the matches Norwich played on their tour were regarded as an extension of the season. Ted subsequently went beyond twenty penalty points for the season, meaning that the ban came into effect at the beginning of the 1976/77 campaign and that he would miss the opening games against Liverpool and Arsenal. Unsurprisingly, the club appealed against the verdict, with his case heard by the FA Commission in London on 3 August. Ted did not, however, ask for the chance to attend the hearing, meaning the decision was confirmed in a letter sent to him at the club.

Minus their goalscoring talisman, Norwich went into the game at Liverpool with a five-man midfield, Boyer left to plough a lonely furrow in attack on his own. Norwich's surprisingly cautious approach to the game may well have been driven by circumstances, but it also meant that they created few chances on the ground where they had scored three the previous season, and Steve Heighway took advantage of a Powell error in the second half, earning Liverpool the points.

Bond had pepped up the Norwich squad in the summer by adding two new recruits in the form of John Ryan and Roger Gibbins. Ryan, signed from Luton Town for £40,000, was an attacking full-back who would allow Jones to move from right-back into the centre of defence permanently, urgently needed now given the pending departure of Stringer and the diminishing presence and role of Forbes. Ryan started his career at Arsenal but had garnished quite a reputation for himself at Luton where he had made nearly 300 senior appearances. As a player he was perfect for Bond – a defender with attacking tendencies. It seemed a perfect deal and, in the fullness of time, turned out to be one of Bond's best as Norwich manager.

The other major summer acquisition for the Canaries, forward Roger Gibbins, was very much an unknown quantity, and few Norwich fans would have been familiar with him when he joined the club from Oxford United in early June. Gibbins had potential, however, and it was that which Bond had seen. He'd started his career at Tottenham, playing for them in the 1974 FA Youth Cup final, as well as appearing for England Schoolboys. He'd spent just one season at Oxford, scoring two goals in nineteen appearances, hardly stellar for a twenty-year-old playing in a struggling Second Division side (they were relegated at the end of the 1975/76 season). But it was enough for Bond and his team of coaches to know that Gibbons was well worth investing in, especially as MacDougall's absence at the beginning of the season meant there was a big hole to fill in the Canary attack. Yet was there more to the signing of Gibbins than that?

In hindsight, yes. Bond would have learnt over the summer of MacDougall's desire to leave Carrow Road, a request that would have shocked him to the core. Hadn't he and Norwich been good for the player? Bond had nurtured him at Bournemouth and had now, at Norwich, turned him into an established First Division striker and a full Scotland international. He was playing alongside someone who complemented him perfectly, in front of fans who adored him and at a club that had just finished tenth in the First Division and was hungry for more of the same. Yet Ted wanted to leave? It didn't make any sense. How could he possibly want to play his football elsewhere now, especially after the tough times he had gone through at Manchester United and West Ham?

It seemed clear now that Ted's frustration had boiled over in Norway, leading to that sending-off and subsequent suspension. He'd gone through a very long, very tough season for Norwich, playing in every one of the club's fifty League and cup games. And just as he'd been looking forward to a break, a chance to be away from the club and the game for a few weeks and an opportunity to focus on his growing interests outside of football, he'd been flown off to Norway for three games with the club there, followed by another two games in Trinidad. Ted's season had started with the Anglo-Scottish Cup back in August and it was not due to end until the club returned from their Caribbean trip in mid-June, over ten months of non-stop football. For Ted, who was now approaching thirty, it was time for a change. He had business interests on the South Coast, an area he'd kept his connections with since leaving Bournemouth, and now wanted the opportunity to give them a little bit more time and attention – a personal decision that he hoped everyone would understand. He certainly had no quarrel with Bond or the Canaries.

With huge reluctance, Bond would have agreed to his star forward's decision, but was adamant that it couldn't be considered until Norwich had got an adequate replacement. Gibbins was potential in abundance but not someone, certainly not yet, who would be able to take Ted's place as an automatic choice. Ted duly returned to the Norwich side at the end of his suspension, Norwich having lost that second game he was banned for at home to Arsenal by three goals to one. Gibbins had made his debut and gone close, while Forbes, perhaps feeling a little frustrated himself, was booked for rugby tackling one of the Arsenal players. He'd earlier tried a shot from 40 yards – a wasted opportunity that, had any of his teammates attempted the same, would have earned them an earful from Forbes himself. With Duncan frustrated and Ted wanting away, it wasn't the sort of opening to a season that Bond would have wanted or expected.

Ever the professional, Ted lined up in the Canaries side for their third League game of the campaign, an away trip to the Hawthorns to play West Bromwich Albion. By now, a certain amount of frustration seemed to be seeping throughout the team. Mistakes were being made, careless ones at that. It didn't help matters when shortly before half-time Ally Brown, ever the opportunist, took a chance on a speculative volley. What's the famous saying? If you don't shoot, you don't score. Brown was rewarded for his daring when the shot skidded its way past the normally reliable Keelan.

Then, a few minutes after half-time, any home truths that Bond might have chosen to pass on to his side were swiftly rendered irrelevant as Steele bundled Tony Brown over in the penalty area. The result was a foregone conclusion. Tony Brown took the penalty himself, wrapping it past Keelan with the sort of confidence that Norwich were now in need of. It sealed a first win of the season for the newly promoted Baggies, and sent Norwich into bottom place. Early days of course but the further any team gets into a poor run, the harder it seems for them to break out of it. MacDougall had played, but the spark seemed to be missing from his eyes. He was on the pitch but his mind seemed elsewhere. A replacement for him now became an absolute necessity.

Replacing a twenty-eight goals in a season man was never going to be easy. And there were not a lot of options available to Bond, not at least for the money he had to spend. Derek Hales would have been the obvious choice to succeed MacDougall. He had outscored Ted the previous season in the Second Division, knocking in twenty-eight goals for Charlton Athletic and helping the Valiants, recently promoted themselves, to finish in a respectable ninth position. Their defence had been the most porous in the League that campaign, yet thanks to Hales they had the fourth-best attack. Did Bond make an enquiry about Hales? It's very probable. He was, like MacDougall, a fast, strong and deadly penalty box predator, one who, again like MacDougall, operated best in tandem with another striker.

In Hales' case, it was Mike Flanagan. Could Hales operate as effectively alongside Boyer? It was worth a shot, and maybe Hales would be interested. Norwich's interest would soon have waned when they learned the sort of transfer fee Charlton were expecting for their star man – nearly double the club's then record outlay. In addition to that, Hales was being watched by other clubs including Derby County, Tottenham and West Ham. And it was Derby who won the race for Hales, their bid of £280,000 securing the deal just before Christmas, an amount that was simply impossible for Norwich to even consider spending on one player.

Such was the harsh economic reality in the game at that time. Clubs were beginning to flex their steadily increasing financial muscles by readily paying big money for the players they wanted. Norwich's record outlay remained the £145,000 they had paid for Phil Boyer, yet Hales, a player from the Second Division, had gone for almost double that. The existing British record transfer fee – £350,000 paid by Everton to Birmingham for Bob Latchford back in 1974 – would be broken a further five times by the end of the decade, and would then stand at just under £1.5 million. Norwich's record transfer fee paid would remain that which they had paid for Boyer some six years previously. Matters weren't helped by the fact that, with MacDougall fixed on returning to the South Coast to see out his career, options for him were limited, with only Southampton able to offer the right package to tempt both player and, reluctantly, club. Norwich therefore ended up selling the previous season's leading Division One goalscorer, someone who had plundered sixty-six goals from 138 first-team appearances for them, for just £50,000; a ludicrously low fee for such a good player, one who would on football's open market been worth at least five times that. The move and the fee, however, had been dictated by circumstances, and Southampton got themselves a bargain while Ted got his dream move, plus the chance to play alongside Mick Channon and Peter Osgood. Everyone, it seemed, had come out of it a winner, except for Norwich City.

Four of MacDougall's previous transfers had been record-breakers. The £195,000 that Manchester United had paid Bournemouth for him had been a record sum for a Third Division player. When he left Old Trafford for West Ham just four months later for £170,000, that sum became both the highest ever received by United for a player as well as the most West Ham had paid for one. And when he joined Norwich for £140,000 that too was, at the time, a record fee paid by Norwich. Three moves in just over a year for a combined cost of £505,000, and now, sixty-six goals later, Norwich had sold him for 10 per cent of that amount. They had, in effect, been mugged. Yet it was hard to hold it against Ted or Southampton. He'd been phenomenal during his time at Carrow Road and no one, least of all the supporters, wanted him to leave. But it wasn't as if he had gone somewhere for money or glory. He'd dropped a division to play for Southampton; a place where he could still play the game and be near his home and business interests.

It was galling, but understandable. No one was surprised to see him back in the First Division though when Southampton, newly promoted, arrived at Carrow Road for the first game of the 1978/79 season. And even fewer were surprised when he scored for the Saints, their consolation goal in a 3-1 defeat. Ted MacDougall, ever the maverick, had chosen to score his last goal at Carrow

Road against the club that he is most readily identifiable with. He scored a further forty-two goals in eighty-six appearances for the Saints before rejoining his main footballing love, Bournemouth, in November 1978.

Ted's last game for Norwich was the trip to Coventry on 9 September. Norwich had finally won their first game of the season the previous week; a scrappy and occasionally bad-tempered victory over Birmingham at Carrow Road, Phil Boyer scoring the only goal. The win hadn't been enough to lift the Canaries from the foot of the table, however, and with Coventry always a tough place to visit, Norwich struggled to make an impression, losing 2-0. The second Sky Blues goal had, unfortunately, come about in somewhat farcical circumstances when Duncan Forbes, attempting a clearing header from a John Beck cross, sent the ball past Keelan and into the goal. Coventry, buoyed by debutants Bobby McDonald (later to play under Bond at Manchester City) and ex-Leeds midfielder Terry Yorath, deserved their win – first to every ball, sharp in the tackle and unerringly accurate with their passing game, in other words, exactly what Norwich had done throughout the previous season.

It wouldn't have escaped Bond's notice that the Sky Blue's two new signings had made a difference to their side. Both were quality players: Yorath in particular, who had played for Leeds in the European Cup final barely a year earlier, was most certainly an upgrade on what they had previously and a player who would definitely merit a starting place in any Norwich line-up. They could only continue to improve as long as they had the means to bring in players of Yorath's obvious quality and big match experience. Norwich, on the other hand, with MacDougall on his way out, Stringer on the verge of leaving and Forbes becoming less and less a prominent figure in the team, were in danger of slipping behind. They could not afford to rest on their laurels and Bond knew it. Norwich needed some quality of their own – and fast.

With MacDougall gone for the criminally low sum of £50,000, Bond knew there wouldn't be much more available than that for a replacement. Fortunately for Norwich, they had a manager who had an uncanny knack of making a little money go a long way, as he would prove later on that season. For now, however, the club needed a short-term fix. And he was pretty good at those as well.

Viv Busby was the man entrusted with the unenviable task of following in MacDougall's footsteps, with the club confirming his signing on 16 September 1976, the same day that MacDougall left for Southampton. Norwich paid out the same amount they'd received for MacDougall in order to secure Busby's signature, and as far as short-term signings went, it was money well spent. Busby was, in many ways, similar to MacDougall – a predatory striker who did all of his work in and around the penalty box while his striking partner did all of the hard work and running in order for him to steal the goalscoring glory, and one who, if he did not get the service he felt he deserved, would not be slow to let his teammates know about it. He was, in short, MacDougall Mark II, though neither he, Ted, or for that matter Bond, would have let anyone get away with saying that in public. What they all would have agreed on was that he was a proven striker. He'd left Fulham after a respectable spell with the Cottagers, during which time he scored twelve goals in the 1973/74 season and eighteen in the following campaign; one of which had been against Norwich in Fulham's 4-0 canter back in September 1974, the Canaries' first defeat of that season. Bond never forgot a player who put in a good performance against his side, and Busby was one of those. He'd bossed the Norwich defence that afternoon, giving the then still imperious Stringer and Forbes as hard a physical battle as they would have all that season, as well as terrorising debutant Norwich 'keeper Roger Hansbury at every set piece, jumping for him as much as he did the ball at every opportunity. It was a classic centre-forward performance, one that the Norwich manager had not forgotten.

Busby made his Norwich debut in the 0-0 draw against Derby County at Carrow Road, doing enough to worry their illustrious central defensive partnership of Roy McFarland and Colin Todd to convince the Norwich support, still smarting at the loss of MacDougall, that he would be a handy acquisition. A week later, Norwich travelled to White Hart Lane, getting their first away point of the season in another 1-1 draw – one Tottenham player in particular impressing with his jinking runs and aggressive wing play on the day. The player in question was Jimmy Neighbour.

Luckily for Norwich, Tottenham were on the verge of signing Peter Taylor from Crystal Palace. He, like Neighbour, was a right-winger, one who had impressed so much during his time at Selhurst Park he had been selected for England on four occasions, even though Palace were a Third Division side at the time.[21] Needless to say, with an international pedigree and potential in abundance, Taylor did not come cheap, and Tottenham ended up paying £200,000 for him – a record for a Third Division player. Bond knew that this might mean that Neighbour would soon be available and started making enquiries. After a quick word with Martin Peters, Neighbour became a Norwich player just a few days after he had played against them.

A busy summer at Carrow Road then. With MacDougall now at Southampton, Stringer at Cambridge United and Forbes on loan at Torquay, joining Johnny Miller and Peter Morris, both of who had left Norwich for Mansfield Town that summer, five previously established first-team players had left the club with four new ones (Ryan, Gibbins, Busby and Neighbour) coming in. The squad, just as Bond had wanted, was being refreshed and given some impetus, the sort of quality that was needed following the defeat at Coventry, and which the manager had identified as being crucial to his ambitions. The signing of Neighbour was perhaps the most exciting of them all. He'd made over 100 appearances for

---

[21] Peter Taylor is now more well known as a football coach, who in his one game as England caretaker manager appointed David Beckham as England captain.

Tottenham, having joined the club as a junior, and made his way up into the first team. He made his first-team debut during the 1970/71 season, winning a League Cup winner's medal that season alongside Peters. He was an old-fashioned winger, the type who got chalk on his boots as he sped up and down the flanks, and either side would do, as he was – as rare a talent for a footballer then as it is today – two-footed and able to twist and torment defenders from either side of the pitch. He was, at twenty-five, coming to the peak years of his career, and it would be at Norwich.

Neighbour's Canary debut was a memorable one. Apart from the fact that he put on a man of the match performance at Carrow Road against Newcastle on 10 October, it also saw Busby score his first goal for Norwich in their 3-2 win, pouncing on a defensive error from the normally reliable Geoff Nulty to put Norwich 2-0 up, after a glorious Peters opener. Two up after fifteen minutes and Carrow Road was purring; Neighbour all tricks and treats on one side, and Suggett on the other, with youngster Billy Steele providing the necessary protection and cover in the centre of the Norwich midfield that allowed Martin Peters to make forward runs in support of the two wide men, plus, of course, the hard-working Boyer and Viv Busby in attack. That team was so typical of Bond – full of attack-minded players with even the full-backs, Mel Machin and Colin Sullivan, encouraged to go forward at every opportunity. Watching that Norwich side in its pomp, as it was for that game, you may even have convinced yourself that John Bond had formulated and reintroduced the classic 2-3-5 formation with that quintet of Neighbour, Boyer, Busby, Peters and Suggett in attack, the swarming Norwich frontline eventually getting a third goal before half-time when Irving Nattrass, more in frustration than anything, obstructed Boyer in his own penalty area. Peters did the honours and Norwich went in at half-time to a standing ovation.

This side, this type of football, was what Bond had wanted for his Norwich side. Playing with freedom and expression, given the opportunity to go forward, create chances and, crucially, take risks. Kevin Bond spoke of a side and players that wasn't afraid to lose the ball, to try things out, be positive and forward-thinking. And if you did lose it? Get it back and try again. Jimmy Neighbour typified this approach – he was the tormentor-in-chief; his brief was to get the ball and run at opposing defenders, to then either cut inside or play a cross into the penalty box. His choice. This had previously been the way Suggett had played the game, but Bond had identified in Suggett a player who had more to offer than 'heads down and run like hell', in due course making Suggett much more of a complete midfielder, utilising his vision with or without the ball to great effect. Playing the two of them in the same side was an indulgence – some managers would have baulked at having to find a place for just one of them – and Newcastle was the first side, but certainly not the last, to suffer for it.

Norwich could not sustain the ferocity of their attacking impetus, nor the discipline that went with it, for the complete game, however, and they paid the price during a fifteen-minute period in the second half when Newcastle pulled two goals back through Tommy Craig (a penalty after Peters, taking a breather in defence, had fouled Micky Burns) and Alan Gowling. They had more than enough to hold on for the win though, the resultant two points lifting the Canaries out of the relegation zone for the first time that season. Three days later, a trip to Loftus Road gave Queens Park Rangers the opportunity to gain revenge on Norwich for so dramatically ending their League title challenge so late on in the previous season. Said opportunity was spurned, Norwich's second consecutive 3-2 win coming via goals from Sullivan, Busby and Peters; the latter's eighty-seventh-minute penalty sealing another well-deserved victory, as well as more despair for the fans of the Hoops.

Busby's performance and goals in those two wins showed what a good player he was, one who was certainly winning over any doubters at Carrow Road. No one was expecting him to score with the sort of alarming regularity that had been the hallmark of MacDougall's spell with the club, but like all good forwards, Busby knew how to bring others into play and to hold the ball up while Norwich's attack-minded midfield moved up in support. It came as a blow to all concerned therefore when, soon after the Queens Park Rangers game, Busby sustained an injury that was bad enough to keep him out the side for a run of eight consecutive League fixtures – a run of games that saw only one win.

One step forward and two back. Bond initially recalled Roger Gibbins to fill the void and he duly delivered his first goal for the Canaries in a 2-1 defeat at home to Leeds. His and Boyer's presence did not offer the sort of physical threat that Norwich had previously utilised, however, and midway through that little run Gibbins was dropped in favour of former Chelsea and England striker Peter Osgood, now at Southampton, who was brought in on a three-game loan to offer the attacking nous and experience that Norwich was missing. It was a gamble worth taking, but while Osgood's class and reputation in the game were unquestionable, for once one of Bond's little left-field punts didn't come off and Osgood failed to score or impress, apart from a few brief cameos, during his loan spell.

Osgood's first match in a Norwich shirt had been that one victory in the barren Busby-less spell; a 1-0 win against West Ham at Carrow Road. The Hammers' midfield on the day included Alan Devonshire, a recent signing from non-League Southall, and Llewellyn Curbishley (better known as Alan), who were adding a little bit of silk and steel to a Hammers side that was steadily reinventing itself at the time. One of the Hammers' players who was missing out as a result of this was former Canary Graham Paddon, the sacrificial lamb in the deal that had seen MacDougall join Norwich. Parting with Paddon had been a hard call for Bond to make at the time, the midfielder's class and talent marking him out, if ever there was one, as a typical Bond player.

The chance to bring him back to Carrow Road was one that Bond could not turn down, even though his squad was not exactly short on gifted midfielders.

Hammers' boss John Lyall was an old teammate and friend of Bond's, and there is little doubt that Paddon's name was mentioned in the lead up to the game, as well as immediately after it. As with Neighbour, Bond worked to get the deal done quickly, and less than twenty-four hours after the end of the match, it was announced that Paddon had rejoined the club for £110,000. Paddon made his second Norwich debut in the 3-1 defeat at Bristol City. Sadly, however, his much-welcomed return to Norwich only lasted two more games before he suffered a broken leg in the game against Sunderland at Roker Park a month later. It was a typically robust challenge from Jim Holton that caused such an appalling injury to Paddon's leg and an enraged Bond took to the pitch in order to confront him. The injury kept Paddon out of the Norwich side for nearly a year, the delicious prospect of watching a midfield that featured him, Peters, Neighbour and Suggett now something the Norwich fans would have to put on hold.

The one redeeming feature of that particular Saturday afternoon had been the return to the fold of Viv Busby. His towering header from a Ryan cross was enough to give Norwich their second away win of the season, some consolation for Bond on his forty-fourth birthday, and an early Christmas present for the doughty band of Norwich fans who had made the near 500-mile round trip. Busby, typically, had led the line in his usual rambunctious manner: making space, holding the ball up and letting others around him play. He had, in only five games (and three goals), become indispensable to Norwich. This fact became all the more evident when he scored in the Canaries' next game, a 2-0 win over old adversaries Queens Park Rangers, before hitting a superb hat-trick[22] on New Year's Day 1977 in the 3-2 win over Leicester City at Carrow Road. Seven goals in seven games for Viv Busby as a Norwich player and not a defeat among them.

Ted MacWho-gall?

Much as he had shared the delight of the Norwich support in Busby's influence and goalscoring prowess, however, Bond knew that his side was still desperately in need of another goalscorer. The Canaries had struggled to score goals during Busby's eight-game absence, and although his class was unquestionable, Boyer was at his most effective playing alongside another striker and carving out the chances for him, just as he had done with MacDougall and was now doing so with Busby. Boyer was, for all his talents, not an out-and-out goalscorer, he was a much more complete forward than that; one who needed a partner to benefit from his hard work, endless running and ability to find space. Busby was now benefiting from those skills, but in the event that he missed another run of games, what was the alternative and where would the goals come from?

Bond believed he had the answer, and if the source was a familiar one, the name in question wasn't.

---

[22] Only the second in the top flight by a Norwich player – the first, of course, had been MacDougall's against Aston Villa the previous August.

The player was known to Bond; he had after all looked on as the then starry-eyed fourteen-year-old signed his schoolboy terms at Bournemouth, the culmination of a South Coast bidding war as both the Cherries and Southampton vied for his signature following an impressive showing in a regional Schools Cup final. And Southampton were probably the favourites, being the club where our aspiring young footballer's cousin had spent eight years as a professional, scoring 145 League goals in 273 League appearances, including thirty-nine during the 1959/60 season – a season total that remains a club record. That player's name was Derek Reeves, Bournemouth-born but a Saints legend to this day. His younger cousin's name was Kevin.

Kevin Reeves. It's a name that resonates with many Norwich City fans, not so much for what he was as a player, though he was without any doubt a very good one. But no, the reason why the name of Kevin Reeves has become an iconic one in recent Canary history is because of what he represented in terms of what was to come; something which became, with predictable regularity, a pattern over the quarter of a century or so that followed.

But back to the young Kevin's schoolboy dilemma.

Southampton was the logical choice. Kevin's brother had already been an apprentice with them. They were, at the time, a First Division club with a stable history and an immensely respected manager in Ted Bates. They also had a reputation for signing up local talent and bringing them through into the first team. Captain Terry Paine had signed for them as a seventeen-year-old and had now made over 600 first-team appearances. He'd been born in Winchester, while Portsmouth-born Bobby Stokes had been rejected by Pompey but not by Saints, and he signed as an apprentice when he was just fifteen and was an established first-team player. Then there was Mike Channon, an England regular and another local lad – born in Christchurch – who'd signed for them when he was seventeen; by the end of the 1972/73 season he'd already scored seventy-nine goals. All the boxes that could be ticked had been ticked and The Dell awaited the arrival of another schoolboy prodigy.

Except that Kevin opted to sign for Bournemouth. For him it was the next logical step of his career. His home town of Burley, nestled on the western edge of the New Forest, no more than a half-hour's drive from the town. And he'd played for Bournemouth Schools. For him it made a lot more sense to join Bournemouth, a place that both he and his family were familiar with. John Bond was still the Cherries' manager at the time Kevin signed, although it wasn't too long afterwards that he upped and left, taking Ken Brown with him and, bit by bit and circuitously if required, a flotilla of his former players. This ultimately caused quite a lot of ill-feeling towards Bond and Norwich from both the club and their supporters; aggrieved that so many of their players were being spirited away to Norfolk for what seemed like, with the exception of Phil Boyer, next to nothing.

It wasn't all one-way though. John Benson, one of those who had left Bournemouth to follow in Bond's footsteps, returned to Dean Court as the

Cherries' new manager after just one year and thirty-seven appearances at Carrow Road. It wasn't long before Reeves made an impression on him and Benson handed Reeves his first-team debut during the 1975/75 season. He never looked back. Seizing the opportunity that had been given to him, Reeves made an immediate impact, going on to score twenty goals in sixty-three appearances. There seems little doubt that if he hadn't already been aware of him, then John Bond would have soon had the exploits of Reeves brought to his attention in one of his chats with Benson. Either way, with Norwich in need of options in attack but having spent pretty much all of their spare cash on Jimmy Neighbour, Bond wasn't slow in following up the lead, especially if there was a bargain to be had.

Kevin himself was completely unaware of Norwich's growing interest in him. This was long before the days of websites, 24/7 sports news and dedicated TV and radio stations. Business, such as it was, was done by telephone and between the respective managers. Agents didn't exist and a player's future would often be mapped up for him long before he knew anything about it. The first Kevin heard about it was during a Thursday morning training session at Bournemouth when John Benson took him to one side and said that Norwich were interested in signing him and wanted to, in the first instance, take him on loan. Yet if that hadn't been unexpected enough, then the fact that he ended up making his Canaries debut two days later at Highbury was even more so. Bond had entered a nightmare scenario whereby he was down to just one fit striker. Boyer and Gibbins were both unavailable so he had no option but to throw Reeves in at the deep end alongside Viv Busby in a game that would be shown later that evening on *Match of the Day*. Welcome to the big time!

He didn't disgrace himself. Norwich lost 1-0 but Reeves acquitted himself well, before coming off with around twenty minutes to go. It was a disappointing result and performance for the Canaries, and the end of a remarkable scoring run for Busby who had found the net in every one of his previous five appearances for the club. Bond rested Reeves for the next game an impressive 2-1 win at Carrow Road against Liverpool that saw Jimmy Neighbour score his first goal for the Canaries, dancing around three hapless Liverpool defenders before placing his shot past Ray Clemence; the only low spot of the afternoon for City being the early departure of the now talismanic Busby because of injury. That meant Norwich would be going into their next game, another home clash this time against Stoke City, minus both Busby and Boyer. It was time for the young guns to deliver, Reeves and Gibbins were both recalled and sent into action against a Stoke side that just happened to boast Peter Shilton in goal. The game did, however, signal the return of a Canary legend to the line-up that afternoon; the indefatigable Duncan Forbes.

Forbes had been away on loan at Torquay, but far from seeing it as a chance to start winding his career down on the English Riviera, he took it upon himself to prove both form and fitness and, in doing so, win his place back in the Norwich side. Upon his return to Trowse, he soon introduced himself to the Norwich new boy as Kevin recalls:

> Forbsey was unbelievable. I remember controlling a few balls and then the next thing I know I'm up in the air. And I say to him, 'What are you doing?' And his classic line was 'I'm going for the ball!' when the ball was about 3 yards in front of him with a pair of legs in between. It didn't bother him.[23]

Forbes was now back in contention at Carrow Road and no doubt itching for the opportunity of 'going for the ball' against a few opposition players again. With David Jones now joining long-term injury concern Graham Paddon, and Boyer on the list of unavailable players for that game, Forbes was a perfect 'minder' for the young duo in the Norwich attack on that day, and his growls of affirmation to that fact would have been heard by most of the 18,408 in attendance, never mind the Stoke players. It was all enough to unnerve Alan Bloor after just two minutes, being dispossessed by Reeves, who having won the ball from a man with fifteen years' experience of top-level football and over 300 League appearances, went on to score his first goal for Norwich in just his second appearance in First Division.

Dreamtime for Reeves. Two games into his loan period and he had already found the net. Not only that, he'd done so within the first few minutes of a game, making an impact among his teammates, the fans and, as he'd hoped, his manager. A good day for a young professional just starting out on his career at the top level. Regrettably for Forbes, it was not such a good one. His attempted clearance shortly after half-time had cannoned into the back of Stoke midfielder Geoff Salmons before rebounding past Keelan and into the Norwich goal for an equaliser that they barely deserved. For Reeves though, his goal and everything about it was a blessing, one of those life-changing moments that we all dream of. His confidence boosted, he began to impose himself on the game, demanding the ball from his more illustrious teammates, making runs, getting in among the Stoke back four and making a nuisance of himself in their penalty area. In other words he was doing exactly what Bond had hoped he would be capable of, albeit long before he had dared hope he would be. The matter of turning Reeves' loan into a permanent move before other clubs began to take an interest – and both Arsenal and West Brom were waiting to pounce should the Canaries have hesitated – was never in question and Bond acted quickly, securing Kevin's services for just £50,000, another steal from his former club.

With Boyer now a long-term injury concern, Kevin became a pivotal member of the Norwich side, playing in every one of the Canaries' remaining nineteen League games that season and adding another eight goals in the process – three of both his and the club's more impressive performances coming in Carrow Road

---

[23] Waghorn, Rick, *12 Canary Greats* (Jarrold Publishing, 2004), p. 103.

160

wins against Coventry City, Manchester United and Everton. Reeves scored in each of those games, the strike against Manchester United in particular being a memorable one; originating from the feet of Peters, his ball to Gibbins allowed the other promising youngster to feed a first-time pass through to Reeves who, with the confident swagger of someone who knew he was a good player, calmly rounded Martin Buchan before coolly passing the ball past Alex Stepney.

Both United men were international players – one was the owner of a European Cup winner's medal, the other a member of Scotland's World Cup squad that had travelled to West Germany in 1974 – and both were made to look thoroughly inadequate by a slip of a lad who, only a few months before, had been turning out at places like Rochdale, Darlington and Stockport County in the Fourth Division.

Far from being brought in with one eye on the future, Kevin had now become a pivotal part of the team, as well as Bond's long-term plans for the club. Following his goal and performance against Stoke he started all of the Canaries nineteen remaining League fixtures, scoring another eight goals in the process and ending the season as the club's second highest scorer, his final total of nine, two short of Busby's eleven. The duo had dovetailed extremely effectively, each playing to their strengths in the games they played together, both finding the net in these matches on three separate occasions Most notably in the 3-0 win over Coventry at Carrow Road on 19 February, a game that saw Busby just miss out on his second hat-trick of the season. That game and the performance that went with it helped ease the pain that the team and supporters had gone through at Portman Road just four days earlier; East Anglian rivals Ipswich Town romping to a 5-0 win in a game that barely saw Reeves and Roger Gibbins get a kick. Indeed, it was more memorable for the fact that the Canaries' central defensive partnership on the day, Duncan Forbes and Tony Powell, were utterly run ragged by the Ipswich forwards. For Powell, the occasional off day was permitted, his quality and consistency since joining the club having been exceptional. For Forbes, it was a different story. He'd struggled in the game against Stoke and now recalled for the crucial Ipswich game, he'd found the going tough again. Admittedly, the quality of the opposition had been very high – better teams and players had found it difficult against the likes of Paul Mariner, Clive Woods and Eric Gates – but even so, it again raised questions about whether there was a future for Forbes, long since replaced as captain by Peters, at the club.

No such questions were being asked about Reeves' future. With Boyer only able to play twice more that season since his injury back in the new year, Reeves had, almost by accident rather than design, become Norwich's first-choice striker; aided and abetted, when available, by Busby, with Gibbins a willing alternative. Reeves' place and prominence in the team typified just how much the dynamics of the side had changed since the last game of the previous season. Only four of the players who had lined up for the Canaries for their 2-0 win over Stoke City on 24 April 1976 had made the starting XI for the game against Sunderland.

Of the remaining seven, Kevin Keelan had been dropped and replaced by Roger Hansbury, David Jones was on the bench, Mick McGuire, Billy Steele and Phil Boyer were all out with long-term injuries, while Ted MacDougall and Peter Morris had left the club – transfers, loss of form and injuries to key players which, despite the quality of some of the incoming players, affected both form and morale in a significant manner.

That catalogue of long-term player injuries was perhaps the most challenging issue that Bond had to deal with that season and, quite probably, of his managerial career to date. Norwich had been without key players for lengthy periods over the whole of the season. Add to that a significant departure or two and it becomes clear just how much of a juggling act, consistency wise, that campaign had been. Among those Canaries who had missed out were the following;

- Mick McGuire – long-term injury; played zero out of a maximum of forty-two League games.
- Phil Boyer – long-term injury; played in twenty-two out of a maximum of forty-two League games.
- Viv Busby – assorted injuries throughout season; played in seventeen out of a maximum of thirty-seven League games.
- Graham Paddon – long-term injury; played in three out of a maximum of twenty-seven League games.

As well as,

- Ted MacDougall – transferred to Southampton; played in three out of a maximum of forty-two League games.
- Dave Stringer – transferred to Cambridge United; played in one out of a maximum of forty-two League games.
- Duncan Forbes – loan to Torquay/injuries/loss of form; played in twelve out of a maximum of forty-two League games.

Imagine the manager of any leading club in the modern-day game having to miss out on the availability of such key players throughout the season – seven in total – all of whom he might reasonably have expected, at the end of the previous campaign, to be the spine of his side for much of the next one. Place the ever-changing selection dilemmas that it would have caused for John Bond and Mel Machin in a modern context and imagine Chris Hughton having the same issues with his Norwich squad throughout the 2013/14 season. That might mean Bradley Johnson being out for the entire season with both Ricky Van Wolfswinkle and Gary Hooper both being out for long spells, along with Robert Snodgrass. It might also have meant Wes Hoolahan, Michael Turner and Sebastien Bassong being unavailable for selection for most, if not all, of the season as well. Would, under those circumstances, Norwich struggle today with such losses on the playing front? Of course they would. The fact that Bond had to react and cope with such losses back then and still manage to keep his side in the First Division was testimony to his managerial and coaching skills, as well as his ability to pluck out unproven youngsters from relative footballing obscurity – in this case Roger Gibbins and Kevin Reeves – long before they might have been considered ready for regular first-team football. To perform as well as they did, the consistency and fast development of Reeves, in particular, was a very large and positive plus to come from what had been an erratic but ultimately satisfactory season that saw Norwich finish in sixteenth position.

9

NO REEVES, NO FANS, NO FUTURE

Despite Bond's previous assurances to Reeves that the club 'didn't need the money', it was clear that a number of big and wealthy clubs wanted to offer Norwich very big money in exchange for him. In time, the club must have realised that, far from being a long-term strike partner for Reeves, Fashanu was now more likely to be his replacement, the obvious allure of a seven-figure sum being offered to the club in exchange for Reeves' services no longer one they could afford to ignore.

When the yellow-and-green dust had settled on Norwich City's 1976/77 season, and everyone connected with the club was able to look back on what had been a reasonably satisfactory campaign, most would have done so with one name on their mind: Kevin Reeves.

For just as the Canaries' celebrated return to the top flight a year earlier had been characterised by the form and fitness, indeed, the very presence of the evergreen Martin Peters, then the one just gone was all about nineteen-year-old Reeves, plucked from relative obscurity at Bournemouth and thrown into the white-hot cauldron of a First Division debut at Highbury, the focus of a crowd of over 30,000 people; most of whom, including just about all of the Norwich fans, would have been saying, 'Kevin who?'.

And no wonder.

In the week leading up to Norwich's approach to take him on loan, Reeves had played in just sixty-three League games for Bournemouth in a little over two and a half seasons. Most of these had been in the Fourth Division, and for a team that had not exactly made its mark on that game or the League in that time; his first season in the first team ending with the ignominy of relegation. By the time the 1976/77 season started, Reeves was just another young player plying his trade in the lower divisions – one of dozens who would have been hoping for that stroke of luck, that moment of genius, that flash of inspiration that might have raised them above the parapet and got them noticed. The harsh truth of that particular dream, however, was that you were just as likely to have the loss of form, the falling out with the manager or the injury that would mean a very premature and unexpected exit from the game before you were even out of your teens. It did happen, and frequently. The game is, and was, littered with the broken bodies and dreams of young players who had, for one reason or another, fallen out of love with the game – or, as was more probable, the game had fallen out of love with them. Football has no compassion, no sense of duty to its own. It is a cruel game at the best of times, swift to weed out the weak and wanting. This was never more evident than in the lower divisions where there was rarely a second chance if you didn't make the grade. Paul Kent, for example, had been lucky. He had arrived at Norwich as an exceedingly promising young player of whom a lot was thought of and expected. Ultimately, it didn't work out for Paul at Carrow Road. Yet at least he had the consolation of being released from a club in the top division – he had that on his playing CV to fall back on. There was, at the time, a very big difference in being released from a club like Norwich to being let go by the likes of Bournemouth. The former said not quite good enough but worth another look further down maybe. The latter? Just plain not good enough.

More often than not, the young players that were signed on as schoolboys for lower division clubs at that time had a near-impossible task to get through to even the rarefied heights of first-team football at that level. A tiny percentage would eventually make it through to the first team of a club like Bournemouth. An even tinier percentage of that number would go on to make a decent career out of the game. Smaller still would be those that got moves to clubs in either one of the top two divisions. Then, right at the top of the pyramid, you got those players that had come through the schoolboy ranks at a lower league team and up into the 'A' team and reserves, there for the seasoned old pros who are dropping out of the game to kick and abuse. Survive that and possess that rare quality that makes someone really stand out and get noticed, and you win the lottery and move to a team in the top division of English football.

Such was the footballing miracle of Kevin Reeves. He did all of that and made it. You can only stand back and admire those that came into the game and succeeded, despite all those odds that were piled mercilessly up against them.

What route had Reeves taken in that circuitous journey that saw him make his debut as a First Division footballer at Highbury barely five years after he had taken part in that Bournemouth Schools Cup final? Reeves was playing for Twynham School from Christchurch in Dorset against Oakfield; a game that he must have made some impression on as Twynham managed to win 5-3, despite being 3-0 down at one point. After the game, Reeves, then only fourteen, was approached by Bournemouth scout Reg Tyrell, who invited him to come along to Dean Court for schoolboy trials – he had been, in effect, cherry-picked from that elite schoolboy crop by the Cherries. No academies or state-of-the-art training facilities for the up-and-coming young players then. Reeves' training at Dean Court involved regular Thursday night sessions in the club's car park, where he began to learn his trade for two years before, again one of the minority, becoming an apprentice for a year. At that time there were some good players at the club, solid pros who would have good careers in the game, either at Bournemouth, and in and around the lower divisions, or in some cases, managing to do what Reeves and all his peers dreamt of, breaking through and playing in the higher leagues. Apart from Reeves, that Bournemouth youth system was also responsible for players of the calibre of Steve Gritt and Mark Nightingale, both of whom went on to do just that – Nightingale including Norwich as one of the three other clubs he went on to play for, Crystal Palace and Peterborough being the two others.

There were some good professionals at the club during this period; players that Reeves could look up to and emulate. Among those who he watched play for the first team were the future Norwich trio of MacDougall, Boyer and Mel Machin, as well as Jimmy Gabriel, once of Everton where he had won League championship and FA Cup winner's medals. Gabriel joined Bournemouth from Southampton, his experience and knowledge of the game having, no doubt, a huge effect on the players around him, much as Peters arrival at Norwich did the same at Carrow Road – he was another masterstroke signing of Bond's.

Reeves trod a very well-worn path south when he joined Norwich in 1976. The Bournemouth squad of players listed in the 1973/74 *Rothmans Football Yearbook* includes seven players who eventually followed their manager to Norwich, plus one member, Ken Brown, of the coaching team. Six of those players[24] went to Carrow Road from Bournemouth, making Reeves the seventh to do so. Reeves himself pointed out the connection between the two clubs in an interview he gave the *Bournemouth Echo* in 2013, admitting that, 'There were a lot of Bournemouth-Norwich connections, and I know it wasn't very well received by the Bournemouth supporters.' Indeed it wasn't, and it probably hadn't been helped that the Bournemouth manager who had helped get the deal arranged was Benson, one of the six who had joined Bond at Norwich only to return as the Cherries' manager. Did Benson tip Bond the proverbial wink about the young prodigy they had at Dean Court, or had the Norwich team of scouts done their job? Understandably, unpopular move or not, Benson was not going to deny Reeves the chance of proving himself at a higher level and with a bigger club, even if it was Norwich. In fact, knowing the club and the manager, it is probable that he was glad it was Norwich that Reeves was joining. That initial loan agreement that first took Reeves to Carrow Road was, no doubt, intended as an 'insurance' in case he was ultimately unable to make the step up, in which case he would have returned to the Cherries to be welcomed, no doubt, with open arms. It only took the seventy-minute appearance he had at Arsenal to convince Norwich otherwise however, especially as he made the most of the opportunities he had to convince his future teammates of his ability off the pitch, as well as on it.

I settled in fairly quickly. I was able to train for a couple of weeks with the players and I think, without blowing my own trumpet, once you've shown them you've got ability and you can train with the best of them, then you get that respect. You're welcomed into the fold a little bit better.[25]

---

[24] Fred Davies, Mel Machin, John Benson, Tony Powell, Phil Boyer and John Sainty. The players who had originally been at Bournemouth but who teamed up with Bond again via other clubs were David Jones, Ted MacDougall and Mark Nightingale. Adding Reeves, the last to do so in 1976, means that ten ex-Bournemouth employees who had been at Dean Court with Bond eventually, in one position or another, joined him at Norwich. This is a figure that is unlikely to have been matched by any other contemporary football manager in England.

[25] Waghorn, Rick, *12 Canary Greats* (Jarrold Publishing, 2004), p. 105–06.

And what was priceless for Reeves was access to the type of quality coaching from the likes of Bond and Brown that, when matched with the type of players he was surrounded by on a day-to-day basis, meant he could only improve.

I think a lot of the ability is natural, but what Bondy gave me was that he opened my eyes to the timing of runs, where to run, things like that. He made me more aware of the game itself. And that was the key for me, because I was bright enough to take it on board and to learn from that.

Learn he most certainly did. Eight goals from twenty-one League appearances to the end of the 1976/77 season were followed by another twelve from thirty-seven League appearances the following season. He wasn't a natural goalscorer perhaps, the sort of penalty box predator that Norwich had been used to, indulged in even with MacDougall, but he did bring others into play and he did work hard for the team, chasing down lost causes and covering most of the pitch as he did so. He earned himself the comparison, made by Kevin Bond in an earlier chapter, that he was more Phil Boyer than MacDougall – and that was probably why, with that in mind, Bond would have felt comfortable with letting Boyer leave the club to rejoin MacDougall at Southampton in the summer of 1977. The King is dead, long live the King?

If Reeves was never quite the 'King' of Carrow Road (that honour remained with Martin Peters), then he was certainly one in waiting – and one who was seeing off a few more striker partners in the process. Boyer had gone, joined just five games (and no goals) into the season by Busby, sold to Stoke for £50,000 – job done and Norwich get their money back. He (Busby) had always been a short-term fix for Norwich, given the paucity of striking quality at the club when he had joined as a hastily signed replacement for MacDougall. But he had not let anyone down, scoring a total of eleven goals in his twenty-two League appearances for Norwich, not a bad ratio for a stopgap. Reeves also continued to play alongside Roger Gibbins, but despite his performing admirably for the club, he was too similar a player to Reeves to have any chance of staying at the club long-term, and after just seven goals in his twenty-seven League games over the 1977/78 campaign, he was moved on, joining the New England Teamen in America's NASL. His last game for Norwich, a 3-3 draw at home to Nottingham Forest, also marked the debut of his replacement, ex-Newcastle United, West Ham and Cardiff City striker Keith Robson. Another short-term solution admittedly, but Bond knew he had a player on his hands who would run through brick walls – and certainly opposing defenders – for the cause, creating as he did so time and space for Reeves to further flourish in the Norwich attack while the club searched for a more long-term partner for their prodigy who was, even now, still reported to be attracting the interest of the man who had witnessed his debut – Terry Neill at Arsenal.

In a Norwich side that wasn't exactly short of strong characters, Robson was no exception. He'd begun his career at Newcastle United, but as is often the case with talented young players coming through the ranks at their local club (Robson was born in nearby Hetton-le-Hole), he found his way through to the first team blocked by an expensive 'import'. In this case it was all £180,000 worth of Malcolm MacDonald, bought from Luton Town only weeks after Robson had signed on as a full-time professional himself. With MacDonald, a big name commanding a big fee (it was only fractionally under the British record at the time), joining an already well-established front line at the club that included the likes of John Tudor, it was always going to be difficult for Robson to establish himself at the club, so he moved on to West Ham where he managed thirteen goals in sixty-eight appearances, one of which was in the 1976 European Cup Winners Cup final against Anderlecht. Ability at the highest level proven therefore, and an easy choice for Bond as far as striking cover was concerned, especially with Robson having shown he could perform at the highest level at Bond's old club.

A deal was soon struck between the two clubs and Robson became a Canary for the surprisingly low fee of £25,000. His arrival at Carrow Road and perceived reputation as being something of a hothead on the pitch drew the now-famous quote from a *Daily Telegraph* sportswriter who, musing the deal, observed of Robson that 'he does not always prefer the cerebral approach'. Whether or not this was intended as a slight on Robson's footballing ability or character remains, enigmatically, uncertain. What is clear, however, is that his exuberant style was seen as being, potentially, a perfect foil for Reeves' more calculated approach, and there is no doubt that there would have been high hopes among the Norwich coaching hierarchy, not least Bond, at seeing how the two of them would be able to work together.

Bought to play alongside Reeves, it is ironic therefore that Robson's debut for the Canaries saw Reeves miss out due to a knock that he had sustained three weeks earlier at Bristol City. The Canaries' 3-0 defeat that day was one of their worse performances of the 1977/78 season. Roger Gibbins took his place for that home game against champions-in-waiting Nottingham Forest, and it is fair to say that neither he nor Robson got a kick in the first half as Forest sauntered into a 3-0 lead within the twenty-five minutes of the game.

This was at least an improvement from the game in Bristol, where Norwich conceded three goals in the first fifteen minutes. It did, however, suggest there were still flaws in the Canaries' back four that needed addressing, either that or the team's expansive type of play and extravagant midfield, that often featured Neighbour, Paddon, Suggett and Peters, needed revising – especially in away games where Norwich's defensive record was the second worse in the League that season, with all of the bottom six clubs conceding fewer goals on their travels. Bond had reacted to the defeat at Bristol by doing the unthinkable in dropping Kevin Keelan, replacing him with the ever-patient Roger Hansbury. In an attempt to soften the blow, or so it must have seemed at the time, he also dropped Kevin from the side.

But it did not seem to make any difference and Forest ran riot, with Peter Withe, Colin Barrett and future Canary Martin O'Neill all making unseasonal hay, and Barrett's goal coming from an uncharacteristic error from Powell. Barrett then made amends by making an error of his own handball in the penalty area. This gave John Ryan, one of the tortured back four of that first half, the chance to give the Canaries a little confidence going into the break, his firmly hit penalty past the not inconsiderable figure of Peter Shilton doing just that.

Norwich was a different team in the second half and should have won the game. As it was they secured a draw, with Robson, already showing that he certainly *would* run through brick walls as well as opposing defenders, scoring the equaliser. It was a debut goal that garnished much acclaim and joy from both his teammates and most of the crowd of just over 26,000. Norwich did have some *cojones* after all. The goal typified by Robson's second-half performance; he was everywhere and anywhere, harrying the Forest midfield and snapping at the heels of their defenders, even the much-feared Kenny Burns didn't escape his ire. The end result and deserved point perfectly illustrating that, as much as it is perhaps football's greatest cliché, the oft trotted-out statement about it being 'a game of two halves' was never more pertinent than it had been on this occasion.

It also showed that, yet again, Bond's eye for a player and a bargain had paid off. Robson had provided much of the energy that characterised that comeback, and the conviction that he and Reeves might turn out to be a striking partnership to match that great one of MacDougall and Boyer was duly strengthened – even though the two had yet to play together. Indeed, that confidence must have been so high that Bond felt he could now dispense with the services of Roger Gibbins. He surprisingly left the club for that USA move shortly after the Forest game, Norwich happily accepting the £60,000 offer from the New England Teamen for a man who never quite seemed to fit at Carrow Road, despite his popularity among the supporters and respectable total of twelve goals from forty-eight League appearances.

Robson's equalising goal in that game against Forest was both the first and the last he scored for Norwich that season. He and Reeves featured together in nine of the Canaries' remaining fourteen League fixtures of the season, with Reeves an ever-present in all of them, scoring a further six goals and ending the season with twelve goals from thirty-six League games. The five games that Robson missed during the run in saw Reeves play alongside youth prospect Phil Lythgoe, with Lythgoe (the son of ex-Norwich player Derrick, a scorer for the Canaries in the 1962 League Cup final) scoring his first goal for the club in the 3-1 home defeat to Manchester United, impressing all with his enthusiasm and willingness to get 'stuck in'. Had Norwich unearthed another striking gem? As it turns out they had, but it wasn't Lythgoe.

Reeves had now, in his short Norwich City career played alongside five different partners in the Norwich attack. He was a constant and, no doubt, one of the first names on the Norwich team sheet, the inconsistencies in finding him a long-term striking partner doing little to stop him scoring goals and impressing. He ended the 1977/78 season with twelve goals from thirty-seven League appearances, not exactly prolific but then he wasn't that sort of player. Establishing his place in the side and his role had never been a problem, what had caused problems was finding the right sort of player to perform the more traditional striker's role alongside him. Robson had offered the most hope, but both his form and goalscoring output were erratic – his final Canaries record of just fourteen goals from seventy-one League and cup appearances illustrating that. He was a good player, that was unquestionable, but not the right one for the role he had been given. Indeed, of all of Reeves' strike partners, the most ideal one had been Busby, the typical penalty box predator who had only lasted for twenty-three games. His departure now seemed a little premature.

The 1978/79 season didn't see the Canaries find a suitable partner for Reeves either. Former Tottenham and England striker Martin Chivers returned from Swiss exile in the summer of 1978 and at first glance he looked the perfect foil for Reeves. Strong, courageous and vastly experienced, he certainly started that campaign in a rich vein of form, scoring in Norwich's opening day win against Southampton (for whom Ted MacDougall reminded Norwich fans of what they had been missing), as did Reeves. Chivers went on to score another three in Norwich's next five matches, and following a 4-0 win over Birmingham in which they had both scored again, the new-look striker partnership had got six between them and Norwich were sixth in the table. Encouraged by Chivers, Bond went out and bought another striker, the equally formidable Davie Robb from Tampa Bay, to replace Chivers when he was injured. Like Chivers, Robb made an immediate impact, scoring Norwich's third goal in an impressive 3-0 win over Derby County on 8 September. The game was one of the featured matches on that night's *Match of the Day*, and Robb, Reeves (who scored the second) and Norwich got some well-deserved plaudits from many sources for their attacking game and all-in impressive performance, even from die-hard Everton fan Ed Stewart on his Sunday morning BBC Radio 2 programme, *Junior Choice*.

Yet the focus remained, inevitably, upon Reeves. The immediate impact he had made at Norwich after signing now stretched beyond the confines of Carrow Road and Norfolk, and the notice that he had served as a player of great potential was officially when he was selected for the England under-21 team to play their Italian counterparts in Rome in a European Championship quarter-final tie on 4 April 1978 – the accolade coming less than eighteen months after he had signed for Norwich. Nine more appearances for the under-21s followed, his most impressive game being in England's 3-1 win in Pernik against a strong Bulgarian side that saw him score two goals. Unsurprisingly, it didn't take long before there were calls for him to be given his chance in the full England team, one which eventually, and deservedly, came about, albeit in somewhat unusual circumstances.

England had been due to play Bulgaria at Wembley in a European Championship qualifying game on 21 November 1979. The game had been earmarked as the one that Tottenham's Glenn Hoddle would make his international debut in but not Reeves, his place and position in the England team occupied by Kevin Keegan. However, when the London fog came down on the night of the game, leading to its abandonment (fog working in a Norwich players favour on this occasion), Keegan's German club, SV Hamburg, refused to allow him to play. Thus, one Kevin's loss became another's gain, Reeves taking Keegan's place and No. 7 shirt on the night. Despite having a fine game, Reeves' debut was overshadowed by a virtuoso performance from Hoddle that included a goal. Not that it mattered to Reeves. He had gone from a virtual unknown to a full England international in a little under three years – if not a meteoric rise to fame then certainly an impressive one that was a credit to both himself and the coaching and guidance he had received since joining Norwich. And while everyone at Carrow Road was delighted for him and the recognition his selection had given Norwich, they were all very well aware of another thing: now that he had played for England, he wouldn't be a Norwich City player for very much longer.

In truth, Norwich had been fending off bids for their most valuable asset for some time, certainly long before Kevin's England bow. Nottingham Forest made Trevor Francis the first million-pound English footballer in February 1979, following up that milestone purchase with one of a similar amount for Reeves very shortly afterwards. Not surprisingly, Bond didn't want his star man to leave, but he felt obliged to let Kevin know of the interest. The response was one he probably didn't expect, with Kevin admitting, 'I didn't want to go at that time. I was happy at Norwich and Bondy was great. He said: "If you don't want to go, don't go!" So there was no: "Look, we need the money!" There was no pressure on me at all, which was great as far as I was concerned.'[26] Thus Norwich fended off Brian Clough's interest and Kevin stayed put. Meanwhile, Reeves' early-season strike partners had long since departed. Chivers' impressive start to the season swiftly ended with an Achilles tendon injury after just seven games. By the time he returned to the side, it was clear his interest in playing for Norwich had dulled somewhat during his spell on the sidelines; a 6-0 humiliation at Liverpool on 21 February 1979 signalling the end of his brief Norwich career and the former England man joined Brighton a month later. Robb, so impressive on his debut, had also gone, returning to the US to join Philadelphia Fury after just four League appearances and that lone goal. Their coming and going meant that Reeves had now played alongside and seen off, through no fault of his own, eight different strike partners. The eighth, Justin Fashanu, made his debut alongside Reeves' in a televised 1-1 draw at home to West Brom on 13 January.

Bond had successfully rebuffed the interest of Brian Clough and Nottingham Forest for Reeves, but rather than send out the message that Reeves was not for sale, it seemed to start up a bidding war for the player. With Forest still

---

[26] Waghorn, Rick, *12 Canary Greats* (Jarrold Publishing, 2004), p. 110.

interested and long-time admirers Arsenal also coming back into the picture, the speculation about his future raged around the club. Inevitable newspaper gossip columns linked with those clubs, and fallen giants Leeds United also came into the picture as potential suitors. Norwich, perhaps surprisingly, managed to resist the temptation to cash in over the summer of 1979, and Reeves started the season in a Norwich shirt; Norwich winning 4-2 at Everton before following that up with another big win, this time at home to Tottenham 4-0, Reeves scoring twice. Three days later, a 2-1 win over Leeds made it three out of three for Bond's team, and for the first time in their history Norwich were top of the First Division, the Reeves and Fashanu combination in attack looking, after so many false starts, to be the real deal.

By the beginning of March 1980, Reeves and Fashanu had scored fourteen goals between them, honours even at seven each. Fashanu's impact at the club had been, if anything, even more dramatic than Reeves' had been, the Doctor Barnardo's boy who had grown up as part of a loving foster family in Norfolk beginning to get his share of the headlines, on and off the pitch, with the majority of the footballing ones citing just what an effective front pairing he and Reeves had become. But despite Bond's previous assurances to Reeves that the club 'didn't need the money', it was clear that a number of big and wealthy clubs wanted to offer Norwich very big money in exchange for him. In time, the club must have realised that, far from being a long-term strike partner for Reeves, Fashanu was now more likely to be his replacement, the obvious allure of a seven-figure sum being offered to the club in exchange for Reeves' services no longer one they could afford to ignore.

Manchester City had remained interested in him throughout, and the League meeting between the clubs at Maine Road on 1 March 1980 gave everyone at Maine Road, including the club's fans, a better chance to take a look at the young Norwich starlet they were rumoured to be in the process of buying, with several bids having already been rejected. A week later, Norwich entertained Brighton at Carrow Road, the disquiet of the fans being clearly illustrated before and during the match with the unfurling of a large banner at the Barclay End of the ground that was brief and to the point: No Reeves, No Fans, No Future. The message was clear. Norwich were in the process of putting together a good team, one that might even be able to challenge for honours in the years to come, something which could not be expected to happen if the club continued its long-held policy of selling its best players. The eventual departure of Kevin Reeves is often cited as the beginning of the club's policy of doing just that – it was, however, merely the continuation of a practice that had existed for much longer at Carrow Road and was down to pure economics, the very simple fact of it being that the only way the club could continue to exist was dependant on the income it could get from player transfers. Reeves was not, therefore, the first in a long line of big money Canary departures – that also included, in time, Fashanu, as well as Dave Watson, Chris Woods, Steve Bruce,

Andy Townsend and Robert Fleck – but the latest in a long list of player sales that could be traced right back to the shock sale of goalkeeper Willie Mellor to Newcastle in 1914 for £765 (then a club record sale), and Alf Kirchen to Arsenal in 1935 for £6,000. Popular players had come and gone in the past (Terry Bly, Hugh Curran, Ron Davies and David Cross for example), just as they always would, a harsh footballing fact of life that Norwich City followers have always found, often understandably, hard to accept, whether it was Mellor for £765 or Dean Ashton for £7 million over a century later.

The more things change, the more they stay the same.

Reeves said his farewells with a goal in the 2-2 draw against the Seagulls and then was gone, the £1 million deal to take him to Manchester City being finalised in the days after that game, leaving Reeves free to make his debut for them, against Arsenal, just as his Norwich one had been, on 15 March. It wasn't the best of debuts for Kevin with his all-new club, Man City losing 3-0; his bad day at the office being compounded by the fact that he gave away a penalty. He remains, for many, one of the iconic figures in Norwich City history. His arrival, swift rise to fame and future fortune and inevitable big money departure, symbolised just how much football and Norwich City had changed in one decade. It had opened with the appointment of the man who ultimately led the Canaries to the top flight of English football for the first time in their history, and had ended with the departure of the player whose goals had done so much to help establish them as regulars in that division. Norwich City supporters meanwhile, ever willing to hang their hat on a good striker – and they'd seen a few – now had the explosive talent of Justin Fashanu to look forward to.

10
THINGS TO COME

It was almost as if the Canaries had decided to keep him in a large glass case at Carrow Road with an accompanying notice that read 'In Case Of Emergency, Break Glass'.

One of Bond's most difficult tasks (and there were many) during his tenure at Carrow Road was working to obtain a certain consistency of good form and results in the Canaries game.

Norwich fans were long used to initial footballing bright spells being followed by a sequence of results that were so tumultuously bad that the side quite often seemed to be reaching out and kissing the damp spectre of relegation when, only weeks previously, the prospect seemed impossible. Take that first season in the top flight for example. The 2-0 win over West Bromwich Albion on 18 November 1972 was the Canaries' eighth win in eighteen games, a spell that had seen only five defeats and good enough, at the end of the day's play, to see Norwich as high as sixth in the Division One table – an achievement that would, no doubt, have been featured and commented upon on the BBC's *Grandstand* as they did their cursory run through of the League tables once all the results of the day had come through. Close your eyes and you can almost hear Frank Bough trying to keep the surprise out of his voice as he talks the viewers through them:

Starting with League Division One and Liverpool stay top after their 3-2 win over Newcastle United, John Toshack among the scorers there, while Arsenal, 1-0 winners over Everton thanks to a John Radford goal, his seventh of the season, stay in second. Chelsea, meanwhile, drop out of the top six, they're replaced in fourth by Tottenham who won at Leicester City with a goal from Martin Chivers. Leeds stay third after their draw at Crystal Palace, who move off the bottom to twentieth with that point thanks to two goals from John Craven; Mick Jones and Johnny Giles scoring for Leeds, they were two down at half-time. Norwich, meanwhile, remain this season's surprise package, they move back up to sixth after a 2-0 win over West Bromwich at Carrow Road, Dave Stringer and Graham Paddon, scorer of a hat-trick at Arsenal in the League Cup in midweek remember, getting the goals there. What a fine job Ron Saunders is doing at Norwich, last season's Division Two champions.

Indeed he was. The Canaries were, forgive the pun, flying – flying, that is, in the face of all the critics who had predicted their immediate demise throughout the summer. Not only were the Canaries in the top six, they had just won their way through to the semi-finals of the League Cup. Their cup runneth over. But as history now shows, it was Norwich's last win in the League until the following April, the terrible sequence of results that followed seeing them lose fourteen of their following eighteen matches. As a consequence of this defeat at Manchester United at Carrow Road on 7 April meant that the team's so-called surprise package were now doing everything that had been expected of them and were bottom of the League.

But being a Norwich City fan has always being about the ups and the downs, that not always nicely intoxicating mixture of footballing heaven and hell. The Canaries could, and often did, throughout the decade have periods where they looked like world-beaters, untouchable, a side who could give anyone a good game and then some. Yet, on others, they looked, and played, like a team of strangers, there to be picked apart and disposed of accordingly. Sometimes this would all happen in the course of one afternoon, or even one half. Such is the lot of the football fan from Norwich. On other, equally frustrating occasions, the Canaries would put a run of results together that would catapult them, an irresistible sporting force that shot up the table, only to lose a game that on paper, that great definer of form the proverbial home banker against the winless team at the bottom of the. This would frequently be a prelude to an equally dazzling run of consecutive defeats that would send them plummeting down the table again, sometimes, in the process, even managing to drop below the side that the initial surprise loss to had precipitated the plunge. Looking back at all of the campaigns that made up the seventies, the club's ability to alternate between fine runs of games and form and those that were anything but, can be seen on numerous occasions.

This was certainly the case during the 1977/78 season which, strangely enough, for all its regular doses of joy and despair, saw at least a little bit of consistency in terms of the club's League position; the Canaries admirably held a place in the top ten from August until early April. They certainly got off to a good start, a difficult-looking opening fixture at West Ham ending in a 3-1 win with David Jones (2) and John Ryan the scorers. For Ryan, it was the start of a stand-out season for him, one that would end with him being both the club's leading goalscorer and the Player of the Year – the latter quite an achievement when you consider it was won despite having to compete with the still massively influential figure of Peters, as well as the up-and-coming Reeves.

Ryan joined Norwich from Luton for just £40,000, and his stand-out ability as an attacking midfielder came to the fore after Bond pushed him into a more advanced role in order to accommodate Kevin Bond at right back. His goalscoring record that season (fifteen in the League plus one in the League Cup) was all the more remarkable because of just how good some of them were, and how they defined him as a player of rare quality who, if said qualities had been identified and worked with earlier in his career, could have very well played for England. They included a 25-yarder against West Ham; a solo run that led to another long-range shot against Tottenham, for whom Pat Jennings was playing; a similar charge forward ending with a goal from 20 yards at Middlesbrough; a free-kick at the Wolves that nearly tore the net from its fixings, such was the venom in the shot; a 20-yarder at Leicester; and a sublime chip over and beyond Kevin Carr in an entertaining 2-2 draw at Newcastle. One can only speculate on how prominent a name and player in the game John Ryan would have been had his performances and goals been the sort of public property they are today. With every piece of action televised and analysed, it is fair to say that he may not have ended up playing as many games for Norwich over the two and a half years he was at Carrow Road (132 with twenty-nine goals scored) as he did.

Ever modest, Ryan refused to take any credit for his run of form, as well as the team's good run in the League that season. He once said of Martin Peters, 'I do all the running while he does all the playing', a typically self-effacing comment that took the credit off him and gave it to the man who had done so much for Norwich. Peters, of course, would have been the first to say that Norwich's success and steady development during the second half of that decade was a team effort above all else, which was absolutely right, as was the important role that Ryan played in it. He remains, for me, one of the most underrated players in the club's history.

John Bond appreciated him, however. Ryan left Norwich for Sheffield United in September 1980, spending two seasons at Bramall Lane before linking up with Bond again at Manchester City two years later in a player-coaching role at the age of thirty-five. He made nineteen appearances for them in the second part of that 1981/82 season, nearly two decades after he had joined Arsenal as a schoolboy. He has since enjoyed a hugely successful period coaching, including a spell as the youth coach at Manchester City, as well as a similar role with a team in Thailand before returning to the UK to take up a position as Regional Director of Coaching for the PFA – in other words, coaching the coaches of tomorrow, including those taking the UEFA 'A' License, the highest coaching qualification in the game. He currently coaches in the USA where he remains one of the most highly qualified and respected coaches in the game.

Just as Ron Greenwood passed on his knowledge and love of the game to many of the younger coaches in his time, including John Bond, so has Bond's own influence spread among many of those who played under him, Ryan taking those first steps as a youth coach under him at Maine Road. It would seem that as good as he was at spotting a good footballer when he was in his mid to late teens, Bond also knew a good coach as a player approached his late twenties to early thirties, John Ryan being one example of many.

The second half of that season was marred somewhat by an injury to the irrepressible and oft thought indestructible Keelan in the Norwich goal. He'd suffered the ignominy of being dropped the previous campaign, his performance drawing the ire of Bond following the Canaries' 3-1 defeat at Everton on 19 April. As Keelan was then thirty-six, many would have thought it was the last they would have seen of him in a Norwich shirt, especially as his ever-willing and ready understudy Roger Hansbury had stepped in and performed with some aplomb in the remaining matches. The 0-0 draw at Stoke City was a highlight, where he was called on to make a series of saves under a side who played, as teams normally do in that situation, with no little verve and attacking flair for George Eastham, their newly appointed manager.

Keelan, however, took his accustomed place in the No. 1 shirt at the beginning of the following season, one that saw boos for John Bond in the Carrow Road clash against Bristol City just five games in. Following their impressive opening day win at Upton Park, Norwich had stuttered somewhat, drawing their next two games; both at Carrow Road, and both, in Middlesbrough and Queens Park Rangers, against opposition they would have been expected to have beaten. This was followed by a savage 4-0 defeat at Manchester City, Mike Channon scoring two and thoroughly enjoying himself in the process. The irony of his performance was not lost on some Norwich supporters – City had, in the close season, felt obliged to temporarily delay another financial crisis by selling Phil Boyer, with a £135,000 bid from Southampton to reunite him with Ted MacDougall gratefully received. Boyer's arrival at Southampton meant, of course, the Saints felt they could recoup some of the money by selling Channon. Thus, in a tenuous and somewhat roundabout way, the sale of Boyer did contribute to that heavy defeat at Maine Road. That run of two draws and one defeat in three games was hardly unusual by Norwich standards, but expectations had been raised at Upton Park on day one and now people felt let down – which they demonstrated by not turning up for Norwich's next game against Bristol City. That same game the previous season (which came after a run of only one win in six games) had seen an attendance of 18,434 at Carrow Road – only 13,940 turned up for the same fixture less than six months later, a sure sign of discontent among the massed ranks of yellow and green. Norwich's subsequent inability to break down a Robins defence that was supposedly there for the taking (despite including such notable footballing luminaries as Norman Hunter and Gerry Sweeney), soon led to sounds of discontent echoing around a half-empty Carrow Road. Those sounds became boos when a clearly frustrated Bond left the director's box midway through the second half in order to reach the dugout, his subsequent action of replacing the ineffective Viv Busby with Roger Gibbins getting the first cheer of what was becoming a long afternoon. Gibbins got a second one with only a few minutes left, his late diving header securing the win and the points that lifted Norwich to ninth. It was Busby's last game for Norwich, and within two months he had joined Bristol City.

Boos for Bond? It seemed inconceivable. He had turned the club around at all levels; winning them an immediate promotion back to the top flight and adding another Wembley final in the process, and it had not been his fault that his team had performed so badly that afternoon. He'd also added a cast of entertainers to the side: Martin Peters for one, Jimmy Neighbour another, as well as returning prodigal son Paddon to his footballing home. Then there was the exciting potential being shown by Kevin Reeves. The club was overachieving; simply staying in the top division was evidence of that. Since Norwich had won their place at the top table back in 1975, they'd stayed put yet, in the same period, big name clubs like Wolves, Sunderland and Tottenham had all dropped down to the Second Division. Norwich had thrived, and that was the problem.

Bond's presence at the club, his media-friendly character and personality had considerably raised his profile, both in the game and sport as a whole – the following summer would see him joining big hitters Lawrie McMenemy and Denis Law as one of the BBC's studio pundits for the 1978 World Cup finals in Argentina. That's just how big a name in the game he was at the time, as were some of his players. The aforementioned Peters and Reeves were being talked about in terms of either an England recall or an England debut, while David Jones, now a Welsh international, was establishing himself as one of the best central defenders in the League. There was also, of course, the media-friendly and easy lead story of Kevin, John Bond's son, now making his way in the game at the club where his father was in charge. So, if Norwich weren't exactly big box office in the way that Brian Clough, Liverpool and Kenny Dalglish were, then they were certainly a more than respectable support act.

With that increased exposure came expectation. And in the minds of those watching the club at the time, the Canaries weren't delivering. The disappointment of Boyer's sale had been tempered by the convincing win at West Ham, but when that hadn't been followed up by results with performances to match in the next three games, the sense of disappointment, however unreasonable it may now seem, was palpable, with Bond bearing the brunt during that game against Bristol City. No fan would have dared question his future at the club or have wanted his removal; neither would anyone in the boardroom. It was a discontent born out of frustration and a desire for the club to push on, something which it either didn't seem capable of doing or, significantly, seemed to want to do. Such was, and is, the price of progress – however much you push on, people still expect more. And this was now the case at Carrow Road.

Yet progress was being made, even if it wasn't being realised in a series of convincing wins in the League. One of the first things Bond had done when he was appointed manager was to shake some life into the club's schoolboy and youth policy, which had been on the verge of disappearing. Now, just a few years later, the fruits of his labour were beginning to blossom. The previous campaign had seen Doug Evans make his senior bow, and during the 1977/78 season, Phil Lythgoe and Greg Downs both made theirs – the latter while well known as a full-back, initially debuted as a striker – while in the 1978/79 campaign, debuts would arrive for Richard Symonds and Justin Fashanu. Some would, inevitably, have better careers in the game than others. The overall worth and success of any club's youth system can be measured not so much by the number of players that pass through it that make it in the game, but those that are deemed good enough to be considered for first-team selection. At that point it is down to the player to succeed, the youth team coaches and set up have done their job and can tick off another success. Evans, Lythgoe, Downs, Symonds and Fashanu all had varying degrees of success in their careers, but the success in bringing them through was constant for the Canaries' youth set-up, and very credible justification for Bond's insistence that money be invested in it upon his appointment.

The other progress that the club made that season was the new and hugely welcome ability to stay in and around the top ten for so much of the season – a season that, for the first time in the Canaries' relatively short five seasons in the top flight, had seen them not even once flirt with the prospect of relegation. Sixth was the highest placing they'd held that season and fourteenth the lowest. The final finishing position of thirteenth was not as high as the one they'd enjoyed two years earlier, but even then, they'd had a spell prior to Christmas when they'd been as low as eighteenth. Likewise the following season had seen Norwich bottom of the table over the opening weeks of that 1976/77 campaign, rallying up to the heights of eleventh in March before slipping down as far as fifteenth, which is where they ended the season. Respectable? Maybe. But in a division that was very tight near the bottom at its conclusion, Norwich had finished it just three points shy of a relegation spot – the eighty-fourth-minute winner scored by Kevin Reeves against Bristol City in mid-April turning out to be quite a crucial goal. Had he not converted that Colin Sullivan cross late in that game, there is a very real chance that Norwich would have gone into their last League game that season against Sunderland needing a win to stay up, it was that close.

Thus a season of mid-table stability was an enormous achievement for the club, players and manager – that very same manager who had been criticised at Carrow Road when Bristol City came to town, booed by the club's lowest top-flight attendance to date of just 13,940.[27] That season also saw average home attendances drop by around nearly 3,000 a match, something that is mystifying even today, given what the side achieved that season. Fortunately, sanity prevailed among those more vociferous Norwich fans and the booing heard at that game was not repeated, nor heard again at Carrow Road for a very long time to come afterwards.

Grounds for optimism therefore as the club prepared for the last full season of 1970s football. Another modestly budgeted pre-season paved the way for the 1978/79 season; participation in the Anglo-Scottish Cup for a fourth successive

---

[27] Low? Putting things into perspective, when Norwich played Vitesse Arnhem in the first round of the UEFA at Carrow Road in 1993, the crowd was just 16,818 – disappointingly low for such a prestige match, and when the club were doing exceedingly well.

summer, and entry in the Willhire Cup, a low-key tournament in which Norwich were joined by local rivals Ipswich Town, Colchester United and Cambridge United. The Canaries beat the latter two but lost to Ipswich in the last match, which constituted the tournament's final.

Low key and low interest, which is probably just how John Bond and Ken Brown wanted that summer to be. The Canaries had ended the previous season by flying off to the United States; a 'jolly' in all but name which included, as well as the inevitable sightseeing, the odd game of football, one of which was that extraordinarily high-scoring game against the Tampa Bay Rowdies mentioned earlier.

A fun break for players and management alike, and a holiday for Bond who, upon his return would be reporting for World Cup duty as part of the BBC's team for the tournament's final stages that were being played in Argentina. No doubt he would have fielded interminable questions from his colleagues in the studio as to whether he'd be looking to bring some of the players he'd seen in action to Norwich, and no doubt he would have loved to have done that. The financial reality for Norwich City in the summer of 1978 was a little more prosaic. The conclusion of that 1978 World Cup, characterised by the masses of ticker tape that heralded the arrival of teams into the field of play and the BBC's annoyingly catchy theme music to its coverage,[28] saw two members of the victorious Argentinians squad in Osvaldo Ardiles and Ricardo Villa head for Tottenham for a joint transfer fee reported to be around £750,000. The Canaries, operating under the radar as usual, also brought an international footballer to England – ex-England international Martin Chivers, who'd been playing for Servette in Switzerland. As well as Chivers, and ever mindful of the need for defensive additions to a squad that had looked a bit shaky at the back on occasions during the season just gone, Bond also signed centre-half Phil Hoadley from Orient.

In signing Hoadley, Norwich had also been the grateful recipients of a first in British football. True, they hadn't shaken the game to its very foundations by signing a couple of Argentinean superstars, but the arrangement was still an historic one in terms of transfer dealings as he was the first player to take advantage of the newly created freedom of contract rule, his transfer free of £110,000 being determined by an independent tribunal. Phil immediately became an integral member of the Norwich team, going straight into the starting XI for the opening day win over Southampton. He'd been signed as a replacement for David Jones, the Canaries' imposing Welsh international centre-back having suffered ligament damage while playing for his country against England that May. That injury kept him out for the entire 1978/79 campaign, and he didn't return to the side until the following December, meaning he'd been out of the game for eighteen months. Once again injury worries meant that Norwich were

---

[28] 'Argentine Melody' (Cancion de Argentina), composed by Andrew Lloyd Webber.

taking two steps back for every one taken forward. Previous seasons had seen the side without several leading players for lengthy periods, including Duncan Forbes, Phil Boyer, Graham Paddon and now Jones.

Injuries, suspensions and myriad other niggles that led to Norwich shuffling the pack throughout the previous season, had also led to the irrepressible Duncan Forbes making playing comebacks on a scale that Frank Sinatra would have approved. He'd been sent packing on loan to Torquay United way back in August 1976, the move being seen by many as the precursor to his leaving Norwich permanently – the loan spell was, in effect, testing the waters for both clubs, as well as the player himself.

As things turned out, Forbes returned to Norwich after playing seven League games during his spell in Devon. Ever the consummate professional, he trained with as much passion and dedication as he had ever done and bided his time. He knew that reputation alone would not get him a call up back into the first team if the chance arose, but maintaining high standards and turning out for the reserves when needed would. Which is exactly how it turned out. He made twelve League appearances during the 1976/77 season, following that up in the following campaign by making another three, stepping into the team when needed, doing his job and performing well before stepping aside again. It was almost as if the Canaries had decided to keep him in a large glass case at Carrow Road with an accompanying notice that read 'In Case Of Emergency, Break Glass'. Thus when Jones missed the last game of the 1977/78 season, Forbes got another recall, three months after his last game for the club and surely, *surely* this time it would be his last Canary hurrah? He'd taken part in and thoroughly enjoyed his testimonial just over a fortnight earlier, a game that had seen the 1971/72 championship-winning side see off Norwich 3-0. But instead of taking his final bow in the celebratory confines of his testimonial, here he was again, a fortnight later, leading the line in the final League game. He even popped up to score the last-minute equaliser for the Canaries in that 1-1 draw against West Brom, a goal and a moment that, as you might expect, raised the Carrow Road roof.

The other great Norwich City survivor from the side that Saunders had inherited was, of course, Kevin Keelan. Like Forbes, he'd had his detractors over the last couple of years or so, including his manager, who had so controversially dropped him in the aftermath of the 3-1 defeat at Aston Villa sixteen months earlier. Keelan had ridden out that affront to his professional dignity and returned to the side in time for the start of the following season, only to break his right hand in the game at Bristol City the following February. That injury kept him out of the side for the remainder of the season, and when Duncan Forbes headed what everyone had assumed to be his last goal in his final game for the club against West Brom, the unfamiliar name of Clive Baker was wearing the No. 1 shirt for Norwich.

Yet Keelan, now thirty-seven, took his place in the Norwich side for the opening game of the 1978/79 season – that impressive 3-1 win over Southampton that had seen both Reeves and Chivers score, as well as a valedictory strike at Carrow Road for Ted MacDougall. It would, however, be one of only four victories in the club's opening twenty-one League games. The Canaries reached the halfway point of that season having drawn twelve of those matches, well on their way to setting a new club and League record of twenty-three draws out of their forty-two League games, including a remarkable sequence of seven drawn in a row from December to March, making Norwich the first team selected on the pools coupon for thousands of punters around the country. They all probably thought it a safe bet when City 'went' for their eighth draw in a row at Anfield on 21 February, but Liverpool were in no mood to play along, winning by six goals to nil in a game that defined the word 'rout' all ends up. Unfortunately for Norwich, that game saw another injury to Keelan, this time a broken thumb, one that was serious enough to see him miss club's remaining games for the third consecutive season. Keelan and Liverpool would meet again, however, for like Forbes, his time at the Carrow Road was not yet at an end.

For Phil Hoadley of course, his Carrow Road career was just beginning. Whether or not he would have been signed had David Jones been fit and available at the start of the season is open to question. He and Tony Powell formed an effective rearguard in the centre of the Norwich defence; part of an impressive collective effort by the rearguard that season that saw only nineteen goals conceded in the club's Carrow Road fixtures, their best since the first season after promotion under the somewhat more diligent, defensively wise, Ron Saunders. Another welcome development, as was their overall defensive record; fifty-seven goals conceded in forty-two League games, their best from the club's six seasons in the top flight. Powell was an ever-present that campaign, one of two. Kevin Bond was the other, the young right-back fully justifying the faith that had been placed in him as a potential first-team player by his father, even when many had questioned that belief. Kevin also made the first of his two appearances for the England 'B' team that year. The obvious consistency and quality that was now at the heart of the Norwich back four was paying off and those three members of the preferred Norwich back four played together in all but the three matches that Hoadley missed that season. Indeed, the only cause for concern in the Norwich defence had been the absence of a regular left-back after Colin Sullivan's surprise move to Cardiff for £60,000 in the new year. Sullivan played in the Canaries' first ten League games of the season, after which duties in the No. 3 shirt were handed over to Ian Davies. Richard Symonds filled in on the occasions Davies wasn't available for all bar two games, which saw the ever-willing Forbes and Doug Evans play one game each in a reshuffled defence. Evans was chosen specifically to mark John Robertson in a game at Nottingham Forest. He did this fairly effectively, so much so that Tony Woodcock was given his two goals with minimal interference from either Evans or any of his teammates. By the time Tottenham arrived at Carrow Road three days later, normal service was resumed with Davies returning to the side and, with him starting to establish an understanding with his three amigos alongside him in the Norwich defence, they kept a clean sheet. This was one of eleven the club managed that season; one more than rivals Ipswich Town, who finished ten places and twelve points ahead of them in the League.

More progress: consistency in the League, a tighter defence, and as the introduction to the team of players like Phil Lythgoe, Greg Downs, Kevin Bond and Ian Davies had shown, positive signs that the youth structure at the club, not so much revamped by John Bond as totally rebuilt from the foundations upwards, was also starting to prove its worth.

The introduction of Justin Fashanu into the first team that season also proved this. Fash's senior debut in the Carrow Road encounter with West Brom was one of the main talking points of that evening's *Match of the Day*. Surprisingly, given his unerring ability to make the headlines, Justin did not score on his debut, but he certainly had enough about him to suggest that Norwich had a future star on their hands, and the experienced and seasoned defensive pairing of John Wile and Ally Robertson got more than they normally bargained for in a fixture against Norwich. Bond, aware of the rich potential that Fashanu had but also aware of the expectation that it would create, sensibly left Fashanu out of Norwich's next game. But Fashanu had done enough to feature in fifteen of the clubs remaining matches that season, the first of the five goals he additionally contributed coming in a 2-2 draw at Leeds. Thus shielded and occasionally admonished by his manager when his on-field enthusiasm threatened to get him into trouble, Fash saw out the season relatively untroubled off or on the pitch, the pressure and expectation on it still resting on the equally inexperienced shoulders of Kevin Reeves. But Fashanu's time would come.

Norwich ended the 1978/79 season again respectably placed in the Division One table, twelve points clear of the first of those three relegation positions – a massive gap, especially when you consider that it was, at this time, still just two points for a League win. The one disappointment of another solid League campaign had been their failure to win a single League game away from home – the Canaries had not been successful on their travels away from Carrow Road since that win at West Ham on the opening day of the previous season. This was, of course, tempered by the number of draws the club had in those away fixtures – thirteen in all – meaning thirteen valuable away points. It was more than they had got over the previous two seasons, the overall away record of just eight defeats as a consequence meaning only eight other clubs in the division lost fewer games on their travels.

So, again, more signs of progress on the pitch, testimony to all of the hard work that John Bond had put into the club since his arrival. Bond's achievements at Norwich were now being noted by other clubs, and there is little doubt that his was a name in the minds of more than one club chairman at the time. It was certainly one that was tossed around by the newspapers when Jimmy Armfield left Leeds United in July 1978 as it was again when his successor at Elland Road,

Jock Stein, left the club only forty-four days after his appointment. Did Leeds United Chairman Manny Cussins enquire about Bond's availability at the time? The answer can only ever be speculation of course, but it is highly likely that he did, or at least someone at Leeds United would have done. Certainly Arthur South would have been aware of the growing commercial interest in his manager, something which led, ultimately, to Bond being offered that ten-year contract, an astonishing offer for any club to make to their manager, no matter what their status in the game.

Ultimately it went unsigned, yet Bond came very close to inking his name on the dotted line and, in doing so, committing the rest of his career to the Canaries. He was so serious about signing it that he demanded the same for Ken Brown. To agree to that condition was a sign the club were equally serious about wanting to ensure Bond stayed put. In the end and for whatever reasons – maybe Bond had become aware of the growing interest in him at other clubs and didn't want to lock himself into a long-term contract – it didn't happen.

Thus we can only wonder how the history of Norwich City would have been different had John Bond remained in charge almost right up to the start of the age of the Premier League.

The impact he made on Norwich City was enormous, so much so that, in taking a snapshot look back at that footballing decade at Carrow Road as I have done so here, I find, invariably, everything comes down to him. His decisions, foresight, vision and desire to see his team not only winning, but doing so in style and putting a smile on people's faces – and there were plenty of smiles in and around Carrow Road at that time, even in the dark days leading up to the departure of Ron Saunders and the relegation that followed – something that even Bond could not prevent happening. Yet you feel that nothing on earth was going to stop him getting the team promoted again straight away, and not only that, but keeping them among the elite of British football for the remainder of his time at the club. His impact was immediate and the vision clear – one of his first decisions being to introduce a properly structured, coached and managed schoolboy and youth policy at the club, one that has been producing first-team players ever since, some of whom have left for vast amounts of money. Think Darren Eadie, Craig Bellamy and Chris Sutton, the network of schoolboy and youth team sides that they would have come through at the club were a legacy of Bond's management. Them and many others.

Think also of the players who graced the Carrow Road turf during that decade – in the case of Martin Peters, 'graced' being exactly the right word. Peters, Ted MacDougall, Phil Boyer, Jimmy Neighbour, Graham Paddon, Kevin Reeves. They were all Bond signings, from World Cup winning superstar to unknown teenage striker who ended up fetching £1 million pounds. What some clubs wouldn't give now for a manager who can, time and time again, pick up such footballing bargains for next to nothing, polish them and sell them on for fortune? John Bond did.

And think, finally, of what I believe to be his greatest legacy; the manner and style of the football that Norwich City has long been identified with. There is no doubt that throughout the 2013/14 Premier League season, whenever Norwich are featured in a live televised game, the pundits or commentator will refer to the Canaries' reputation for 'playing good football' and being 'attractive', a team that 'likes to pass the ball around'. Who do we have to thank for that? Bond again. It's a legacy that all of the managers who have followed him into the top job at Norwich have known they are expected to emulate. Some have done so; others have not been so successful. But it is expected, nonetheless.

A stretch of ten games in the autumn of 1978 illustrated this and his overall policy perfectly – ten games played, forty-one goals scored, of which Norwich had conceded twenty; an average of two goals a game, something which few managers or coaches today would regard as acceptable. Yet the fact that Norwich ended up scoring twenty-one over the same period would have been enough to satisfy the manager, the fans, and the boardroom. The game was much simpler then, part of the entertainment industry as Kevin Bond observed on more than one occasion when we met. And he is right, as was his father. Because, while we may tend to look back on the seventies in a footballing sense through yellow-and-green-tinted spectacles, there is little doubt that, for much of that decade, it was what came first, second and third at Carrow Road. The game had its darker side even then, the rise of organised football hooliganism in England for example, as well as the continued failings of England at international level. Yet these were all of secondary importance to Norwich City supporters.

Because we had Kenny, Kenny Foggo, Kenny Foggo on the wing.

Kevin Keelan and Duncan Forbes. They started the decade at the club, and were both still there when it finished.

And we had Jimmy Bone, scorer of our first-ever goal in the First Division.

And Graham Paddon, hat-trick hero at Highbury and in possession of a left foot that could shell peas.

We had Ted MacDougall. Supermac: 138 appearances, 66 goals.

Phil Boyer. First Norwich City player to be selected for England.

Martin Peters. A World Cup winner and Canary legend.

Jimmy Neighbour. A different player to Kenny Foggo but the same song!

Kevin Reeves. The £1-million man.

Justin Fashanu. Scorer of one of the greatest goals to ever be seen at Carrow Road, and certainly one of the coolest celebrations.

And John Bond.

Cheers gents. And thanks Bondy. It was an unforgettable ride.

ACKNOWLEDGEMENTS

My huge and never-ending thanks to everyone who has helped or indulged me during the planning and writing of this project, without whom it would not have happened.

Tom Furby and all at Amberley Publishing.

Peter Rogers and Norwich City Football Club. The Mothership. Think the final moments of *Close Encounters of the Third Kind*.

Kevin Bond.

Paul Kent.

Mick Dennis.

Gerry Harrison.

Gary Gowers.

Russell Saunders.

Andrew Harrison, creator and webmaster of the phenomenal 'Sing Up The River End' website.

Chris Bethell, club historian at Millwall Football Club.

Paul King.

Rob Butler, Paul McVeigh and Chris Goreham on BBC Radio Norfolk for their indulgences and support throughout this and all of my other work. All top gents.

Everyone at the Holiday Inn at Carrow Road, a home from home!

To Rick Waghorn, author of *12 Canary Greats* – an invaluable resource. Also to Rob Hadgraft, author of *Norwich City – The Modern Era: A Complete Record* and Mike Davage, author, alongside John Eastwood, of *Canary Citizens*, and sole author of *Glorious Canaries – Past and Present*, recommended reading for any Norwich fan.

And to Sarah, my wife, for putting up with the bleary-eyed reclusive and somewhat obsessive monster that I become whenever I am writing a book. What's it like outside?

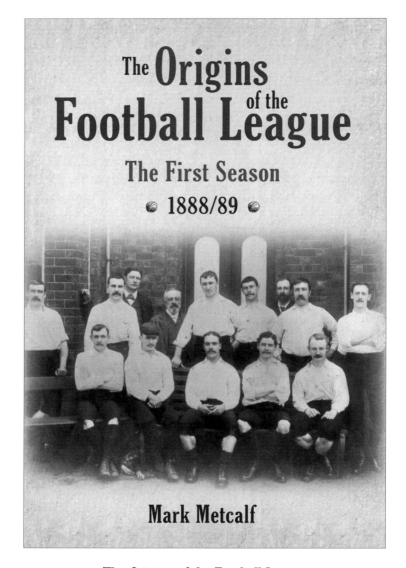